PEOPLE'S BIBLE COMMENTARY

LUKE

VICTOR H. PRANGE

CONCORDIA PUBLISHING HOUSE · SAINT LOUIS

Revised edition first printed in 2004.
Copyright © 1992 Concordia Publishing House
3558 S. Jefferson Ave., St. Louis, MO 63118-3968
1-800-325-3040 · www.cph.org

Manufactured in the United States of America
ISBN 0-7586-0441-6

1 2 3 4 5 6 7 8 9 10   13 12 11 10 09 08 07 06 05 04

CONTENTS

ILLUSTRATIONS

EDITOR'S PREFACE

The *People's Bible Commentary* is just what the name implies—a Bible and commentary for the people. It includes the complete text of the Holy Scriptures in the popular New International Version. The commentary following the Scripture sections contains personal applications as well as historical background and explanations of the text.

The authors of the *People's Bible Commentary* are men of scholarship and practical insight gained from years of experience in the teaching and preaching ministries. They have tried to avoid the technical jargon which limits so many commentary series to professional Bible scholars.

The most important feature of these books is that they are Christ-centered. Speaking of the Old Testament Scriptures, Jesus himself declared, "These are the Scriptures that testify about me" (John 5:39). Each volume of the *People's Bible Commentary* directs our attention to Jesus Christ. He is the center of the entire Bible. He is our only Savior.

We dedicate these volumes to the glory of God and to the good of his people.

The Publishers

Introduction to Luke

Jesus Christ is the heart and center of the Bible. The story of his life, death, and resurrection is told in the four gospels: Matthew, Mark, Luke, and John. None of the writings which came to be called "gospels" had titles originally. But as collections of the New Testament books were made, each received a title.

The title "gospel according to Luke" is found at the end of the oldest existing papyrus Greek copy of Luke, dating from A.D. 175–225. Early Christian writers regularly spoke of Luke as the author of this third gospel. His name does not, however, appear in the writing itself.

Luke is named three times in the New Testament, all in letters of Paul. In Philemon verse 24, he is named with three other "fellow workers." Paul sends greetings to the Christian church at Colosse from "our dear friend Luke, the doctor" (Colossians 4:14). Paul was in prison when he wrote his second letter to Timothy. He mentions that "only Luke is with me" (2 Timothy 4:11). Luke was obviously one who worked closely with Paul.

In considering the authorship of the third gospel, one must take into account the writing titled "The Acts of the Apostles." Both of these writings are addressed to Theophilus (Luke 1:3; Acts 1:1). Reference is made in Acts to "my former book." This can only refer to the third gospel.

In Acts there are a number of sections in which the author includes himself as he tells the story, the so-called "we sections" (16:10-17; 20:5-15; 21:1-18; 27:1–28:16). Here an eyewitness is reporting what he personally experienced with the apostle Paul.

Yet the writer of the third gospel explicitly disclaims his being an eyewitness of the events in the life of Jesus (Luke 1:2). He could not have been one of the twelve apostles. His reports come as a result of his having "carefully investigated everything from the beginning" (verse 3). Paul was in this same position of having to hear second-hand about the earthly ministry of Jesus.

Putting these facts together and accepting the universal testimony of the early church, there can be little doubt that Luke was the author of the gospel that bears his name. He likely was a Gentile, though one cannot be certain about this. He was a learned person, gifted as a writer, a physician by profession.

Luke, no doubt, intended his writing especially for the people whom Paul had reached in his mission journeys. These were predominantly Gentiles. Some were quite wealthy; many were women. Early church tradition suggests that Luke did his writing in the large and important city of Antioch, the home base for Paul in his mission journeys. It was in this city that the disciples of Jesus were first called "Christians" (Acts 11:26).

Luke himself does not call his writing a gospel. In his book he speaks of others who have "undertaken to draw up an account of the things that have been fulfilled among us" (Luke 1:1). The Greek word that the NIV translates as "account" refers to various kinds of writings, especially the narration of historical events. The word literally means "a written composition that leads through to an end." That is exactly what Luke did: beginning with the birth of Jesus, he leads through to the end, to Jesus' death and resurrection.

Note especially that Luke speaks of "the things that have been fulfilled among us." When Jesus appeared on

Easter Sunday to the two disciples on the road to Emmaus, "he explained to them what was said in all the Scriptures concerning himself" (24:27). Later that evening Jesus told his assembled disciples that "everything must be fulfilled that is written about me in the Law of Moses, the Prophets and the Psalms" (verse 44). Luke's purpose was to show the early Christians, who "examined the Scriptures every day" like the Bereans (Acts 17:11), that Jesus Christ was truly the fulfillment of the Old Testament. This was a point of controversy for the Jewish religious teachers.

Luke was presenting to the Roman world a person proclaimed by the Christians to be the Savior from sin and yet a person who had been crucified by order of the Roman governor Pontius Pilate. Luke argues the case that Jesus was innocent of all crimes deserving of death and that Jesus' death was the result of scheming by the Jewish religious leadership. Yet ultimately the death of Jesus was the result of "God's set purpose and foreknowledge" (Acts 2:23). The death of Jesus was divinely necessary, "as it has been decreed" (Luke 22:22), though caused by human beings. The Roman world needed to know the real reason for the death of Jesus on a Roman cross.

This gospel was written for a mission church. Luke includes many of the statements of Jesus that detail the responsibilities of those who will carry on the mission of preaching the good news in all the world. Many of the words and actions of Jesus were directed to his own disciples. His earthly ministry was their time of schooling in theology and mission.

Luke's gospel abounds with familiar stories found nowhere else in the Bible: the Good Samaritan, the Prodigal Son, the Pharisee and the Tax Collector, Zacchaeus, and more. Luke takes special note of the importance of women in telling the story of Jesus: Elizabeth, Mary (mother of

Jesus), Anna, Mary and Martha, the widow of Nain, and others. The opening chapters resound with songs the church has continued to sing over the centuries: the Magnificat, the Benedictus, the Gloria in Excelsis, the Nunc Dimittis.

In presenting a brief outline, the word *servant* has been chosen to characterize the entire life of Jesus. On the night before his death on the cross, Jesus said to his disciples, "I am among you as one who serves" (22:27). Jesus trained a body of servants and sent them into the world as his witnesses. Every believer is a servant of the greatest of all servants, Jesus Christ. Reading the gospel of Luke will help one appreciate more fully the service which Jesus rendered. It will help all who follow Jesus to become better servants.

Outline

Theme: Jesus Christ, the Servant of God

    I. Preparation for service (1:1–4:13)

        A. Preface to Luke's gospel (1:1-4)

        B. The births of John and Jesus (1:5–2:40)

        C. The introduction of God's Servant (2:41–4:13)

    II. The Servant at work, getting people ready for God's kingdom: preaching, teaching, healing, reaching, training (4:14–19:27)

        A. Service in Galilee (4:14–9:50)

        B. Service on the way to Jerusalem (9:51–19:27)
            1. Jesus urges people to get ready for the coming kingdom (9:51–13:21)
            2. Jesus reveals some surprises as to who will inherit the kingdom (13:22–17:10)

3. Jesus wants people to be aware that the work of the kingdom is going on right now (17:11–19:27)

III. The Servant at work, opening the doors of the kingdom: suffering, dying, rising again (19:28–24:53)

A. Jesus arrives in Jerusalem (19:28–21:38)

B. Jesus suffers and dies (22:1–23:56)

C. Jesus rises and ascends into heaven (24:1-53)

Luke

PART ONE

Preparation for Service (1:1–4:13)

Preface to Luke's gospel

Introduction

1 **Many have undertaken to draw up an account of the things that have been fulfilled among us, ²just as they were handed down to us by those who from the first were eyewitnesses and servants of the word. ³Therefore, since I myself have carefully investigated everything from the beginning, it seemed good also to me to write an orderly account for you, most excellent Theophilus, ⁴so that you may know the certainty of the things you have been taught.**

Luke is the only one of the four evangelists who introduces his gospel with a kind of personal foreword. He clearly states the purpose of his writing: "that you may know the certainty of the things you have been taught." Luke does not want his readers to be in doubt about the truth concerning Jesus Christ, the Servant of God. By the time Luke wrote his gospel, other reports of the life and teachings of Jesus were beginning to circulate. Luke assures his readers that he has investigated everything from the beginning and now provides this orderly account of the truth.

Who is Theophilus, to whom Luke addresses this gospel? The name literally means "lover of God." Perhaps Theophilus was a prominent Christian in the early church; some suggest he may have paid for the parchment on which this gospel was written. However, it is possible that the name could be symbolic and refer simply to any believer, any lover of God. The name occurs again in the second volume of Luke's writings, the book of Acts. That book begins, "In my former book, Theophilus, I wrote about all that Jesus began to do and to teach." Each person who reads this gospel must hear himself addressed as the lover of God who seeks to know the truth about Jesus Christ.

The births of John and Jesus

The birth of John the Baptist foretold

⁵In the time of Herod king of Judea there was a priest named Zechariah, who belonged to the priestly division of Abijah; his wife Elizabeth was also a descendant of Aaron. ⁶Both of them were upright in the sight of God, observing all the Lord's commandments and regulations blamelessly. ⁷But they had no children, because Elizabeth was barren; and they were both well along in years.

⁸Once when Zechariah's division was on duty and he was serving as priest before God, ⁹he was chosen by lot, according to the custom of the priesthood, to go into the temple of the Lord and burn incense. ¹⁰And when the time for the burning of incense came, all the assembled worshipers were praying outside.

¹¹Then an angel of the Lord appeared to him, standing at the right side of the altar of incense. ¹²When Zechariah saw him, he was startled and was gripped with fear. ¹³But the angel said to him: "Do not be afraid, Zechariah; your prayer has been heard. Your wife Elizabeth will bear you a son, and you are to give him the name John. ¹⁴He will be a joy and delight to you, and many will rejoice because of his birth, ¹⁵for he will be great in the sight of the Lord. He is never to take wine or other fermented drink, and he will be filled with the Holy Spirit even from birth. ¹⁶Many of the people of Israel will he bring back to the Lord their God. ¹⁷And he will go on before the Lord, in the spirit and power of Elijah, to turn the hearts of the fathers to their children and the disobedient to the wisdom of the righteous—to make ready a people prepared for the Lord."

¹⁸Zechariah asked the angel, "How can I be sure of this? I am an old man and my wife is well along in years."

¹⁹The angel answered, "I am Gabriel. I stand in the presence of God, and I have been sent to speak to you and to tell you this good news. ²⁰And now you will be silent and not able to speak until the day this happens, because you did not believe my words, which will come true at their proper time."

²¹Meanwhile, the people were waiting for Zechariah and wondering why he stayed so long in the temple. ²²When he came out, he could not speak to them. They realized he had seen a vision in the temple, for he kept making signs to them but remained unable to speak.

²³When his time of service was completed, he returned home. ²⁴After this his wife Elizabeth became pregnant and for five months remained in seclusion. ²⁵"The Lord has done this for me," she said. "In these days he has shown his favor and taken away my disgrace among the people."

Luke parallels the births of John and Jesus. In each case the angel Gabriel makes the announcement foretelling the birth; both the mother of Jesus and the father of John sing hymns of praise—one before and one after the births of their sons; then comes the description of the two births and the rite of circumcision that follows. While there are some parallels between John and Jesus, above all we must recognize how much greater Jesus is than John. Both are servants of God, but the service that Jesus renders is far superior to anything John does. Above all, Jesus is the Son of God; John is only the blessed offspring of two very pious and aged human parents.

Zechariah and Elizabeth prayed earnestly to the Lord that he would grant them a child. However, Elizabeth had reached the point in her life when women normally no longer can conceive children. So when the angel Gabriel announces to Zechariah that he would father a child, this old man is dumbfounded—and he does not believe. As a chastisement from God, Zechariah is unable to speak for the entire nine months of his wife's pregnancy.

Gabriel describes the special role this John (which means "the Lord has shown favor") is to fulfill: "He will be a joy and delight to you, and many will rejoice because of his birth, for he will be great in the sight of the Lord. . . . Many of the people of Israel will he bring back to the Lord their God." John would be like the great Old Testament prophet Elijah; his calling was "to make ready a people prepared for the Lord."

Zechariah was serving his turn as priest in the temple when the angel appeared to him. Aaron had 24 grandsons; one was named Abijah (1 Chronicles 24:10). John was born from this priestly family. He grew up very conscious of the requirements of the law. In the plan of salvation, he was just the right person to serve as the forerunner of the Savior.

The birth of John took place in the time of Herod king of Judea. This is the same Herod who slaughtered many innocent boys after the birth of Jesus. The announcement of John's birth is linked to the reign of a king who was quite insignificant in comparison to the great Caesar in Rome. The birth of Jesus will be related to the actions of the great world leader Caesar Augustus (2:1).

We dare not leave this story without mentioning the joy of Elizabeth and her acknowledgement of the Lord's gracious action: "The Lord has done this for me. . . . He has shown his favor and taken away my disgrace among the people." Here is a mother-to-be who truly anticipates the birth of her child as a blessed gift of the Lord!

The birth of Jesus foretold

²⁶In the sixth month, God sent the angel Gabriel to Nazareth, a town in Galilee, ²⁷to a virgin pledged to be married to a man named Joseph, a descendant of David. The virgin's name was Mary. ²⁸The angel went to her and said, "Greetings, you who are highly favored! The Lord is with you."

²⁹**Mary was greatly troubled at his words and wondered what kind of greeting this might be.** ³⁰**But the angel said to her, "Do not be afraid, Mary, you have found favor with God.** ³¹**You will be with child and give birth to a son, and you are to give him the name Jesus.** ³²**He will be great and will be called the Son of the Most High. The Lord God will give him the throne of his father David,** ³³**and he will reign over the house of Jacob forever; his kingdom will never end."**

³⁴**"How will this be," Mary asked the angel, "since I am a virgin?"**

³⁵**The angel answered, "The Holy Spirit will come upon you, and the power of the Most High will overshadow you. So the holy one to be born will be called the Son of God.** ³⁶**Even Elizabeth your relative is going to have a child in her old age, and she who was said to be barren is in her sixth month.** ³⁷**For nothing is impossible with God."**

³⁸**"I am the Lord's servant," Mary answered. "May it be to me as you have said." Then the angel left her.**

Six months have passed since Gabriel's announcement to Zechariah. Now the Lord sends his messenger on another mission. This time Gabriel goes not to the holy city of Jerusalem but to a humble town in Galilee; not to a temple but to a house; not to an aged man but to a young and vibrant maiden. The promised child to Zechariah and Elizabeth was in answer to many prayers; the promised child to Mary was a total and complete surprise. A child born of a virgin—here is something altogether new. Not an old couple finally having their first son, but a maiden bearing an infant conceived by the Holy Spirit—this is surely the greater miracle!

Mary was pledged to be married to Joseph, a descendant of David. She herself also came from that royal family; her son would be given the throne of his father David. But more than that—the promised child would be Son of the Most High, the Son of God. His kingdom would never end.

Hard to believe? Without a doubt! Yet the faith of Mary shines brightly in contrast to the doubts of the priest Zechariah: "I am the Lord's servant. . . . May it be to me as you have said." Zechariah was also a servant; he did his duty in the temple. Mary's service was special and unique: to be the mother of God.

Mary visits Elizabeth

³⁹At that time Mary got ready and hurried to a town in the hill country of Judea, ⁴⁰where she entered Zechariah's home and greeted Elizabeth. ⁴¹When Elizabeth heard Mary's greeting, the baby leaped in her womb, and Elizabeth was filled with the Holy Spirit. ⁴²In a loud voice she exclaimed: "Blessed are you among women, and blessed is the child you will bear! ⁴³But why am I so favored, that the mother of my Lord should come to me? ⁴⁴As soon as the sound of your greeting reached my ears, the baby in my womb leaped for joy. ⁴⁵Blessed is she who has believed that what the Lord has said to her will be accomplished!"

When the angel Gabriel announced to Mary that she was to become the mother of a child, Mary was also told that Elizabeth had conceived. Mary wasted no time but hurried to pay a visit to her aged relative. She journeyed from her own city of Nazareth to the hill country of Judea. She hardly expected the kind of welcome she received from Elizabeth.

Luke tells us that the Holy Spirit filled the soul of Elizabeth, and she exclaimed, "Blessed are you among women, and blessed is the child you will bear!" She goes on to wonder at the great favor shown to her that "the mother of my Lord" should come to visit. Elizabeth knew this truth because of a special revelation by the Holy Spirit. The child in her womb joins the praise by leaping for joy. Later in the gospel, Jesus urges his disciples to do the same: "Rejoice in that day and leap for joy, because great is your reward in heaven" (6:23).

Above all, Elizabeth praises the faith of Mary. Remember that at this time no sounds were coming from the lips of Zechariah because of his unbelief. Elizabeth had good reason to marvel at the faith of Mary.

To honor Mary in the way that Elizabeth does is certainly God pleasing. Her praise was motivated by the Holy Spirit. We Christians today also honor Mary as an example of faith and service. But we do not go beyond this and regard Mary as someone more holy than us, for she too was sinful. The child to be born of Mary was as much her Savior from sin as he is our Savior from sin.

Mary's song

⁴⁶And Mary said:

> **"My soul glorifies the Lord**
> ⁴⁷ **and my spirit rejoices in God my Savior,**
> **⁴⁸for he has been mindful**
> **of the humble state of his servant.**
> **From now on all generations will call me blessed,**
> ⁴⁹ **for the Mighty One has done great things for me—**
> **holy is his name.**
> **⁵⁰His mercy extends to those who fear him,**
> **from generation to generation.**
> **⁵¹He has performed mighty deeds with his arm;**
> **he has scattered those who are proud in their**
> **inmost thoughts.**
> **⁵²He has brought down rulers from their thrones**
> **but has lifted up the humble.**
> **⁵³He has filled the hungry with good things**
> **but has sent the rich away empty.**
> **⁵⁴He has helped his servant Israel,**
> **remembering to be merciful**
> **⁵⁵to Abraham and his descendants forever,**
> **even as he said to our fathers."**

⁵⁶Mary stayed with Elizabeth for about three months and then returned home.

The Magnificat

Mary had heard Elizabeth heap praise on her. She responds with her own hymn of praise to the Lord. She points away from herself; she had no special merit or worth. She has been favored by the Lord and breaks into this marvelous hymn magnifying him.

The Latin Bible translation of the song of Mary begins, "Magnificat anima mea Dominum." The opening word, "Magnificat," has named this canticle (song), which early found a place in the daily evening (vespers) worship of the church. Composers, including Bach, have set these words to exalted music. Here are words for every Christian to sing.

Verses 46 to 49 center on the personal blessings that have come to Mary. Notice the personal pronouns "my" and "me." Mary recognizes her humble status as a servant. She will be praised by future generations because of what the Mighty One has done for her. However, not the name of Mary but the name of the Lord is holy. It is as if Mary foresees the excessive adoration that some would heap on her in the coming centuries, and she seeks to defuse such adulation.

In verse 50 Mary turns her attention to "those who fear him." The word "fear" is a common biblical term. It refers to the holy awe and respect one has for the Mighty One of whom Mary has just spoken. Such fear will call forth worship and obedience. Mary herself is an example of one who fears the Lord. The Lord's mercy surrounds those who reverence him.

Mary continues by recalling some of the Lord's great acts of mercy, how he works in contrasting ways. The proud he brings down, but he lifts up the humble. The hungry he fills with good things, but the rich he sends away empty. His mercy to Israel, his servant, goes back to the time of Abraham. The theme of Mary's Magnificat will be fully developed in the ministry of her son. In a way far surpassing anything of Old Testament history, the saving work of Jesus Christ unfolds the mercy of God "to those who fear him, from generation to generation."

Mary stayed with Elizabeth for three months, right up to the time when John was to be born. She was a good companion for her aged relative and took the place of Zechariah in household conversation. What happy times these two women must have spent together, each looking forward to the birth of sons totally unexpected!

The birth of John the Baptist

⁵⁷**When it was time for Elizabeth to have her baby, she gave birth to a son.** ⁵⁸**Her neighbors and relatives heard that the Lord had shown her great mercy, and they shared her joy.**

⁵⁹**On the eighth day they came to circumcise the child, and they were going to name him after his father Zechariah,** ⁶⁰**but his mother spoke up and said, "No! He is to be called John."**

⁶¹**They said to her, "There is no one among your relatives who has that name."**

⁶²**Then they made signs to his father, to find out what he would like to name the child.** ⁶³**He asked for a writing tablet, and to everyone's astonishment he wrote, "His name is John."** ⁶⁴**Immediately his mouth was opened and his tongue was loosed, and he began to speak, praising God.** ⁶⁵**The neighbors were all filled with awe, and throughout the hill country of Judea people were talking about all these things.** ⁶⁶**Everyone who heard this wondered about it, asking, "What then is this child going to be?" For the Lord's hand was with him.**

At last the time came for the child of Zechariah and Elizabeth to be born. Neighbors and relatives shared the mother's joy; Zechariah hardly seems to be in the picture. But his time is coming.

The Old Testament law decreed that sons were to be circumcised on the eighth day. God had said to Abraham, "Every male among you shall be circumcised. You are to undergo circumcision, and it will be the sign of the covenant between me and you" (Genesis 17:10,11). No uncircumcised male was to eat of the passover (Exodus 12:48). Circumcision took place in the home, and the child was named at the same time.

On the day of circumcision, the eighth day after birth, the neighbors and relatives again gather. They propose to Elizabeth that she give her child the name of his father (perhaps to cheer up old Zechariah?). But Elizabeth needed no advice from others as to what name this child should have. The name had already been given by the angel: "You are to give him the name John" (verse 13). No amount of persuasion could change her mind.

Having failed to budge mother, the well-meaning family friends turn their attention to the long silent Zechariah, hoping that he might overrule his wife. To the astonishment of all, Zechariah writes the words on a tablet: "His name is John."

At once the tongue of Zechariah is loosed, and words of praise flow from his mouth. Here is conversion—doubt turned to faith, skepticism replaced by adoration. No wonder the people of the hill country of Judea talked of hardly anything else for quite a spell. "What then is this child going to be?" It was a question the new father would answer.

Zechariah's song

⁶⁷**His father Zechariah was filled with the Holy Spirit and prophesied:**

⁶⁸**"Praise be to the Lord, the God of Israel,**
  because he has come and has redeemed his people.
⁶⁹**He has raised up a horn of salvation for us**
  in the house of his servant David
⁷⁰**(as he said through his holy prophets of long ago),**
⁷¹**salvation from our enemies**
  and from the hand of all who hate us—

⁷² to show mercy to our fathers
  and to remember his holy covenant,
⁷³ the oath he swore to our father Abraham:
⁷⁴ to rescue us from the hand of our enemies,
  and to enable us to serve him without fear
⁷⁵ in holiness and righteousness before him all our days.

⁷⁶ And you, my child, will be called a prophet of the
    Most High;
  for you will go on before the Lord to prepare the way
    for him,
⁷⁷ to give his people the knowledge of salvation
  through the forgiveness of their sins,
⁷⁸ because of the tender mercy of our God,
  by which the rising sun will come to us from heaven
⁷⁹ to shine on those living in darkness
  and in the shadow of death,
  to guide our feet into the path of peace."

⁸⁰And the child grew and became strong in spirit; and he lived in the desert until he appeared publicly to Israel.

For too long Zechariah had been unable to speak; now he is filled with the Holy Spirit to voice his faith. The song of Zechariah also gets it name from the Latin: "Benedictus Dominus"; the NIV translates it as "Praise be to the Lord." This canticle has been used for centuries in the daily morning service (matins) of the church.

We need to take the word "prophesied" in verse 67 very seriously. Zechariah speaks of the salvation that will come through Jesus as a fact which has already been accomplished. And this before Christ is even born! We are at the very end of the Old Testament, the time of promise. With Luke chapter 2 we enter the New Testament, the time of fulfillment.

Zechariah praises the Lord "because he has come and has redeemed his people. He has raised up a horn of salvation for us in the house of his servant David." David himself in Psalm 18 said of the Lord, "He is my shield and the horn of my salvation, my stronghold" (verse 2). Now Zechariah uses this same term, "horn of salvation," to refer to the Messiah. Jesus came from the house of David, and as the Servant of the Lord, he will bring salvation from all enemies. The rescue effected by Christ will enable God's people to serve him. The priest Zechariah had devoted his life to serving the Lord by representing the people in the temple. Now he sees a new era when all believers as priests will worship their Savior.

After speaking of the coming Messiah and the Messiah's work, the father turns his attention to his newborn son and the task that will fall to John. John's ministry will be one of preparing the way before the Lord. By his preaching he will give to people the knowledge of salvation through the forgiveness of sins. On those living in darkness, on those in the shadow of death, the sun is rising. And John is sent to make the way ready. His calling is to guide feet into the path of peace. So sang old Zechariah.

Chapter 1 of Luke's gospel concludes with the note that the child grew and became strong in spirit. John's growth is more than just physical; his spiritual fibers were toughened for the task before him. He made his home in the desert till his time of service came. No doubt, his father and mother had died before that ministry began. But they had seen with the eyes of faith, and that was sufficient.

The birth of Jesus

2 **In those days Caesar Augustus issued a decree that a census should be taken of the entire Roman world. ²(This was the first census that took place while Quirinius was governor of Syria.) ³And everyone went to his own town to register.**

19

⁴So Joseph also went up from the town of Nazareth in Galilee to Judea, to Bethlehem the town of David, because he belonged to the house and line of David. ⁵He went there to register with Mary, who was pledged to be married to him and was expecting a child. ⁶While they were there, the time came for the baby to be born, ⁷and she gave birth to her firstborn, a son. She wrapped him in cloths and placed him in a manger, because there was no room for them in the inn.

No event in the history of the world has been so celebrated in word and song as the birth of Jesus Christ! Yet this story is told by Luke in a totally undramatic fashion. The significance of what happens here in Bethlehem's manger was already revealed in chapter 1 with the angel's announcement to Mary. The actual birth of the babe is told in the simplest words: "she gave birth to her firstborn, a son." So the Son of God enters our world in utter humility and without fanfare.

It was a census ordered by Caesar Augustus, ruler of the Roman Empire from 27 B.C. to A.D. 14, which brought Mary and Joseph from Nazareth to Bethlehem. The purpose of this census is indicated by the translation in the King James Version: "to be taxed." Everyone went to his own town to register on the tax rolls. Mary and Joseph made this journey of about 80 miles from their home city in Galilee to the ancient city of Bethlehem, family home of the famous King David. Here this child, whose kingdom would be far greater than that of his ancestor, was born. It was to fulfill God's Old Testament promise that the Messiah was born in Bethlehem, not Nazareth.

Critics of the Bible have found fault with Luke's mention of Quirinius as being governor of Syria when this census was taken. Historical records list Quirinius as the governor of Syria about 10 years *after* the death of King Herod; a census was taken at that time (A.D. 6/7). Since Jesus was born while Herod was king (who died about 4 B.C.), some claim that Luke makes a mistake here. But before coming to this conclusion, one must take into account several possibilities: (1) Luke calls this the "first" census while Quirinius was governor of Syria; Quirinius may have had an earlier tour of duty in Syria, a hint of which is found in an ancient document. (2) Some learned Greek scholars suggest that the word *first* might better be translated as "prior"; the translation would then be: "this census was *prior to* Quirinius being governor of Syria." We moderns hardly have all the facts available to us from two thousand years ago; we dare not stand in judgment of Luke, who writes by inspiration of God's Spirit and has "carefully investigated everything from the beginning" (1:3).

After the birth of Jesus, his mother wrapped him in cloths and placed him in a manger. The Old English word *swaddle* (found in the KJV) means to bind an infant in lengths of bandage. This was the normal way of clothing an infant; today we would "diaper" a child. Only at the end of the story do we find out that the inns were all full in Bethlehem. This necessitated their using a less suitable place for shelter. So it was among the animals that Jesus was born; he was bedded in a manger, a feeding trough for cattle. Is it any wonder that this scene has captured the imagination of artists and poets! But we must not be so fascinated by romanticized versions of this event that we miss its true significance: here is the Word of God made flesh for us and for our salvation. Glory be to God on high!

The shepherds and the angels

⁸And there were shepherds living out in the fields nearby, keeping watch over their flocks at night. ⁹An angel of the Lord appeared to them, and the glory of the Lord shone around them, and they

were terrified. ¹⁰But the angel said to them, "Do not be afraid. I bring you good news of great joy that will be for all the people. ¹¹Today in the town of David a Savior has been born to you; he is Christ the Lord. ¹²This will be a sign to you: You will find a baby wrapped in cloths and lying in a manger."

¹³Suddenly a great company of the heavenly host appeared with the angel, praising God and saying,

¹⁴"Glory to God in the highest,
> and on earth peace to men on whom his
> favor rests."

¹⁵When the angels had left them and gone into heaven, the shepherds said to one another, "Let's go to Bethlehem and see this thing that has happened, which the Lord has told us about."

¹⁶So they hurried off and found Mary and Joseph, and the baby, who was lying in the manger. ¹⁷When they had seen him, they spread the word concerning what had been told them about this child, ¹⁸and all who heard it were amazed at what the shepherds said to them. ¹⁹But Mary treasured up all these things and pondered them in her heart. ²⁰The shepherds returned, glorifying and praising God for all the things they had heard and seen, which were just as they had been told.

We must assume that very few people in Bethlehem were aware of that baby lying in a manger; only Mary and Joseph were in on the secret of his divine origin. That all changes as God goes public with the good news. His salvation is not just for Zechariah and Elizabeth and Mary. Jesus Christ is the Savior of all people. The first audience to hear the good news is a band of shepherds living out in the fields near Bethlehem. King David had been a shepherd out on those same fields. Now news of the birth of one greater than David is broadcast to shepherds.

The darkness of night is shattered by the bright light of angelic beings. This is the third appearance of angels in Luke's gospel. Angels serve as messengers of God to interpret events that would otherwise go unnoticed or be mis-understood. The shepherds are told that the baby wrapped in such ordinary cloths and lying in a manger is none other than the Savior, Christ the Lord!

This is the first occurrence of the name *Christ* in Luke's gospel. This is a Greek translation of the Hebrew word *Messiah,* meaning "Anointed One." The word is found, for example, in Psalm 2:2, where we are told that the kings of the earth take their stand against the Lord and against "his Anointed One." In the Greek translation, one would find the word *Christ* here. Since it was customary to anoint kings in the Old Testament, the word *Christ* has reference to the fact that Jesus is a king, descended from David and destined to rule forever. The birth of Jesus fulfilled the Old Testament promise that God would send a king, a messiah, to save his people.

This good news of great joy is amplified by the sudden appearance of a multitude of the heavenly host singing praises to God. Their song is familiar to us from our Sunday worship, where we continue to sing the *Gloria in Excelsis* (Glory in the Highest). The song of the angels has a double focus: in the highest heavens there is resounding glorious praise to God for his generous gift of a Savior; on earth there is peace for people on whom God's favor rests. This last phrase differs from the familiar translation of the KJV: "good will toward men." The ancient Greek texts of the New Testament account are divided here, which leads the NIV to translate it as "on whom his favor rests."

As suddenly as the angels had come, so suddenly they left. The shepherds are once more alone with their flocks. But they can hardly go on with their night watch as if nothing had happened. They hurry off to Bethlehem to see this thing that the Lord had told them about.

The angel had given them a sign so that they could recognize the baby: one lying in a manger. What they searched for, they found. We don't know how long they stayed. We don't know what was said. But we do know that the shepherds did not keep the news to themselves; they spread the word. Their message was not so much about the baby in a manger; rather, they shared the angel's message: "A Savior has been born to you; he is Christ the Lord." No wonder the people who heard the shepherds' talk were amazed. They may have questioned whether perhaps these sheep herders were not a bit unhinged. Yet the shepherds knew what they had heard and seen. And they echoed the angels' praise with their own earthly songs as they returned to their waiting flocks.

Mary's reaction to all these happenings is much more subdued. We are told that she "treasured up all these things and pondered them in her heart." Her treasures were not any earthly relics—a bit of straw from the manger, the cloth in which the baby was wrapped, or one of the shepherds' staffs left behind. Her scrapbook of this event was carried within her heart. She turned over again and again in her mind what had happened and was amazed at what a great thing God had done.

Here are the two sides of Christmas: one is very public; the other, private. Both are necessary. We need to go public with the good news; we need to celebrate with word and song; we need to witness to others. But Mary's example is also for us to follow: what a marvelous thing God has done for me! This child is my Savior from sin and death and Satan and hell. Here is our priceless treasure!

Jesus presented in the temple

²¹On the eighth day, when it was time to circumcise him, he was named Jesus, the name the angel had given him before he had been conceived.

²²When the time of their purification according to the Law of Moses had been completed, Joseph and Mary took him to Jerusalem to present him to the Lord ²³(as it is written in the Law of the Lord, "Every firstborn male is to be consecrated to the Lord"), ²⁴and to offer a sacrifice in keeping with what is said in the Law of the Lord: "a pair of doves or two young pigeons."

²⁵Now there was a man in Jerusalem called Simeon, who was righteous and devout. He was waiting for the consolation of Israel, and the Holy Spirit was upon him. ²⁶It had been revealed to him by the Holy Spirit that he would not die before he had seen the Lord's Christ. ²⁷Moved by the Spirit, he went into the temple courts. When the parents brought in the child Jesus to do for him what the custom of the Law required, ²⁸Simeon took him in his arms and praised God, saying:

> ²⁹"Sovereign Lord, as you have promised,
>   you now dismiss your servant in peace.
> ³⁰For my eyes have seen your salvation,
> ³¹which you have prepared in the sight of all people,
> ³²a light for revelation to the Gentiles
>   and for glory to your people Israel."

³³The child's father and mother marveled at what was said about him. ³⁴Then Simeon blessed them and said to Mary, his mother: "This child is destined to cause the falling and rising of many in Israel, and to be a sign that will be spoken against, ³⁵so that the thoughts of many hearts will be revealed. And a sword will pierce your own soul too."

³⁶There was also a prophetess, Anna, the daughter of Phanuel, of the tribe of Asher. She was very old; she had lived with her husband seven years after her marriage, ³⁷and then was a widow until she was eighty-four. She never left the temple but worshiped night and day, fasting and praying. ³⁸Coming up to them at that very moment, she gave thanks to God and spoke about the child to all who were looking forward to the redemption of Jerusalem.

³⁹When Joseph and Mary had done everything required by the Law of the Lord, they returned to Galilee to their own town of Nazareth. ⁴⁰And the child grew and became strong; he was filled with wisdom, and the grace of God was upon him.

Just as John was circumcised and named on the eighth day, so it is with Jesus. Saint Paul takes special note of the fact that Jesus was "born under law, to redeem those under law" (Galatians 4:4,5). The circumcision is a part of Christ's active obedience: he fulfilled the law perfectly in our place. And his circumcision brings to an end the need for us New Testament Christians to practice circumcision as a religious rite in fulfillment of the Old Testament law. In this sense, Christ is truly the end of the law (Romans 10:4).

The angel Gabriel had revealed to Mary what she was to name her child (1:31). The name "Jesus" comes from two Hebrew words: *the Lord* (Jehovah) plus *save*. Matthew 1:21 gives this interpretation of the name *Jesus:* "He will save his people from their sins." Truly an appropriate name for this child!

Circumcision took place in the home of the parents. We don't know just where Mary and Joseph might have stayed while they remained in Bethlehem. Undoubtedly, they were able to find more suitable shelter than the stable after the rush of people had left Bethlehem following the census registration.

When Jesus was 40 days old, they made the short trip to Jerusalem for the purification of Mary and the presentation of the child in the temple. The law of the purification of a mother is found in Leviticus chapter 12. A poor person was required to bring two doves or young pigeons as her sacrificial offerings. The law also required that a firstborn male was to be consecrated to the Lord (Exodus 13:2). If the child was not given into the service of the Lord, the parents needed to redeem him by a payment of five shekels (Numbers 3:46,47). Mary and Joseph did not make this payment since Jesus was consecrated to the Lord in the fullest possible way. On the 40th day of his life, Jesus is presented to the Lord.

We are now introduced to two very pious and aged persons, Simeon and Anna. They remind us of those other two persons, Zechariah and Elizabeth, whom we met at the beginning of this story of the births of John and Jesus. And just as Zechariah sang a hymn of praise, so does Simeon.

Simeon had been promised by the Holy Spirit that he would not die before he had seen the Lord's Christ. When Mary and Joseph come into the courts of the temple, the Spirit directs Simeon to do the same. Seeing the child Jesus, he takes the infant in his arms and praises God with the song commonly called the *Nunc Dimittis* (from the opening words of the hymn in Latin). We continue to sing this song as part of our communion liturgy and in our evening worship (vespers).

Simeon is not really making a request of the Lord—he is making a statement of fact: "You now dismiss your servant in peace." Simeon's service in the temple as a watchman waiting for the fulfillment of the Old Testament promises is at an end. The watch is over; the servant can retire in peace. With the eyes of faith, Simeon sees more than a babe in arms; he sees a Savior dying on the cross; he sees salvation for all people, both Israelite and Gentile.

Joseph and Mary marveled at the words spoken by Simeon. But the old man is not finished. He shows insight that could come only by special revelation of the Spirit concerning the destiny of this child. Israel would be divided over Jesus—he would cause some to fall and some to rise. For some, Jesus would be a rock of offense over which they would stumble; for others, he would be the living stone of salvation. Mary would herself witness his suffering on the cross; her own soul would be pierced with the sword.

Simeon passes from the scene to be replaced by Anna, a widow of 84. She had faithfully served the Lord for many years with worship, fasting, and prayer. Now she adds her thanksgiving to that of Simeon's and speaks of the child to all who were looking forward to the redemption of Jerusalem.

Joseph and Mary had much to discuss as they proceeded on their way back to Bethlehem following their visit to the temple. For the time being, they decided to stay in Bethlehem. Luke skips over the story of the coming of the wise men and the flight into Egypt (Matthew 2). He simply reports that after doing everything required by the law of the Lord, Mary and Joseph returned to Galilee, to their own town of Nazareth. Here Jesus grew up, becoming stronger day by day, filled with wisdom and the grace of God.

The introduction of God's Servant

The boy Jesus at the temple

⁴¹**Every year his parents went to Jerusalem for the Feast of the Passover. ⁴²When he was twelve years old, they went up to the Feast, according to the custom. ⁴³After the Feast was over, while his parents were returning home, the boy Jesus stayed behind in Jerusalem, but they were unaware of it. ⁴⁴Thinking he was in their company, they traveled on for a day. Then they began looking for him among their relatives and friends. ⁴⁵When they did not find him, they went back to Jerusalem to look for him. ⁴⁶After three days they found him in the temple courts, sitting among the teachers, listening to them and asking them questions. ⁴⁷Everyone who heard him was amazed at his understanding and his answers. ⁴⁸When his parents saw him, they were astonished. His mother said to him, "Son, why have you treated us like this? Your father and I have been anxiously searching for you."**

⁴⁹**"Why were you searching for me?" he asked. "Didn't you know I had to be in my Father's house?" ⁵⁰But they did not understand what he was saying to them.**

⁵¹**Then he went down to Nazareth with them and was obedient to them. But his mother treasured all these things in her heart.**

The youth of Jesus

⁵²And Jesus grew in wisdom and stature, and in favor with God and men.

The time between the birth of Jesus and the beginning of his early ministry is sometimes called "the silent years." There is only one break in this silence, the story of the boy Jesus at the temple. Though this story is included in the second chapter of Luke, it really fits better with what follows in chapter 3. Already as a 12-year-old, Jesus is introduced as the Servant of the heavenly Father. The child who was presented in the temple now takes a seat among the teachers of the Word of God, much to the amazement of the onlookers.

Luke tells us that Mary and Joseph regularly went up to Jerusalem for the annual feast of the Passover. This feast celebrated the redemption of the people of Israel from Egypt and was observed in the spring of the year. It was the most important of the Jewish festivals, and the law required all males to attend.

At the conclusion of the Passover feast, Mary and Joseph started back to Nazareth, thinking that Jesus was among the group of pilgrims who were traveling together. But at nightfall the boy was nowhere to be found. A frantic search began for the missing son, one which ended three days later when Jesus was discovered in the temple courts. These courts surrounded the temple sanctuary and were used as a place for instruction and study of God's Word.

Jesus was making quite an impression on the crowd that had gathered. Here was no ordinary boy; his questions and answers showed superior knowledge and understanding. Mary and Joseph were also astonished—and a bit perturbed—when they found him. This is evident from the words spoken by Mary: "Son, why have you treated us like this? Your father and I have been anxiously searching for you."

Any parent who has suffered the trauma of a missing child can well imagine what Mary and Joseph experienced. How guilty Mary must have felt for failing to keep closer watch over the whereabouts of this son entrusted to her care by the Lord.

The words that Jesus speaks to his mother here are the first recorded in any of the gospels. Mary had addressed a question to him. He responds with a double question: "Why were you searching for me? Didn't you know I had to be in my Father's house?" There is in these questions a gentle rebuke for Mary. She was tempted at times to think of Jesus as an ordinary child, one over whom she had complete control.

Mary had to learn, as also later at the wedding at Cana, that Jesus was directed by a greater will, the will of the heavenly Father, in a way no other child was directed. This was something that Mary and Joseph did not understand. For them it was a learning experience. And for all who witnessed this 12-year-old in the temple, it was a dramatic introduction to the Servant of God.

What Jesus did was not an act of rebellion over against his parents. His complete obedience to them continued to be demonstrated on their return to Nazareth. For Mary this incident added to the treasure stored in her heart. Already she was learning what those words of Simeon meant, "a sword will pierce your own soul too."

Luke closes out this story by telling us that Jesus grew in wisdom and stature and in favor with God and men. One assumes that Jesus spent the next 18 years of his life in and around Nazareth working as a carpenter (see Mark 6:3, where the question is asked, "Isn't this the carpenter?"). We will next hear of Jesus when he is baptized by John in the Jordan River at about 30 years of age (3:23).

John the Baptist prepares the way

3 In the fifteenth year of the reign of Tiberius Caesar—when Pontius Pilate was governor of Judea, Herod tetrarch of Galilee, his brother Philip tetrarch of Iturea and Traconitis, and Lysanias tetrarch of Abilene—²during the high priesthood of Annas and Caiaphas, the word of God came to John son of Zechariah in the desert. ³He went into all the country around the Jordan, preaching a baptism of repentance for the forgiveness of sins. ⁴As is written in the book of the words of Isaiah the prophet:

> "A voice of one calling in the desert,
> 'Prepare the way for the Lord,
>   make straight paths for him.
> ⁵Every valley shall be filled in,
>   every mountain and hill made low.
> The crooked roads shall become straight,
>   the rough ways smooth.
> ⁶And all mankind will see God's salvation.'"

⁷John said to the crowds coming out to be baptized by him, "You brood of vipers! Who warned you to flee from the coming wrath? ⁸Produce fruit in keeping with repentance. And do not begin to say to yourselves, 'We have Abraham as our father.' For I tell you that out of these stones God can raise up children for Abraham. ⁹The ax is already at the root of the trees, and every tree that does not produce good fruit will be cut down and thrown into the fire."

¹⁰"What should we do then?" the crowd asked.

¹¹John answered, "The man with two tunics should share with him who has none, and the one who has food should do the same."

¹²Tax collectors also came to be baptized. "Teacher," they asked, "what should we do?"

¹³"Don't collect any more than you are required to," he told them.

¹⁴Then some soldiers asked him, "And what should we do?"

He replied, "Don't extort money and don't accuse people falsely—be content with your pay."

¹⁵The people were waiting expectantly and were all wondering in their hearts if John might possibly be the Christ. ¹⁶John answered them all, "I baptize you with water. But one more powerful than I will come, the thongs of whose sandals I am not worthy to untie. He will baptize you with the Holy Spirit and with fire. ¹⁷His winnowing fork is in his hand to clear his threshing floor and to gather the wheat into his barn, but he will burn up the chaff with unquenchable fire." ¹⁸And with many other words John exhorted the people and preached the good news to them.

¹⁹But when John rebuked Herod the tetrarch because of Herodias, his brother's wife, and all the other evil things he had done, ²⁰Herod added this to them all: He locked John up in prison.

We last heard of John son of Zechariah in 1:80. There Luke reported that "he lived in the desert until he appeared publicly to Israel." That public appearance is initiated not by John but by the word of God that came to him. One is reminded of similar calls to service received by the Old Testament prophets. Jeremiah reports, "The word of the LORD came to me" (1:4). God calls John to prepare the way for Jesus.

The public nature of John's ministry is emphasized by the setting given it by Luke. He notes that the word of God came to John in the 15th year of the reign of Tiberius Caesar. This Roman emperor was the successor of Caesar Augustus, who died in A.D. 14. The 15th year of Tiberius would be A.D. 28/29. At that time Pontius Pilate, who would condemn Jesus to death, was the governor of Judea. The capital city of Jerusalem was located in the province of Judea and was under the direct rule of Rome. Pilate served as governor in the years A.D. 25–36.

Other parts of the country of Palestine remained under the control of the family of Herod the Great, who was king of all Palestine when Jesus was born. Herod the Great had ten wives. Two of his many sons are mentioned by Luke: Herod tetrarch of Galilee and his brother Philip tetrarch of Iturea and Traconitis. The Herod mentioned here became the ruler of Galilee and Perea on the death of his father in 4 B.C. He is the Herod we will hear about several times in Luke's gospel. He is also known as Herod Antipas. The title *tetrarch* originally meant the governor of one of the four divisions of a country or province; in time it became simply a stereotyped title for any petty prince.

Luke mentions two religious leaders, the high priests Annas and Caiaphas. Annas was high priest during the years A.D. 6–15. He also continued to exert great influence in temple affairs during the high priesthood of his son-in-law Caiaphas (A.D. 18–36). This is the political and religious setting for the public ministries of both John and Jesus.

John's father, Zechariah, had said that his son "will go on before the Lord to prepare the way for him, to give his people the knowledge of salvation through the forgiveness of their sins" (1:76,77). John did exactly that in the country around the Jordan River. The words written in the book of Isaiah the prophet are fulfilled: "A voice of one calling in the desert, 'Prepare the way for the Lord.'" The quotation ends on this significant note: "All mankind will see God's salvation." The preaching of John prepared the way for the Savior of all people.

John was a preacher of repentance. The word *repent* is used in two senses in the Bible. Sometimes the word means only "to be sorry for sins." An example of this use is the summary of Jesus' message: "Repent and believe the good news!" (Mark 1:15). John's preaching of repentance included the call to faith in the coming Savior. This is evident from Luke's statement that John "exhorted the people and preached the good news to them." Response to John's preaching of repentance included both sorrow for sins and faith in the good news of forgiveness of sins.

John did not only preach; John also baptized (hence the designation "John the Baptist"). His was a baptism of repentance for the forgiveness of sins. The people who were baptized made confession of their sins (see Matthew 3:6). The word of God that came to John no doubt included the command to baptize. This was an added means by which John made ready the way for the coming of Jesus. John recognized that his baptism was only preparation for what was to come: "I baptize you with water. But one more powerful than I will come. . . . He will baptize you with the Holy Spirit and with fire." John's baptism was an effective means of grace for the forgiveness of sins, but it was only preparatory for the baptism of Jesus that would follow.

Luke includes some examples of the preaching of John. He certainly does not mince words as he addresses the crowd coming out for baptism as a "brood of vipers." A brood refers to a group of young offspring such as birds, fish, or snakes. John's words are a reflection on the religious leadership that brought forth such spiritual children. They sense the coming judgment but are like sheep without a shepherd. They don't know how to escape the wrath to come. John points the way: produce fruit in keeping with repentance. The fruits of faith show the genuineness of repentance. Being the physical children of Abraham is no guarantee that a barren tree will escape the ax and fire of judgment.

The preaching of John moved the crowd to ask, "What should we do then?" John points out to them some of the fruits of genuine repentance. He urges them to share their garments and food with the poor and needy. He tells the tax collectors to be fair and honest. Soldiers are directed to refrain from extorting money from people through false accusations; rather, they should be content with the pay they receive. Notice that John suggests fruits of faith which bring benefits to other people. Here is preparation for him who would give the commandment to love one another.

The ministry of John raised in the hearts of people the thought that he possibly was the promised Messiah, the Christ. John would, of course, have none of this. His ministry was to prepare the way for the Coming One—one infinitely more powerful, one who would baptize with the Holy Spirit, one who would ultimately be the judge of the living and the dead. John did not feel himself worthy even to untie the sandal strings of this Coming One.

The ministry of John came to a grinding halt when he was locked up in prison by Herod. John had rebuked Herod for the evil things Herod had done; above all, John had spoken out against the adultery of Herod in divorcing his own wife and taking his brother's wife, Herodias. The Word of God is not well received by the sinful world. John made this discovery. His imprisonment for speaking the Word is an ominous introduction to the ministry of Jesus and foreshadows the cross on which he will die.

The baptism and genealogy of Jesus

[21]When all the people were being baptized, Jesus was baptized too. And as he was praying, heaven was opened [22]and the Holy Spirit descended on him in bodily form like a dove. And a voice came from heaven: "You are my Son, whom I love; with you I am well pleased."

[23]Now Jesus himself was about thirty years old when he began his ministry. He was the son, so it was thought, of Joseph,

the son of Heli, ²⁴the son of Matthat,
the son of Levi, the son of Melki,
the son of Jannai, the son of Joseph,
²⁵the son of Mattathias, the son of Amos,
the son of Nahum, the son of Esli,
the son of Naggai, ¹⁶the son of Maath,
the son of Mattathias, the son of Semein,
the son of Josech, the son of Joda,
²⁷the son of Joanan, the son of Rhesa,
the son of Zerubbabel, the son of Shealtiel,
the son of Neri, ²⁸the son of Melki,
the son of Addi, the son of Cosam,
the son of Elmadam, the son of Er,
²⁹the son of Joshua, the son of Eliezer,
the son of Jorim, the son of Matthat,
the son of Levi, ³⁰the son of Simeon,
the son of Judah, the son of Joseph,
the son of Jonam, the son of Eliakim,
³¹the son of Melea, the son of Menna,
the son of Mattatha, the son of Nathan,
the son of David, ³²the son of Jesse,
the son of Obed, the son of Boaz,
the son of Salmon, the son of Nahshon,
³³the son of Amminadab, the son of Ram,
the son of Hezron, the son of Perez,
the son of Judah, ³⁴the son of Jacob,
the son of Isaac, the son of Abraham,
the son of Terah, the son of Nahor,
³⁵the son of Serug, the son of Reu,
the son of Peleg, the son of Eber,
the son of Shelah, ³⁶the son of Cainan,
the son of Arphaxad, the son of Shem,
the son of Noah, the son of Lamech,
³⁷the son of Methuselah, the son of Enoch,
the son of Jared, the son of Mahalalel,
the son of Kenan, ³⁸the son of Enosh,

**the son of Seth, the son of Adam,
the son of God.**

After describing the ministry of John, Luke once again introduces Jesus. He is among the people who come to be baptized by John. Jesus identifies with the people whom he came to save. Matthew tells us that the association of Jesus with sinners coming for baptism brought forth a protest from John. Jesus' answer points to his work of fulfilling the entire will of God for us: "It is proper for us to do this to fulfill all righteousness" (Matthew 3:15). The Sinless One does not separate himself from sinners but becomes one with them in his baptism.

The way in which Luke reports the baptism of Jesus makes it a flashback into the ministry of John. Jesus was, of course, baptized before John was locked up in prison. Here the chronological order of events is not being followed, but rather the theological. Luke wants to finish the ministry of John before introducing Jesus. So he saves the report of the baptism of Jesus till this point in the story.

Jesus was a person of prayer. This is especially emphasized in Luke's gospel. It was while Jesus was praying after his baptism that heaven was opened and the Holy Spirit descended upon Jesus in bodily form like a dove. In Acts 10:38 Peter, preaching in the home of Cornelius, makes reference to the fact that "God anointed Jesus of Nazareth with the Holy Spirit and power." The visible descent of the dove is public witness to the fact that here truly is the Messiah, the Christ, the Anointed One. For John, this was God's sign that made the Messiah known to him (John 1:32,33).

The climax to the baptismal scene comes with the declaration that Jesus is none other than the Son of God. The voice of the Father from heaven introduces his Son: "You are my Son, whom I love; with you I am well pleased." Before Jesus begins his public ministry, the Father puts his seal of approval on him. Everything that is reported about Jesus in this gospel must be seen from this perspective: here is the Son of God. To read the gospel simply as the story about a man who dies on the cross is to miss the point completely. It is the Son of God who dies for sinners.

We don't want to leave this event without pointing out the presence of the Holy Trinity: the voice of the Father from heaven, the Son being baptized, and the Holy Spirit descending in the form of a dove. When Jesus gave the command to baptize all nations, he told us that we should baptize "in the name of the Father and of the Son and of the Holy Spirit" (Matthew 28:19). Our baptisms today continue to confess the Holy Trinity, who was revealed at the baptism of Jesus.

We are told that Jesus was about 30 years old when he began his ministry. He had fully matured physically; spiritually, he was ready to undertake that arduous service which would ultimately lead to the cross.

But before going on with the story of that ministry, Luke pauses to demonstrate that Jesus is both Son of God and Son of Man, both divine and human. To teach this truth, Luke makes use of a long list of names, the genealogy of Jesus. As we today read Luke's gospel, we might be inclined simply to skip over all these names. They don't mean much to us.

Altogether, there are 78 names in the genealogy. The first name is Joseph, thought to be the father of Jesus (the reader of the gospel knows differently, of course, because of what was said in chapter 1). The last name is that of God. In contrast to Matthew, who begins his genealogy of Jesus with Abraham (Matthew 1:1-17), Luke traces the roots of Jesus back to God himself.

The next-to-last name is Adam. His fall into sin made it necessary for the second Adam (1 Corinthians 15:45-47), Jesus Christ, to come into this world. Adam was created by God from the dust of the earth. Jesus is not the Son of God by creation; rather, in the words of Luther's explanation to the Second Article of the Apostles' Creed, Jesus Christ is *"begotten* of the Father from eternity."

Yet though he is the only begotten Son of God, Jesus also has a human genealogy. He is the descendant of many famous Israelites. It would appear that Luke has given us the family tree of Joseph. However, in Matthew 1:16 Jacob is listed as the father of Joseph. In Luke, Joseph's father is named Heli. The other names from Joseph back to David in the two lists also differ completely.

Several suggestions have been made to explain this different listing of names. Some believe that what Luke records is actually the family tree of Mary, starting with her husband's name. Others explain the different names as the result of the Jewish law of levirate marriage: a child receives the legal name of a woman's dead husband though physically being the child of the man's brother with a different name. We may finally have to admit that with our present knowledge of the way genealogies were constructed in ancient times, we simply are not able to explain why the names differ in the lists of Luke and Matthew.

This genealogy shows that Jesus is the culmination of Israel's history. He numbers among his ancestors men like Noah, Abraham, Jacob, Judah, and David. He comes from the people. But at the same time he comes from God. Here is one uniquely qualified to carry out the work of saving all people. Here is God's Servant.

The temptation of Jesus

4 Jesus, full of the Holy Spirit, returned from the Jordan and was led by the Spirit in the desert, ²where for forty days he was tempted by the devil. He ate nothing during those days, and at the end of them he was hungry.

³The devil said to him, "If you are the Son of God, tell this stone to become bread."

⁴Jesus answered, "It is written: 'Man does not live on bread alone.'"

⁵The devil led him up to a high place and showed him in an instant all the kingdoms of the world. ⁶And he said to him, "I will give you all their authority and splendor, for it has been given to me, and I can give it to anyone I want to. ⁷So if you worship me, it will all be yours."

⁸Jesus answered, "It is written: 'Worship the Lord your God and serve him only.'"

⁹The devil led him to Jerusalem and had him stand on the highest point of the temple. "If you are the Son of God," he said, "throw yourself down from here. ¹⁰For it is written:

"'He will command his angels concerning you
to guard you carefully;
¹¹they will lift you up in their hands,
so that you will not strike your foot against a stone.'"

¹²Jesus answered, "It says: 'Do not put the Lord your God to the test.'"

¹³When the devil had finished all this tempting, he left him until an opportune time.

Testing by the devil is the final episode in the preparation of Jesus for his ministry. In the Garden of Eden, Adam and Eve were tested by the cunning serpent and failed. In the wilderness of Sinai, the people of Israel lusted after the worldly pleasures of Egypt and murmured against the Lord's leadership. But Jesus Christ shows himself to be the true Servant of the Lord in triumphing over the devil.

The devil was once an obedient angel serving his Maker. But this role was not satisfactory; he rebelled against the will of God and was cast down from heaven. With God's permission Satan tests the faith of believers. The ultimate clash between two wills is the contest fought by Christ and the devil.

Jesus is directed by the Holy Spirit to enter into this contest. After his baptism in the Jordan River, he is led by the Spirit into the desert, a location reminiscent of the wilderness through which Israel was guided by Moses. The temptation lasted 40 days; this again reminds one of the 40 years of the exodus from Egypt. The 40 days that Jesus spent in the desert are the origin of the 40-day period of Lent.

During these 40 days, Jesus fasted; he ate nothing and was terribly hungry. Israel also experienced hunger and thirst in the wilderness. The devil seizes upon this situation by suggesting to Jesus, "If you are the Son of God, tell this stone to become bread." The devil is not so much challenging Jesus to prove his divine sonship as tempting him to use the power of that sonship for his own selfish purpose: to provide bread for himself. Jesus responds by quoting a portion of Deuteronomy 8:3. These are words of Moses addressed to Israel: "He [God] humbled you, causing you to hunger and then feeding you with manna, which neither you nor your fathers had known, to teach you that *man does not live on bread alone* but on every word that comes from the mouth of the LORD." The devil had focused attention on the bread alone; Jesus directs attention to the one who stands behind the bread. Jesus would fail in his mission if he used his divine power for his own selfish purposes to satisfy his earthly needs.

The next temptation reported by Luke (the order of the temptations varies from Matthew 4:1-11) is political in nature. The devil led Jesus to a high place and showed him in an instant all the kingdoms of the world. Then the test: "I will give you all their authority and splendor . . . if you worship me." As the Son of God, Jesus had almighty power. He could easily have become a great world leader and controlled nations. But in seeking this end, he would have been rejecting the will of his Father (even as Satan had done). Jesus overcomes Satan with a quotation from Deuteronomy 6:13: "Worship the Lord your God and serve him only."

Now the devil led Jesus to the highest point of the temple in Jerusalem. He urges Jesus to jump down from this height, assuring him by a quotation from Psalm 91:11,12 (though omitting the key phrase "in all your ways") of the angels' guarding care. Israel in the wilderness had put the Lord to the test in similar ways. Jesus refused this course by once more quoting the Scriptures (Deuteronomy 6:16).

Jesus won the victory over the devil by using the sword of the Spirit, which is the Word of God. He did what Adam and the people of Israel had failed to do. Like us, he was tempted (Hebrews 4:15), but he was not overcome. He supplies us with the example of how we can use the Word of God to win victories over the temptations that come to us from Satan.

This defeat of Satan in the desert is not, however, the end of the story. Luke closes with the rather foreboding comment: "When the devil had finished all this tempting, he left him until an opportune time." Jesus would be faced with various tests during his earthly ministry. The most serious of these was the cross. Through all the testings, Jesus continued to do the Father's will. We find comfort in the fact that although we do at times give in to the devil, Christ did not. He is our champion; by faith in Jesus, we are assured of the final victory over sin, death, and the power of the devil.

PART TWO

The Servant at Work, Getting People Ready for God's Kingdom: Preaching, Teaching, Healing, Reaching, Training (4:14–19:27)

Service in Galilee

Jesus rejected at Nazareth

¹⁴Jesus returned to Galilee in the power of the Spirit, and news about him spread through the whole countryside. ¹⁵He taught in their synagogues, and everyone praised him.

¹⁶He went to Nazareth, where he had been brought up, and on the Sabbath day he went into the synagogue, as was his custom. And he stood up to read. ¹⁷The scroll of the prophet Isaiah was handed to him. Unrolling it, he found the place where it is written:

¹⁸ "The Spirit of the Lord is on me,
   because he has anointed me
   to preach good news to the poor.
He has sent me to proclaim freedom for the prisoners
   and recovery of sight for the blind,
   to release the oppressed,
¹⁹   to proclaim the year of the Lord's favor."

²⁰Then he rolled up the scroll, gave it back to the attendant and sat down. The eyes of everyone in the synagogue were fastened on him, ²¹and he began by saying to them, "Today this scripture is fulfilled in your hearing."

²²All spoke well of him and were amazed at the gracious words that came from his lips. "Isn't this Joseph's son?" they asked.

²³Jesus said to them, "Surely you will quote this proverb to me: 'Physician, heal yourself! Do here in your hometown what we have heard that you did in Capernaum.'"

²⁴"I tell you the truth," he continued, "no prophet is accepted in his hometown. ²⁵I assure you that there were many widows in Israel in Elijah's time, when the sky was shut for three and a half years and there was a severe famine throughout the land. ²⁶Yet Elijah was not sent to any of them, but to a widow in Zarephath in the region of Sidon. ²⁷And there were many in Israel with leprosy in the time of Elisha the prophet, yet not one of them was cleansed—only Naaman the Syrian."

²⁸All the people in the synagogue were furious when they heard this. ²⁹They got up, drove him out of the town, and took him to the brow of the hill on which the town was built, in order to throw him down the cliff. ³⁰But he walked right through the crowd and went on his way.

The time of preparation has been completed; the Servant of the Lord is ready to go to work. That work is first of all to get people ready for God's kingdom. By preaching, teaching, healing, reaching, and training, Jesus heralds the coming of God's rule. When asked when the kingdom of God would come, Jesus responds, "The kingdom of God is within you" (17:21). He himself brings the kingdom. He invites all to enter by trusting in him as the Savior.

Galilee is the scene of this early ministry. Jesus had grown up in this northern province ruled by Herod. In many ways it had felt the influence of the Romans and other Gentiles much more than the Jewish area around Jerusalem. Consequently, Galileans were treated with some disdain by the religious leadership in the south.

The Jesus who returned to Galilee was charged with the power of the Spirit. At his baptism he had heard the voice of his Father, and the Spirit rested upon him; in the desert he had defeated Satan. In no time at all, news about him and his activities spread through the whole countryside. He went into the village synagogues to teach the people. These synagogues were the buildings where the people assembled for worship and study of the Old Testament. Everywhere Jesus was praised.

After reporting in general on the beginnings of Jesus' ministry in Galilee, Luke tells of one specific incident in Nazareth that provides a contrast to the usually favorable response. Nazareth had only one claim to fame: it was the insignificant village where Jesus was brought up. Mary probably continued to live here; Joseph seems to have died, since no mention is made of his activity after the story of the 12-year-old Jesus in the temple.

Jesus was in Nazareth on the Sabbath Day. As he had so often done in the past, Jesus went into the village synagogue on that day. The synagogue service included the reading of the Old Testament law and prophets. Jesus was handed the scroll of the prophet Isaiah, and he read Isaiah 61:1,2. The words were those of the servant of the Lord who declared that the Spirit was on him. He had been anointed to preach good news to the poor, to open the eyes of the blind, to release the oppressed, to proclaim the year of the Lord's favor.

When Jesus had finished the reading, he rolled up the scroll and handed it back to the attendant. Already his reading of this passage must have deeply impressed the people, for their eyes were fixed on him as he sat down to expound this Scripture. His words at first pleased them: "Today this scripture is fulfilled in your hearing." The age of the Messiah has dawned; the Servant of the Lord has come.

But gradually the implications of what Jesus was saying struck home. He himself was that servant of the Lord who had been anointed with the Spirit. His ministry was to preach and teach and heal. This was too much for these people; they knew the identity of the one saying these things—"Isn't this Joseph's son?"

The hometown people had not known this man to be a miracle worker when he was among them. Rumors had come of some healings performed by Jesus in Capernaum, but these people of Nazareth needed convincing that Jesus was anything more than a rather precocious Bible student. Jesus makes reference to their doubts in a well-known proverb that asks the doctor to prove his wares by doing some healing.

No healings were forthcoming from Jesus. Rather, he declared that his ministry is one much wider than simply to impress people back home. He cited two well-known Old Testament stories about the prophets Elijah and Elisha. Elijah was sent to help a non-Israelite widow survive the severe famine, though there were many suffering widows at home (1 Kings 17:7-24). Elisha healed the gentile general Naaman, though there were many lepers in Israel (2 Kings 5:1-19).

The people at once caught the implications of what Jesus was saying. They needed to break out of the narrow view of the Messiah as coming only to establish an earthly kingdom for the Jews. The Servant of the Lord came to seek and to save the lost wherever they might be and whoever they were. This was too much for the Nazarenes. Filled with fury, they drove their native son from the town and took him to the brow of the hill on which the town was built, intent on throwing him down the cliff (we are reminded of the devil's temptation asking Jesus to jump from a height).

But the time for Jesus to die had not yet arrived. Making use of his divine power, he walked right through the crowd and went on his way. Jesus does not go elsewhere because he rejected the people of Nazareth. Rather, the people reject him because of his implied announcement that he is going elsewhere. Later, the people of Capernaum had the same reaction when Jesus left their presence; they tried to keep him for themselves (4:42). The response of Jesus: "I must preach the good news of the kingdom of God to the other towns also, because that is why I was sent."

This story of the rejection in Nazareth is a preview of a whole series of rejections that Jesus would experience. "He came to that which was his own, but his own did not receive him" (John 1:11). The stubborn self-centeredness and pride of people continues to resist the good news of the kingdom of God. Only the power of the Spirit through the Word of God overcomes this resistance and leads to faith in Jesus Christ as Savior.

Jesus drives out an evil spirit

[31]Then he went down to Capernaum, a town in Galilee, and on the Sabbath began to teach the people. [32]They were amazed at his teaching, because his message had authority.

[33]In the synagogue there was a man possessed by a demon, an evil spirit. He cried out at the top of his voice, [34]"Ha! What do you want with us, Jesus of Nazareth? Have you come to destroy us? I know who you are—the Holy One of God!"

[35]"Be quiet!" Jesus said sternly. "Come out of him!" Then the demon threw the man down before them all and came out without injuring him.

[36]All the people were amazed and said to each other, "What is this teaching? With authority and power he gives orders to evil spirits and they come out!" [37]And the news about him spread throughout the surrounding area.

Leaving Nazareth behind, Jesus went down to the city of Capernaum, situated on the Sea of Galilee. This was a more culturally important place than Nazareth. The Romans had a company of soldiers here. Many incidents from the life of Jesus took place in Capernaum. We may regard it as his home during his earthly ministry (see Mark 2:1). Peter and Andrew lived here, plying their fishing trade on the nearby sea.

On the Sabbath, Jesus is again in the synagogue teaching the people. His message possesses a power and authority that amazes those who hear. Throughout this section of his gospel, Luke will be stressing the power of Jesus in word and deed.

While in the synagogue, Jesus is confronted by a man possessed by a demon, an evil (or unclean) spirit. All disease and illness, both mental and physical, is the result of sin, which came into the world because Adam and Eve obeyed the devil. Throughout his ministry, Jesus shows himself to be the opponent of every form of sickness. The devil recognizes that Jesus is the enemy, naming him "the Holy One of God." The devil knows also that his ultimate end will be destruction.

Jesus shows his present power and authority in healing this man instantly by commanding the demon to come out. This is the first of 21 miracle stories included by Luke in his gospel. These miracles benefit those who are afflicted and troubled; they also reveal the divine sonship of Jesus.

The devil understood Christ's true nature, but the people in the Capernaum synagogue can only ask questions. They are amazed at the power of Jesus, which allows him even to order evil spirits around. The news continues to spread. The popularity of Jesus is on the rise.

Jesus heals many

38Jesus left the synagogue and went to the home of Simon. Now Simon's mother-in-law was suffering from a high fever, and they asked Jesus to help her. 39So he bent over her and rebuked the fever, and it left her. She got up at once and began to wait on them.

⁴⁰When the sun was setting, the people brought to Jesus all who had various kinds of sickness, and laying his hands on each one, he healed them. ⁴¹Moreover, demons came out of many people, shouting, "You are the Son of God!" But he rebuked them and would not allow them to speak, because they knew he was the Christ.

⁴²At daybreak Jesus went out to a solitary place. The people were looking for him and when they came to where he was, they tried to keep him from leaving them. ⁴³But he said, "I must preach the good news of the kingdom of God to the other towns also, because that is why I was sent." ⁴⁴And he kept on preaching in the synagogues of Judea.

From the synagogue Jesus goes to the house of Simon. This is the same person who in 5:8 is called Simon Peter; it was Jesus who gave him the name *Peter* (6:14). Jesus had known Simon from previous conversation (John 1:42), so we are not surprised that he goes to the home of Simon.

Upon arriving, Jesus finds that Simon's mother-in-law was suffering from a high fever. For the first time in this gospel, a request for help comes to Jesus. His response is to rebuke the fever (the use of the word "rebuke" seems to indicate the handiwork of the devil), and this woman was healed. Immediately, she begins to wait on Jesus and the others who were present. Perhaps she was one of the women whom Luke mentions in 8:2,3 as helping to support the ministry of Jesus.

At the end of the Sabbath, as the sun is going down, the streets leading to Peter's home are filled with people bringing their sick to Jesus. What miracles were worked! What joy was experienced! What power was demonstrated! Truly here is evidence of God's rule over the ravages of sin. It is a scene that will be repeated on the Last Day.

These people, also including Peter and his family, did not fully understand the divine nature of Jesus. They were

51

familiar with the Old Testament stories of healings worked by God through prophets and thought of Jesus in the same way. Only the demons (showing their angelic roots) fully recognize Jesus. They know that he is the Son of God and shout it out. They know that Jesus is the Messiah, the Christ.

Jesus did not want the witness of these evil spirits. They witnessed from evil intent and with the purpose of undermining the true purpose of Christ's mission. Too easily people would come to think of the Messiah only as a miracle worker and not as the Servant of God come to redeem sinners from eternal death and hell.

Early Sunday morning Jesus went out to a solitary place. The Sabbath had been long and hard; he had been engaged in bitter warfare with the devil. Now he needed time for meditation and prayer. But the people would not leave him alone. They surged out of Capernaum, begging him to come back. But Jesus could not answer their prayers; for his ministry *must* take him into other towns to preach of God's kingdom.

The word "Judea" in verse 44 is found in the oldest copies of the Greek New Testament. Later copies have the word "Galilee," which also appears in the KJV. Here is evidently a case where a later copyist changed the Greek word to make it better fit his idea of where Jesus was preaching. Luke's use of the word "Judea" no doubt referred to the Roman name for the entire country (as in 1:5), which would also include Galilee. This broadens the extent of Christ's preaching.

The calling of the first disciples

5 **One day as Jesus was standing by the Lake of Gennesaret, with the people crowding around him and listening to the word of God, ²he saw at the water's edge two boats, left there by**

the fishermen, who were washing their nets. ³He got into one of the boats, the one belonging to Simon, and asked him to put out a little from shore. Then he sat down and taught the people from the boat.

⁴When he had finished speaking, he said to Simon, "Put out into deep water, and let down the nets for a catch."

⁵Simon answered, "Master, we've worked hard all night and haven't caught anything. But because you say so, I will let down the nets."

⁶When they had done so, they caught such a large number of fish that their nets began to break. ⁷So they signaled their partners in the other boat to come and help them, and they came and filled both boats so full that they began to sink.

⁸When Simon Peter saw this, he fell at Jesus' knees and said, "Go away from me, Lord; I am a sinful man!" ⁹For he and all his companions were astonished at the catch of fish they had taken, ¹⁰and so were James and John, the sons of Zebedee, Simon's partners.

Then Jesus said to Simon, "Don't be afraid; from now on you will catch men." ¹¹So they pulled their boats up on shore, left everything and followed him.

Up to this point, Luke has pictured Jesus as going it alone in proclaiming the good news of the kingdom. He seems to have no companions as he makes his way through the synagogues. This solitary ministry, however, comes to an end rather quickly as the first permanent disciples are called.

If we only had the gospel of Mark, the call of the first disciples would appear to have happened out of the blue (Mark 1:16-20). But by reading the gospels of Luke and John, we realize that Jesus and the first disciples were rather well acquainted even before their call to follow. In the previous section we heard how Jesus had gone to the home of Simon and healed Simon's mother-in-law. When he now makes use of Simon's boat, it does not seem at all strange. Simon was simply returning a favor.

Jesus needed to use Simon's boat because of the people crowding around him at the Lake of Gennesaret as they listened to the Word of God. Gennesaret is the name of a small district west of the body of water more commonly named the Sea of Galilee. The multitude of listeners points to the popularity of Jesus as a teacher and the authority with which he spoke. The need for helpers in this ministry was becoming more evident all the time.

When Jesus had finished speaking, he told Simon to row out into deep water and let down his nets for a catch of fish. Simon protests that a night of fishing had yielded nothing; to catch fish in deep water in the heat and light of the day seemed highly unlikely. But Simon followed Jesus' instructions. Why? "But because you say so, I will let down the nets." Simon was yielding to the word of this person whom he knew to speak and act with a strange and mysterious authority.

The catch was awesome! The nets began to break; the cry went out to bring another boat to help; both boats were so full of fish that they began to sink. Simon had never seen anything like this in all his life. It was truly a fisherman's delight.

And now Luke uses this man's full name, Simon Peter, as he falls down before Jesus, saying, "Go away from me, Lord; I am a sinful man!" Peter spoke truthfully about himself. He was a sinful man. The miracle that he experienced overwhelmed him and made him aware that he was in the presence of the Holy One. The sinner dare not remain in such company; Peter begs the Lord to go away.

Jesus does not go away. Instead, he tells the sinner Peter that a new occupation awaits: "From now on you will catch men." Peter's last catch was the most impressive one he ever had as a fisherman. It was a preview of things to come. On Pentecost Sunday, Peter preached a sermon that led to the conversion and baptism of three thousand persons. Here was a catch greater even than the one on the Lake of Gennesaret.

Peter and his partners, James and John, the sons of Zebedee, pulled their boats up on shore, left everything, and followed Jesus. It was quite a sacrifice to turn one's back on equipment and a business that had furnished the living for several families. The powerful word of Jesus compelled these men to follow. They become the first disciples, destined to be with Jesus on the Mount of Transfiguration, in the Garden of Gethsemane, and in that room with bolted doors on Easter Sunday evening. Then again they would hear encouraging words from Jesus: "Don't be afraid. Be my witnesses in all the world."

The man with leprosy

¹²**While Jesus was in one of the towns, a man came along who was covered with leprosy. When he saw Jesus, he fell with his face to the ground and begged him, "Lord, if you are willing, you can make me clean."**

¹³**Jesus reached out his hand and touched the man. "I am willing," he said. "Be clean!" And immediately the leprosy left him.**

¹⁴**Then Jesus ordered him, "Don't tell anyone, but go, show yourself to the priest and offer the sacrifices that Moses commanded for your cleansing, as a testimony to them."**

¹⁵**Yet the news about him spread all the more, so that crowds of people came to hear him and to be healed of their sicknesses. ¹⁶But Jesus often withdrew to lonely places and prayed.**

Peter had fallen at Jesus' knees acknowledging his sinfulness. The man with leprosy fell to the ground begging Jesus to make him clean.

The English word *leprosy* comes directly from the Greek and here does not necessarily refer to what modern medicine describes as leprosy, an affliction caused by Hansen's bacillus. It seems that in biblical times various kinds of skin diseases—such as psoriasis, lupus, and ringworm—were included under the term *leprosy*. Skin diseases were very common, and lepers are often mentioned in the gospels.

The Old Testament law ostracized a person who had an infectious skin disease. "The person with such an infectious disease must wear torn clothes, let his hair be unkempt, cover the lower part of his face and cry out, 'Unclean! Unclean!' As long as he has the infection he remains unclean. He must live alone; he must live outside the camp." (Leviticus 13:45,46)

This outcast knows that Jesus is able to make him clean; he only questions the willingness of Jesus to do so. His prayer is a model for us Christians. There should never be any doubt in our minds that God is able to help, but our prayer must always be "Your will be done." In humility we submit ourselves to the will of God.

The reply of Jesus is music to the ears of this man: "I am willing. . . . Be clean!" At once the man is cleansed from his leprosy. In the very same way, God's word of forgiveness cleanses us from all sin. Here is cause for rejoicing!

Jesus sends this man off at once to the priest to offer the proper sacrifices commanded by Moses (Leviticus 14:1-7). By this action Jesus wants to show the religious authorities that he had not come to overthrow law and order. Jesus recognized that there is indeed a proper place for the law in the lives of people. The law concerning the examination for leprosy was meant to protect public health, and Jesus heeds this law. In several stories that follow, we will hear how Jesus comes into conflict with the Pharisees and the teachers of the law over some of his activities which they regard as sinful.

In 4:37 Luke notes how the news about Jesus was spreading; now this information is repeated to emphasize the increasing popularity of Jesus. Just as in Capernaum when the crowds came to hear him and be healed (4:40), so again lines of people stream to Jesus. But often Jesus needed time alone to pray, which provided spiritual refreshment and renewal from his strenuous life of service.

Jesus heals a paralytic

¹⁷**One day as he was teaching, Pharisees and teachers of the law, who had come from every village of Galilee and from Judea and Jerusalem, were sitting there. And the power of the Lord was present for him to heal the sick. ¹⁸Some men came carrying a paralytic on a mat and tried to take him into the house to lay him before Jesus. ¹⁹When they could not find a way to do this because of the crowd, they went up on the roof and lowered him on his mat through the tiles into the middle of the crowd, right in front of Jesus.**

²⁰**When Jesus saw their faith, he said, "Friend, your sins are forgiven."**

²¹**The Pharisees and the teachers of the law began thinking to themselves, "Who is this fellow who speaks blasphemy? Who can forgive sins but God alone?"**

²²**Jesus knew what they were thinking and asked, "Why are you thinking these things in your hearts? ²³Which is easier: to say, 'Your sins are forgiven,' or to say, 'Get up and walk'? ²⁴But that you may know that the Son of Man has authority on earth to forgive sins. . . ." He said to the paralyzed man, "I tell you, get up, take your mat and go home." ²⁵Immediately he stood up in front of them, took what he had been lying on and went home praising God. ²⁶Everyone was amazed and gave praise to God. They were filled with awe and said, "We have seen remarkable things today."**

This story is the first of several that describe the growing conflict between Jesus and the religious leadership of his day. Luke here mentions the Pharisees and the teachers of the law for the first time in his gospel. The name *Pharisee* likely means "separated ones." They were non-priestly interpreters of the law and advocated a rigorous practice of all the commandments, both those written and those handed down (as they believed) by oral tradition from the fathers of Israel. They separated themselves from the society of people whose observance of the law they considered too lax.

The teachers of the law are also called *scribes* or *lawyers* in some Bible translations. They may have been a specific group among the Pharisees who were specialists in the study and teaching of the law. This is a gathering of these law observers from all over the country to scrutinize the activities of the Galilean teacher and healer who was making such a sensation among the people.

As Jesus is teaching with the Pharisees sitting in the audience, four men come carrying a paralytic on a mat and attempt to enter the house to lay him before Jesus. Finding this impossible because of the crowd, they remove a part of the loosely constructed flat roof, lowering the disabled man directly in front of the Savior.

The faith of this paralytic and his friends is evident to Jesus. At once he says, "Friend, your sins are forgiven." Jesus had accepted the sinner Peter as one of his disciples. Jesus had healed the unclean leper. Now he declares this paralyzed man free from sin simply on the basis of faith. But this is more than the Pharisees and teachers of the law can take.

Nothing is said in protest, but Jesus knows what the Pharisees are thinking: "This is blasphemy! This man is making himself the equal of God, for only God has the right to forgive sins."

Jesus questions their thoughts and then proposes to validate his divine power to forgive by making this paralyzed man walk. Without waiting for the Pharisees to answer, Jesus orders the man to take up his mat and walk home. Immediately, the man stood up in front of them and went on his way, praising God. Everyone echoes the praise. Here was another remarkable event. The Greek word that Luke uses for "remarkable" is our English word *paradox*. It is sometimes translated as "contrary to opinion, unexpected, strange."

It was contrary to Jewish opinion that human beings had the power with a word to declare the forgiveness of sins to someone who had made no kind of sacrificial offering. Jesus demonstrates that "the Son of Man has authority on earth to forgive sins." The title "Son of Man" is quite common in the gospels. When applied to Jesus, his human nature is being emphasized. As a human being, Jesus has the power to forgive sins. This is a power Jesus passed on to his disciples (John 20:23) and likewise to the entire church. It is evident from what follows that the Pharisees who questioned the authority of Jesus to forgive remain unconvinced; their opposition to Jesus will grow fiercer and finally lead him to the cross.

The calling of Levi

²⁷**After this, Jesus went out and saw a tax collector by the name of Levi sitting at his tax booth. "Follow me," Jesus said to him, ²⁸and Levi got up, left everything and followed him.**

²⁹**Then Levi held a great banquet for Jesus at his house, and a large crowd of tax collectors and others were eating with them. ³⁰But the Pharisees and the teachers of the law who belonged to their sect complained to his disciples, "Why do you eat and drink with tax collectors and 'sinners'?"**

³¹**Jesus answered them, "It is not the healthy who need a doctor, but the sick. ³²I have not come to call the righteous, but sinners to repentance."**

The association of Jesus with sinners continues in this story of the call of Levi to become a disciple. Matthew 9:9 gives the name of this man as "Matthew," which suggests that either he originally had two names or perhaps his name was changed by Jesus.

Levi is a tax collector. The Latin translation uses the term "publicanus," a revenue agent, from which comes the familiar "publican" of the KJV. It might be more accurate to designate Levi's occupation as that of "toll collector," one engaged in the collection of indirect taxes such as tolls, tariffs, and customs. Such persons were generally looked down on by the Jews because they were working for the heathen Romans and had a reputation for dishonesty by overcharging.

At the call of Jesus, Levi, like Peter, left everything and followed. To celebrate his new life, Levi held a great banquet for Jesus, inviting a large crowd of his old friends in the toll collecting business. The Pharisees and scribes were offended, making their complaint to the disciples of Jesus. The Pharisees strictly observed the law of Leviticus 10:10: "You must distinguish between the holy and the common, between the unclean and the clean." Jesus was obviously not following this biblical precept.

Jesus answers the charge of guilt by association by comparing himself to a doctor. The doctor's work calls for him to associate with the sick; they are the ones who require his skilled care. Likewise with Jesus: he needs to be with sinners in order to bring them to repentance. With their self-righteous attitude, the Pharisees did not understand this loving concern that Jesus had for sinners.

Jesus questioned about fasting

³³They said to him, "John's disciples often fast and pray, and so do the disciples of the Pharisees, but yours go on eating and drinking."

³⁴Jesus answered, "Can you make the guests of the bridegroom fast while he is with them? ³⁵But the time will come when the bridegroom will be taken from them; in those days they will fast."

³⁶He told them this parable: "No one tears a patch from a new garment and sews it on an old one. If he does, he will have torn the new garment, and the patch from the new will not match the old. ³⁷And no one pours new wine into old wineskins. If he does, the new wine will burst the skins, the wine will run out and the wineskins will be ruined. ³⁸No, new wine must be poured into new wineskins. ³⁹And no one after drinking old wine wants the new, for he says, 'The old is better.'"

The word "they" that begins this section might seem to refer to the Pharisees from the previous story. Comparing Matthew 9:14 and Mark 2:18 makes it clear that the reference is to the people and the disciples of John. They are the ones who question Jesus about the custom of fasting. However, the answer of Jesus is directed not only to the questioners but also to the Pharisees who found the teaching of Jesus concerning the practice of fasting very deficient.

Fasting means to abstain from food and at times even from drinking water. Religious people would choose to fast for various reasons: to concentrate on prayer and meditation, as a form of self-punishment for some sin committed, or to evidence a disdain for the body and its needs. Luke 7:33 suggests that John was recognized as one who practiced fasting and who taught the same to his disciples. So did the Pharisees. How different Jesus and his disciples were! Many times we are told that Jesus attended banquets; many of his parables compare the kingdom of God to a banquet. The question put to Jesus is a valid one.

Jesus answers with a question of his own plus a parable. The question compares the time of the earthly presence of Jesus to that of the groom at the wedding banquet. Obviously, the guests don't do any fasting while they are all together for this joyous meal. But once the groom is gone, then they may fast. Jesus is saying that there will come a time when his disciples will fast—after his ascension into heaven. Jesus neither forbids nor commands his disciples to fast but simply states that they will do it. There may be good reasons why believers today will fast. But they dare not look down on others who refuse to fast.

The parable that Jesus tells illustrates a general truth about his teaching. Using the examples of mending a garment and putting wine in skins for storage, Jesus contrasts the old with the new. Jesus is a minister of the new covenant. This is the covenant of forgiveness. The new life in the Spirit breaks loose from the old mentality, which thrives on fault finding and concentration on meritorious observance of the law. The new cannot be patched onto the old; the new cannot be poured into the old. Applying this parable to the specific question about fasting, Jesus seems to indicate that fasting is included among those old practices that can't very well be patched with the new life of faith in the Spirit.

The closing comment made by Jesus in verse 39 reflects a fact so often observed: people like to keep the old and familiar. The old wine is better than the new. The new that Jesus brings is fiercely opposed by those who cling to the old. It is a truth also observed in the lives of Christians: the old self fights against the new self. But make no mistake—Jesus is on the side of the new.

Lord of the Sabbath

6 **One Sabbath Jesus was going through the grainfields, and his disciples began to pick some heads of grain, rub them in their hands and eat the kernels. ²Some of the Pharisees asked, "Why are you doing what is unlawful on the Sabbath?"**

³Jesus answered them, "Have you never read what David did when he and his companions were hungry? ⁴He entered the

house of God, and taking the consecrated bread, he ate what is lawful only for priests to eat. And he also gave some to his companions." ⁵Then Jesus said to them, "The Son of Man is Lord of the Sabbath."

⁶On another Sabbath he went into the synagogue and was teaching, and a man was there whose right hand was shriveled. ⁷The Pharisees and the teachers of the law were looking for a reason to accuse Jesus, so they watched him closely to see if he would heal on the Sabbath. ⁸But Jesus knew what they were thinking and said to the man with the shriveled hand, "Get up and stand in front of everyone." So he got up and stood there.

⁹Then Jesus said to them, "I ask you, which is lawful on the Sabbath: to do good or to do evil, to save life or to destroy it?"

¹⁰He looked around at them all, and then said to the man, "Stretch out your hand." He did so, and his hand was completely restored. ¹¹But they were furious and began to discuss with one another what they might do to Jesus.

Keeping the Sabbath as a day of rest was one of the fundamental laws of the Jews. From the holy mountain of Sinai, Israel had heard the Lord God say, "Remember the Sabbath day by keeping it holy. For in six days the LORD made the heavens and the earth, but he rested on the seventh day. Therefore the LORD blessed the Sabbath day and made it holy" (Exodus 20:8,11). In Exodus 34:21 this prohibition of labor is applied specifically: "Even during the plowing season and harvest you must rest." The Saturday rest was meant to remind the believing Israelite of God's gracious and wondrous creation of the world and everything in it.

Over the years the priests and teachers of the law had worked out a very elaborate set of rules to help the people determine what could and could not be done on the Sabbath, what activities were within the law and which were forbidden. Jesus and his disciples are caught doing two of those forbidden activities: harvesting grain and giving aid to someone whose life was not in danger.

To answer the first charge, Jesus refers to the story in 1 Samuel 21:1-6 that relates how David ate of the consecrated bread in the tent of God at Nob. This was bread that only the priests were to eat, but it was the chief priest who gave the bread to David and his companions. The law was broken to satisfy human hunger. Moreover, Jesus claims an authority even greater than judicial precedent for what the disciples had done: Jesus had permitted his disciples to harvest the grain because "the Son of Man is Lord of the Sabbath."

After this claim of lordship over the Sabbath, it is no wonder that the Pharisees and teachers of the law were on the watch to discover other violations. On another Sabbath, while they were with Jesus in the synagogue, they got what they were looking for. Jesus healed a man whose hand was shriveled. The help Jesus gave might just as well have waited till a day other than the Sabbath. But Jesus showed that one should not wait to do good.

The Pharisees and teachers of the law are furious; the Greek says, "they were filled with madness." One is reminded of the people in the synagogue at Nazareth who attempted to kill Jesus by pushing him over the cliff (4:28,29). Discussions among the enemies of Jesus now centered upon this topic: What are we going to do about Jesus? You will notice the cross always looms in the background as Jesus identifies more and more with the sinner and the hurting.

Before leaving this story, an additional comment is necessary about the keeping of the Third Commandment. This is the only one of the Ten Commandments that is not repeated in the New Testament by Jesus or his apostles as binding on Christians. Rather, Paul writes to the Colossians,

"Therefore do not let anyone judge you by what you eat or drink, or with regard to a religious festival, a New Moon celebration or a Sabbath day" (2:16). Nor should we regard Sunday as a kind of New Testament Sabbath. Sunday is the first day of the new week and celebrates not the old creation but the new life initiated by the resurrection of Christ from the dead.

The twelve apostles

¹²**One of those days Jesus went out to a mountainside to pray, and spent the night praying to God. ¹³When morning came, he called his disciples to him and chose twelve of them, whom he also designated apostles: ¹⁴Simon (whom he named Peter), his brother Andrew, James, John, Philip, Bartholomew, ¹⁵Matthew, Thomas, James son of Alphaeus, Simon who was called the Zealot, ¹⁶Judas son of James, and Judas Iscariot, who became a traitor.**

With this section Luke turns our attention away from the conflicts with the Pharisees and teachers of the law to report on the training of the twelve apostles. The enemies of Jesus were intent on getting rid of him. By choosing the twelve apostles, Jesus guaranteed that even after his service on this earth was completed, the mission of carrying the gospel into all the world would go on.

The choice of the apostles came after Jesus had spent a night in the hills praying to God. As there were 12 tribes in Israel, so Jesus selects 12 men from the larger number of his disciples to be leaders of the new Israel, the holy Christian church.

The word *disciple* means "one who learns." The word *apostle* means "one who is sent out, a missionary." The list of names as given by Luke differs only slightly from those in Mark 3:16-19. Judas son of James is given the name Thaddaeus by Mark. Perhaps this alternate name is to distinguish him from the traitor Judas.

Blessings and woes

¹⁷He went down with them and stood on a level place. A large crowd of his disciples was there and a great number of people from all over Judea, from Jerusalem, and from the coast of Tyre and Sidon, ¹⁸who had come to hear him and to be healed of their diseases. Those troubled by evil spirits were cured, ¹⁹and the people all tried to touch him, because power was coming from him and healing them all.

²⁰Looking at his disciples, he said:

> "Blessed are you who are poor,
> for yours is the kingdom of God.
> ²¹ Blessed are you who hunger now,
> for you will be satisfied.
> Blessed are you who weep now,
> for you will laugh.
> ²² Blessed are you when men hate you,
> when they exclude you and insult you
> and reject your name as evil, because of the
> Son of Man.

²³"Rejoice in that day and leap for joy, because great is your reward in heaven. For that is how their fathers treated the prophets.

> ²⁴ "But woe to you who are rich,
> for you have already received your comfort.
> ²⁵ Woe to you who are well fed now,
> for you will go hungry.
> Woe to you who laugh now,
> for you will mourn and weep.
> ²⁶ Woe to you when all men speak well of you,
> for that is how their fathers treated the
> false prophets.

Having chosen the twelve apostles, Jesus now begins to give them intensive training. First of all, he introduces them to the masses in need of their ministry. After coming down from the hills where they had been (6:12), Jesus and the

Twelve stand on a level place to receive the multitudes. Not only does a large crowd of disciples gather; a great number of people from all over Judea, from Jerusalem, and from the seacoast of Tyre and Sidon come to hear and to be healed. This is Luke's first mention of Tyre and Sidon, cities located along the Mediterranean Sea, largely inhabited by gentile people. The narrow confines of the Jewish synagogue are left behind as Jesus faces this throng of people from all over. Those troubled by evil spirits are cured; all with illnesses press around him seeking only to touch him that they might be healed. This is truly an awesome experience for the apostles (much like Peter's great catch of fish).

It is in this context that Luke records words of Jesus which must have been spoken by him on a number of occasions. Very similar words are found in Matthew chapters 5 to 7, the Sermon on the Mount. The teaching is addressed specifically to his disciples who are addressed with the personal pronoun "you." These are words for the apostles to hear for themselves; these words also serve as a model for apostolic preaching in the future.

The teaching begins with contrasting blessings and woes. Each of the eight statements is a paradox, an assertion that is contrary to what people generally think. The world hardly regards the poor, the hungry, those who weep, and those who are hated as being blessed. But that is the declaration Jesus makes. The world does not think of the rich, the well-fed, those who laugh, and those whom all speak well of as being unfortunate. Yet that is the woe pronounced by Jesus.

The term *beatitude* is used to describe the sentences that begin "blessed are . . ." This is a very familiar form in the Bible. Psalm 1 begins, "Blessed is the man who . . ." Proverbs 3:13 says, "Blessed is the man who finds wisdom, the man who gains understanding." Seven beatitudes are found in Revelation, including these words: "Blessed are those who are invited to the wedding supper of the Lamb!" (19:9). Beatitudes may describe the happiness one enjoys in this life or in the life to come.

Jesus is speaking about the happiness his disciples will enjoy in heaven. In this life they may be poor and hungry and sad and hated. Yet when days like that come, he urges them to rejoice and leap for joy because "great is your reward in heaven." Before teaching them anything about how they are to conduct themselves in this world, Jesus sets the ultimate goal before the disciples.

Each of these four beatitudes is matched with that striking word of warning: "woe." Luke 11:42-52 has a series of woes pronounced against the Pharisees and other opponents of Jesus. But in this section of Luke, the woes are meant as warnings for the disciples. They are warned against taking comfort in riches, good food and entertainment, and a reputation gained by avoiding genuine commitment to Christ. Earthly pleasures can so easily replace striving for true blessedness. Jesus warns his disciples so that they will be on guard.

Each section of beatitudes and woes closes out with a reference to the way in which "their fathers" treated the prophets, both those true and false. By "their fathers" Jesus means Old Testament Israel, who often listened to false prophets but rejected the warnings of the true prophets. Preaching before the Jewish Sanhedrin, Stephen shouted, "You stiff-necked people . . . ! You are just like your fathers: You always resist the Holy Spirit!" (Acts 7:51). Jesus was preparing his disciples for the persecution that was coming, often from fellow countrymen of the house of Israel. How important for the followers of Jesus always to keep the ultimate goal in mind—the blessedness of life in the kingdom of God.

Love for enemies

²⁷"But I tell you who hear me: Love your enemies, do good to those who hate you, ²⁸bless those who curse you, pray for those who mistreat you. ²⁹If someone strikes you on one cheek, turn to him the other also. If someone takes your cloak, do not stop him from taking your tunic. ³⁰Give to everyone who asks you, and if anyone takes what belongs to you, do not demand it back. ³¹Do to others as you would have them do to you.

³²"If you love those who love you, what credit is that to you? Even 'sinners' love those who love them. ³³And if you do good to those who are good to you, what credit is that to you? Even 'sinners' do that. ³⁴And if you lend to those from whom you expect repayment, what credit is that to you? Even 'sinners' lend to 'sinners,' expecting to be repaid in full. ³⁵But love your enemies, do good to them, and lend to them without expecting to get anything back. Then your reward will be great, and you will be sons of the Most High, because he is kind to the ungrateful and wicked. ³⁶Be merciful, just as your Father is merciful.

In the fourth of the previous beatitudes, Jesus alerted his disciples to the fact that they would be hated, excluded, and insulted (6:22). A person who experiences such treatment might be tempted to respond in a similar manner. Jesus, however, commands an altogether different kind of behavior, one totally unexpected in this world. He says to his listeners: "Love your enemies, do good to those who hate you, bless those who curse you, pray for those who mistreat you."

A Greek writer living some years before the birth of Jesus expresses what was the common sentiment: "I considered it established that one should do harm to one's enemies and be of service to one's friends." How very different is the advice Jesus gives! Jesus cites three cases, or situations, and describes a loving response for each: what to do when someone hits you on the cheek, what to do when someone takes your cloak, what to do when someone takes what belongs to you.

Is Jesus being serious? Can a person live this way in the real world? Isn't this kind of idealism impossible to carry out? Obviously, Jesus is much in touch with the real world. He knows the way people generally react in the situations described. What he is saying, in a way which shocks us, is that disciples need to act differently from the world. A loving person will not automatically respond in the usual manner. The specific command of Jesus is not so much a rule of behavior to be followed mechanically as it is a stimulus for the mind to draw out the implications for life in general. As disciples of Jesus, we need to think lovingly in our dealings with people, even with our enemies.

The three situations described by Jesus are followed by three questions all concluding with the same words: "What credit is that to you?" To love those who love you, to do good to those who do good to you, to lend to those from whom you expect repayment—these are all things which even "sinners" (non-disciples) do. Jesus is looking for a higher standard of behavior. He teaches his disciples to break the pattern of reciprocity, the pattern of doing either bad or good based on what others do to us. He is saying, "Don't do bad because you are treated badly; don't just do good to those who treat you well."

Two motives are cited for this kind of behavior. The first is the so-called Golden Rule. One who experiences totally undeserved love knows how wonderful it is and treats others in just that way. The second motive is the manner in which the heavenly Father treats people: he is kind to the ungrateful and the wicked. Be merciful as he is.

Jesus promises a great reward for those who act in this manner. He used the same word in 6:23 ("reward in heaven"). This mention of reward does not at all imply that we are saved by our good works, by our love. Rather, this is a reward that Jesus promises freely and graciously to console his hated and persecuted disciples. It is a reward that comes to them totally unexpectedly, not a reward for which they consciously work.

Judging others

³⁷"Do not judge, and you will not be judged. Do not condemn, and you will not be condemned. Forgive, and you will be forgiven. ³⁸Give, and it will be given to you. A good measure, pressed down, shaken together and running over, will be poured into your lap. For with the measure you use, it will be measured to you."

³⁹He also told them this parable: "Can a blind man lead a blind man? Will they not both fall into a pit? ⁴⁰A student is not above his teacher, but everyone who is fully trained will be like his teacher.

⁴¹"Why do you look at the speck of sawdust in your brother's eye and pay no attention to the plank in your own eye? ⁴²How can you say to your brother, 'Brother, let me take the speck out of your eye,' when you yourself fail to see the plank in your own eye? You hypocrite, first take the plank out of your eye, and then you will see clearly to remove the speck from your brother's eye.

Love and generosity go together. It takes a very generous person to love an enemy, a loving person to give without expecting any return. The opposite of such a person is one who is constantly finding fault with others and condemning their actions.

The temptation to judge and condemn others is very real for the disciple of Jesus. The person who truly seeks to practice love may become more conscious of how others fail to love. Hence the warning: "Do not judge. . . . Do not condemn." Jesus links this prohibition with the promise "You will not be judged. . . . You will not be condemned." This could perhaps refer to human judgment: those critical of others will themselves often experience much criticism. Or the reference might be to God's final judgment.

The negatives are balanced by a double positive: forgive and give. Jesus uses a figure of speech drawn from the commerical world. The merchant first pours grain into a measuring jar, presses it down, shakes it together, and lets it overflow; then he empties the jar into the customer's "lap," into the loose-fitting garment that serves as the sack to carry the grain home. Such is the generosity enjoyed by the disciple who is generous. Here is another application of the Golden Rule (6:31).

The teaching of Jesus here concludes with four parables (6:39-49), four illustrations from life. The first concerns the importance of being able to see before presuming to lead others. Those who are blind don't make good guides. The disciple who is not himself enlightened should not dare to take on the responsibility of being a teacher. In verse 40 one senses that perhaps Jesus is directing some words against students of his who imagined they knew more than the teacher. No student of Jesus should ever dare to correct the teacher but must continually seek to be like the teacher.

The second parable is very familiar and often quoted. It is directed against the disciple who is oblivious to his own failings but eagerly takes on the role of inspecting the lives of other disciples for defects. The extreme contrasting terms used by Jesus—speck of sawdust versus plank—provoke a chuckle. But the term "hypocrite" being applied to such a person shows how serious Jesus is when he warns against fault-finding. As used by Jesus, this word has a more general meaning than just one who pretends to be what he is not. It is a strong term of condemnation often applied to Pharisees; here it is directed to one claiming to be a disciple of Jesus. Any disciple who desires to be a teacher of others must see very clearly before daring to correct the lives of others. The blind can't lead the blind.

A tree and its fruit

[43]"No good tree bears bad fruit, nor does a bad tree bear good fruit. [44]Each tree is recognized by its own fruit. People do not pick figs from thornbushes, or grapes from briers. [45]The good man brings good things out of the good stored up in his heart, and the evil man brings evil things out of the evil stored up in his heart. For out of the overflow of his heart his mouth speaks.

After a parable about a speck of sawdust and a plank, Jesus directs attention to the live tree. John the Baptist had warned that "every tree that does not produce good fruit will be cut down and thrown into the fire" (3:9). Jesus also uses the tree and its fruit as an illustration of a person's life. He draws two lessons: the quality of the fruit demonstrates the worth of the tree; the kind of fruit borne identifies the tree. One can judge a tree by its fruits. This lesson is illustrated by two additional examples: people do not pick figs from thornbushes or grapes from briers. Again Jesus makes his two points: good (figs, grapes) doesn't come from bad (thornbushes, briers); a plant is identified by the kind of fruit it bears.

These lessons from nature are now applied to people. The good man brings good things out of the good stored in the heart; the evil man brings evil things out of the evil stored in the heart. One can't expect anything else, as nature also testifies. The kind of fruit a person bears identifies the quality of the person.

All actions, including the words one speaks, originate in the heart. For a disciple to bring forth the fruits of faith, a life characterized by love and generosity, the heart must first of all be good. A good heart is one that in all humility confesses sin and clings to Christ for pardon and peace. Such a heart will bring forth good fruit.

The wise and foolish builders

⁴⁶"Why do you call me, 'Lord, Lord,' and do not do what I say? ⁴⁷I will show you what he is like who comes to me and hears my words and puts them into practice. ⁴⁸He is like a man building a house, who dug down deep and laid the foundation on rock. When a flood came, the torrent struck that house but could not shake it, because it was well built. ⁴⁹But the one who hears my words and does not put them into practice is like a man who built a house on the ground without a foundation. The moment the torrent struck that house, it collapsed and its destruction was complete."

In this fourth parable, which concludes his section of teachings, Jesus talks about two men who build houses. The one laid the foundation on rock; the other simply built his house on the ground. The first house withstood the torrent of water that struck when a flood came; the other collapsed in total ruin.

These two builders are like two kinds of listeners: the one hears the words of Jesus and puts them into practice; the other only hears without putting the words into practice. We are reminded of a beatitude that Jesus speaks later in this gospel: "Blessed rather are those who hear the word of God and obey it" (11:28). Jesus does not only want to be called "Lord"; he wants his disciples to do what he says. To do so is to build a house that withstands the floods of life.

When we Christians examine our lives, we will find ourselves falling short of doing what Jesus says. His teaching in this part of Luke is primarily law. One of the purposes of the law of God is to reveal our sinfulness and drive us into the arms of the Savior. When we consider the teachings of Jesus concerning love and generosity, we will become conscious of our own shortcomings; we will confess our sins and ask for forgiveness.

The law also serves as a guide for the Christian, giving us direction for our lives. There is much we can learn from frequent review of these teachings of Jesus: the blessings and woes, the command to love, and the warnings against judging others. A good life starts in the heart; here faith must rest on the solid foundation of Christ and his love. The builder of such a house will withstand whatever floods may come.

This sermon of Jesus was spoken on a level place in the presence of a large crowd of disciples and a great number of people from various places (6:17). At the conclusion Luke says nothing about any crowd response. Often when Jesus had performed some miracle, Luke notes the amazement and praises of the people. It is almost as if these teachings of Jesus leave the disciples and the people in stunned silence. That may well be our response when we give serious thought to what Jesus here teaches about our lives as disciples.

The faith of the centurion

7 When Jesus had finished saying all this in the hearing of the people, he entered Capernaum. ²There a centurion's servant, whom his master valued highly, was sick and about to die. ³The centurion heard of Jesus and sent some elders of the Jews to him, asking him to come and heal his servant. ⁴When they came to Jesus, they pleaded earnestly with him, "The man deserves to have you do this, ⁵because he loves our nation and has built our synagogue." ⁶So Jesus went with them.

He was not far from the house when the centurion sent friends to say to him: "Lord, don't trouble yourself, for I do not deserve to have you come under my roof. ⁷That is why I did not even consider myself worthy to come to you. But say the word, and my servant will be healed. ⁸For I myself am a man under authority, with soldiers under me. I tell this one, 'Go,' and he goes; and that one, 'Come,' and he comes. I say to my servant, 'Do this,' and he does it."

⁹When Jesus heard this, he was amazed at him, and turning to the crowd following him, he said, "I tell you, I have not found such great faith even in Israel." ¹⁰Then the men who had been sent returned to the house and found the servant well.

After finishing his teaching to the multitudes, Jesus returns once more to the city of Capernaum. Luke had mentioned Capernaum previously in 4:31. On that occasion Jesus had gone to the synagogue, where he cured a man possessed by a demon. That very synagogue had been built by the Roman centurion who figures into the present story.

The word *centurion* means "captain of a company of one hundred soldiers." Since Herod Antipas was the ruler of Galilee, in which province Capernaum was located, this centurion may have been in Herod's service in some official capacity. A warm feeling had developed between this centurion and the Jewish elders who had charge of the synagogue.

Several times Luke has reported Jesus healing numbers of sick without going into detail (4:40; 6:18,19). Here he gives us the full story for several reasons: this centurion was no doubt a Gentile, and this man shows great faith in the power of Jesus' word. He is a model for the many gentile believers who would be coming into the church in future years.

The delegation of Jewish elders, sent by the centurion to beg help for his critically ill servant, told Jesus that "this man *deserves* to have you do this." They were thinking of the love this man had shown to the Jewish nation.

But the centurion felt no worthiness. As Jesus came near his home, he sent friends to say, "I *do not deserve* to have you come under my roof." Because of his feelings of unworthiness, he had not come to Jesus originally; he had sent the delegation of Jewish elders. (Here Luke gives a fuller account of this story than we find in Matthew 8:5-13.)

The centurion goes on to declare his great confidence in the word of Jesus. It was not necessary for Jesus to touch the sick servant (as the sick had sought to touch Jesus in 6:19). Even as the centurion commanded those under him with a word, so Jesus need only speak the word and the servant would be healed.

Now it is Jesus' turn to be amazed! Many had been astonished at what Jesus had said and done. The faith of this centurion causes Jesus to marvel (Luke uses a Greek word which has that meaning). The faith of this Gentile was greater than any Jesus had found among the people of Israel. The healing that Jesus effects is not nearly so celebrated in this story as the marvelous faith of the centurion. Here also is a miracle! We would do well today to likewise celebrate the marvelous miracle of faith that the Spirit works through the Word.

Jesus raises a widow's son

¹¹Soon afterward, Jesus went to a town called Nain, and his disciples and a large crowd went along with him. ¹²As he approached the town gate, a dead person was being carried out—the only son of his mother, and she was a widow. And a large crowd from the town was with her. ¹³When the Lord saw her, his heart went out to her and he said, "Don't cry."

¹⁴Then he went up and touched the coffin, and those carrying it stood still. He said, "Young man, I say to you, get up!" ¹⁵The dead man sat up and began to talk, and Jesus gave him back to his mother.

¹⁶They were all filled with awe and praised God. "A great prophet has appeared among us," they said. "God has come to help his people." ¹⁷This news about Jesus spread throughout Judea and the surrounding country.

The help that Jesus gave to the centurion by healing his servant is now extended to a woman whose only son had

Raising of the widow's son at Nain

died. Both Gentiles and women were on the fringes of Jewish society. Jesus shows himself to be the Savior of all people.

Nain is a town in southern Galilee situated a few miles southwest of Nazareth. It is located 25 miles from Capernaum. Jesus journeyed there accompanied by his disciples and a large crowd. All of them will witness this very public and amazing miracle.

As Jesus approaches the town gate, he is met by a funeral procession. Burials took place outside towns, and graves have been found to the southeast of Nain. The body of the dead man was being carried on an open coffin similar, no doubt, to a stretcher.

Jesus at once takes command of the situation. A mother is weeping bitterly; he says to her, "Don't cry." Then with the voice of authority, he puts his hand on the coffin, and the procession halts. His words ring out clearly: "Young man, I say to you, get up!" One does not ordinarily speak such words to a corpse, but Jesus is no ordinary person. In response to this order, the dead man sits up.

It is noteworthy that Luke introduces the word "Lord" into this story. It is the Lord whose heart goes out to this widow. Jesus is the Lord who had authority to forgive sins (5:24). He is Lord of the Sabbath (6:5). Here he shows himself Lord even of death itself. The centurion testified to the power of that word; here it is fully evidenced.

As so often happened when Jesus performed a public miracle, the crowd is filled with awe and praises God. They call Jesus "a great prophet." They were perhaps comparing him to the great Old Testament prophet Elijah, remembering what Elijah had done.

In 1 Kings 17:17-24 there is an account of how Elijah raised to life a boy who had died. Elijah did this by stretching himself three times over the boy and crying out to the Lord: "O LORD my God, let this boy's life return to him!"

His prayer was answered, and we read that Elijah "gave him to his mother." Luke uses similar words to describe how Jesus gave the now living son back to his mother.

But the way in which Jesus worked this miracle is altogether greater than in the case of Elijah. By his own word, with no prayer to any higher being, Jesus commanded the young man to get up. Truly, here is the Lord, true God and true man. Even death must bow before him!

Jesus and John the Baptist

¹⁸John's disciples told him about all these things. Calling two of them, ¹⁹he sent them to the Lord to ask, "Are you the one who was to come, or should we expect someone else?"

²⁰When the men came to Jesus, they said, "John the Baptist sent us to you to ask, 'Are you the one who was to come, or should we expect someone else?'"

²¹At that very time Jesus cured many who had diseases, sicknesses and evil spirits, and gave sight to many who were blind. ²²So he replied to the messengers, "Go back and report to John what you have seen and heard: The blind receive sight, the lame walk, those who have leprosy are cured, the deaf hear, the dead are raised, and the good news is preached to the poor. ²³Blessed is the man who does not fall away on account of me."

²⁴After John's messengers left, Jesus began to speak to the crowd about John: "What did you go out into the desert to see? A reed swayed by the wind? ²⁵If not, what did you go out to see? A man dressed in fine clothes? No, those who wear expensive clothes and indulge in luxury are in palaces. ²⁶But what did you go out to see? A prophet? Yes, I tell you, and more than a prophet. ²⁷This is the one about whom it is written:

"'I will send my messenger ahead of you,
who will prepare your way before you.'

²⁸I tell you, among those born of women there is no one greater than John; yet the one who is least in the kingdom of God is greater than he."

²⁹(All the people, even the tax collectors, when they heard Jesus' words, acknowledged that God's way was right, because they had been baptized by John. ³⁰But the Pharisees and experts in the law rejected God's purpose for themselves, because they had not been baptized by John.)

³¹"To what, then, can I compare the people of this generation? What are they like? ³²They are like children sitting in the marketplace and calling out to each other:

" 'We played the flute for you,
    and you did not dance;
we sang a dirge,
    and you did not cry.'

³³For John the Baptist came neither eating bread nor drinking wine, and you say, 'He has a demon.' ³⁴The Son of Man came eating and drinking, and you say, 'Here is a glutton and a drunkard, a friend of tax collectors and "sinners." ' ³⁵But wisdom is proved right by all her children."

We heard in the previous section how the crowd evaluated Jesus: they took him to be "a great prophet." Many miles away from the event that took place in Nain, a prisoner heard reports of what was happening in Galilee. The prisoner was John the Baptist. Herod Antipas had locked him up (3:20) in the fortress Machaerus, located on a solitary peak on the east side of the Dead Sea. Its ruins can still be seen today.

John sent two of his disciples to the Lord Jesus with the question "Are you the one who was to come, or should we expect someone else?" This question has been interpreted in two ways. Some hold that John himself was still convinced that Jesus was the promised Messiah, the Coming One, but he wanted to renew the faith of his disciples and therefore sent them to Jesus to be strengthened.

Others see this question as an example of how even such a person as John, the messenger called to prepare the way of the Lord, could waver. As a prisoner, isolated and cut off from the events taking place, he might have fallen prey to doubts. John had spoken of the role Jesus would fulfill as fiery judge (3:17). Up to this point, John's disciples were reporting much popular acclaim accorded to Jesus but little signs of his coming role as judge of the world. John may well have been confused.

The question John asks through his disciples gives Jesus the opportunity to again point out his role as the Messiah, the Servant of God. He had done this in the synagogue at Nazareth (4:18,19) quoting words of Isaiah 61:1,2. Now Jesus again refers to these words and shows how he is fulfilling them. He sends the disciples back to John, instructing them to report what they had heard and seen. Jesus points to his miracles, including also the raising of the dead at Nain, as evidence that he is the one promised in the Old Testament. His message to John: Don't look for any other messiah.

Jesus' response to the disciples of John concludes with a beatitude: "Blessed is the man who does not fall away on account of me." The words "fall away" are a translation of a Greek verb which pictures a person stumbling over a stone. Jesus is that stone over which some do stumble (1 Peter 2:8). The Pharisees and experts in the law did stumble over Jesus; so did the people at his home synagogue in Nazareth. Jesus is urging John and his disciples not to fall away. We need the same encouragement.

Jesus had spoken about his work as the Messiah. After the departure of John's messengers, he begins speaking about the work of John. He wants his listeners to realize the importance of John in God's plan of salvation and to appreciate John.

Three times Jesus challenges the crowd with the question: "What did you go out into the desert to see?" The use of the word "see" creates the impression that for many, John was a kind of curiosity, a spectacle. People certainly did not go out expecting to see someone frail and fickle, one like a thin reed swaying in the wind. Nor did they go into the desert for a fashion show; the palace is the place for expensive clothes.

Jesus answers his own question by telling the people what they expected of John: they took him for a prophet. And so he was. But he was, Jesus adds, "more than a prophet." John was a very special prophet, the prophet promised in Malachi 3:1, the messenger sent to prepare the way of the Lord. The people at Nain had called Jesus a great prophet. Such a title in the case of Jesus falls short of describing his true identity. But such a title is clearly appropriate for John. In fact, Jesus pays John the highest compliment: there is no greater human being than John. John receives such high praise because of the role assigned to him: he was the messenger who prepared the way for God's chosen Servant, Jesus Christ.

Yet as great as John was, Jesus adds that the least in the kingdom of God is greater than he. Jesus is talking about the eternal glory that all believers will enjoy in heaven. By referring to the glory enjoyed even by the least person in heaven, Jesus does not want to detract from the praise he has given to John. Rather, he directs us away from questions about earthly greatness to the surpassing joys of heaven. This was a lesson that his own apostles had a hard time learning.

What follows in verses 29 and 30 is put into parentheses because this is commentary by Luke and not words of Jesus. All the people who had been baptized by John, tax collectors included, agreed with what Jesus had said about John, that he truly was the prophet through whom God was working. On the other hand the Pharisees and experts in the law refused to be baptized by John, thus rejecting God's way of salvation.

Following the parentheses, Jesus' words continue. He criticizes the people living at that time because they found fault both with John and with him. Jesus refers to children who shout to one another: we played flute music for you, but you did not dance; we played a dirge, but no one cried. Nothing seemed to move these people. John was too strict and sober for them; Jesus was criticized for advising against fasting and even attending banquets with tax collectors and sinners. Though the crowds praised the mighty deeds of Jesus, they had not turned over their hearts to him.

Jesus concludes with a brief proverb: "Wisdom is proved right by all her children." That's similar to our saying "Time will tell." In the end, people will find out that both John and Jesus had roles to fulfill in God's plan of salvation. John's work was to prepare the way of the Lord by warning of the coming judgment; Jesus' work was to embody God's love and mercy for sinners, to seek and to save the lost. It was this role which led him ultimately to the cross.

Jesus anointed by a sinful woman

36Now one of the Pharisees invited Jesus to have dinner with him, so he went to the Pharisee's house and reclined at the table. 37When a woman who had lived a sinful life in that town learned that Jesus was eating at the Pharisee's house, she brought an alabaster jar of perfume, 38and as she stood behind him at his feet weeping, she began to wet his feet with tears. Then she wiped them with her hair, kissed them and poured perfume on them.

39When the Pharisee who had invited him saw this, he said to himself, "If this man were a prophet, he would know who is touching him and what kind of woman she is—that she is a sinner."

40Jesus answered him, "Simon, I have something to tell you."

"Tell me, teacher," he said.

41"Two men owed money to a certain moneylender. One owed him five hundred denarii, and the other fifty. 42Neither of them had

the money to pay him back, so he canceled the debts of both. Now which of them will love him more?"

⁴³Simon replied, "I suppose the one who had the bigger debt canceled."

"You have judged correctly," Jesus said.

⁴⁴Then he turned toward the woman and said to Simon, "Do you see this woman? I came into your house. You did not give me any water for my feet, but she wet my feet with her tears and wiped them with her hair. ⁴⁵You did not give me a kiss, but this woman, from the time I entered, has not stopped kissing my feet. ⁴⁶You did not put oil on my head, but she has poured perfume on my feet. ⁴⁷Therefore, I tell you, her many sins have been forgiven—for she loved much. But he who has been forgiven little loves little."

⁴⁸Then Jesus said to her, "Your sins are forgiven."

⁴⁹The other guests began to say among themselves, "Who is this who even forgives sins?"

⁵⁰Jesus said to the woman, "Your faith has saved you; go in peace."

It seems that Jesus did not turn down many invitations to a meal. He went to the wedding at Cana (John 2:1-11). He accepted the invitation of the tax collector Levi to attend the banquet in his home (Luke 5:29). At that banquet the Pharisees and teachers of the law found fault with Jesus for eating with tax collectors and sinners. This was the complaint against Jesus voiced by many of the people of his generation, as we heard in the previous portion of Luke's gospel (7:34).

In view of his ready acceptance of invitations, it does not surprise us that Jesus was willing to have dinner at the house of a Pharisee named Simon. One is more surprised that this Pharisee would extend such an invitation. There is the likelihood that it was not out of love for Jesus or with the desire to learn from him. Rather, the Pharisee may actually have wanted to add to that list of items for which Jesus might be criticized. The unsocial reception that Jesus received from the Pharisee (verses 44-46) indicates that he felt no deep affection for Jesus.

The incident reminds us of what is reported back in 6:7: "The Pharisees and the teachers of the law were looking for a reason to accuse Jesus, so they watched him closely to see if he would heal on the Sabbath." The presence of the sinful woman provided a similar opportunity for this Pharisee to accuse Jesus.

The woman who had lived a sinful life is not identified by name. Tradition seems to think she was Mary Magdalene, from whom seven demons had come out (8:2), but there is no proof for that. The woman's sinful life may have been that of a harlot. Learning that Jesus was at the home of the Pharisee, she brought an alabaster jar of perfume. Alabaster is a kind of soft stone, yellow or cream colored.

Those attending a banquet in Bible times would recline on a couch while eating, their feet and legs extended. This permitted the woman to stand behind Jesus at his feet. She began to wet his feet with her tears and then wipe them with her hair; she kissed them and poured perfume on them. We cannot judge this action by modern conventions. In Palestine, where washing of feet with water was customary, her action would not seem to have been quite so out of place—though still unusual. We need to note the gracious way in which Jesus received this sign of love and affection.

The Pharisee also takes note and is offended. He says nothing aloud, but his thoughts are filled with disgust. The crowds judged Jesus to be a great prophet (7:16). This Pharisee draws another conclusion: If Jesus were a prophet, he would know that this was a sinful woman and not allow her to even touch him.

Knowing what the Pharisee was thinking, Jesus tells him a story. Two men owed money, one man ten times as much as the other. (A denarius was a coin worth about a day's wages.) Neither could pay the moneylender; in mercy he canceled the debts of both. Simon caught the point of the parable: the man with the bigger debt would have more love for the moneylender.

Jesus now applies this parable to the Pharisee and the sinful woman. The Pharisee had shown no love for Jesus; on the other hand, the woman had shown an abundance of love. By her love she demonstrated the abundance of the forgiveness that she had received.

Verse 47 could seem to say that this sinful woman was forgiven because she had shown such great love. But the parable of Jesus clearly shows that forgiveness had come prior to the show of love: first the debt was canceled, and this then resulted in love for the moneylender. First this woman had received forgiveness from Jesus; then she showed her love for him. The NEB translation of the verse makes this point clear: "Her great love proves that her many sins have been forgiven."

In order to reassure this woman and for the sake of the Pharisee and his guests, Jesus says to her: "Your sins are forgiven." This provokes the same kind of question that was raised in the case of the paralytic (5:21). Jesus does not respond to the question but rather speaks a final word of blessing to the sinful woman: "Your faith has saved you; go in peace."

Jesus had praised the great faith of the centurion (7:9). Here another person on the fringe of society, a woman who had lived a sinful life, proves her great faith by her love. Faith saves, but faith is never alone. A living faith will demonstrate itself by love for the Savior. This woman chose to show her love in a unique and unusual way. Everyone who has truly experienced the forgiveness of sins will find ways to show love for Jesus.

The parable of the sower

8 After this, Jesus traveled about from one town and village to another, proclaiming the good news of the kingdom of God. The Twelve were with him, ²and also some women who had been cured of evil spirits and diseases: Mary (called Magdalene) from whom seven demons had come out; ³Joanna the wife of Cuza, the manager of Herod's household; Susanna; and many others. These women were helping to support them out of their own means.

⁴While a large crowd was gathering and people were coming to Jesus from town after town, he told this parable: ⁵"A farmer went out to sow his seed. As he was scattering the seed, some fell along the path; it was trampled on, and the birds of the air ate it up. ⁶Some fell on rock, and when it came up, the plants withered because they had no moisture. ⁷Other seed fell among thorns, which grew up with it and choked the plants. ⁸Still other seed fell on good soil. It came up and yielded a crop, a hundred times more than was sown."

When he said this, he called out, "He who has ears to hear, let him hear."

⁹His disciples asked him what this parable meant. ¹⁰He said, "The knowledge of the secrets of the kingdom of God has been given to you, but to others I speak in parables, so that,

> "'though seeing, they may not see;
> though hearing, they may not understand.'

¹¹"This is the meaning of the parable: The seed is the word of God. ¹²Those along the path are the ones who hear, and then the devil comes and takes away the word from their hearts, so that they may not believe and be saved. ¹³Those on the rock are the ones who receive the word with joy when they hear it, but they have no root. They believe for a while, but in the time of testing they fall away. ¹⁴The seed that fell among thorns stands for those who hear, but as they go on their way they are choked by life's worries, riches and pleasures, and they do not mature. ¹⁵But the seed on good soil stands for those with a noble and good heart, who hear the word, retain it, and by persevering produce a crop.

In a number of passages Luke includes general summaries of the activities of Jesus. One of these is found in 4:44, where specific mention is made of the fact that Jesus preached in the synagogues. In the summary that begins chapter 8, there is no mention of the synagogues. It seems that more and more, Jesus is doing open-air preaching (see 6:17). His message remains the same as that proclaimed in the synagogue at Nazareth (4:18): the good news of the kingdom of God.

On this preaching tour Jesus is accompanied by the twelve apostles and some women. For the apostles this is practical training for the time when they would be sent out (9:1,2). Three women are named: Mary, who came from the village of Magdala on the west shore of the Sea of Galilee; Joanna, whose husband held an important position in the household of Herod Antipas; and Susanna. In addition, there are other women not named. The mention of Herod indicates that the message of Jesus was reaching into the homes of some prominent families of the land. These women helped to support the ministry of Jesus with their money. In this they furnish an excellent example for Christian men and women today.

Luke pays special attention to women in his gospel. One thinks of Elizabeth, Mary, Anna, Simon's mother-in-law, the widow at Nain, and the sinful woman of the last section. The women named here will be important witnesses to the resurrection. They are mentioned as observing the place of the burial of Christ (23:55); Mary Magdalene and Joanna are named by Luke as being among the women who went to the tomb on Easter morning (24:10).

The preaching tours of Jesus met with considerable success when judged by the numbers who gathered to listen. But from the parable which Jesus tells, it is obvious that not all who came were truly listening. As Jesus experienced this in his ministry, he wanted the disciples to understand this fact as well.

The parable of the sower is a familiar one and is recorded also by Matthew and Mark. Jesus tells about a farmer sowing seed. The seed fell in various places: along the path running through the field, on rocky soil, among thorns, and on good soil. The seed that fell on good soil yielded a crop a hundred times more than what was sown. The seed that fell elsewhere did not produce a crop, for reasons given in the parable.

When Jesus had finished the parable, he issued a challenge: "He who has ears to hear, let him hear." This appeal to listen is repeated in 14:35 and is also found in a slightly altered form at the conclusion of each of the seven letters to the churches in Revelation chapters 2 and 3. Jesus knows how hard it is for people to really listen to his Word, how many distractions and temptations there are that keep the Word from bearing fruit. Therefore this challenge is for all those with ears: Listen!

We who have heard the parable of Jesus explained so often might find it hard to understand why his disciples would have to ask what this story of the sower and his seed was all about. Jesus answers by first giving his reasons for speaking in parables at all. To the disciples the knowledge of the secrets of the kingdom of God is given; to others (nondisciples) everything will remain a parable, a riddle. People generally are charmed by the simplicity of the parables told by Jesus. Yet without the enlightenment of the Holy Spirit, people will not understand. The parable becomes a form of God's judgment upon listeners who refuse to really listen.

Jesus quotes Isaiah 6:9 to support what he has said about the Word of God that comes in parables. Isaiah was commissioned by the Lord to preach to Israel. But as part of the commissioning speech, the Lord tells Isaiah that people will hear but not understand; they will see but not perceive. The results of preaching the Word are not universally successful, as Isaiah, Jesus, and the apostles found. We make the same discovery today.

In explaining the parable of the sower, Jesus divides listeners into four classes: (1) some have the devil take away the Word they have heard before it even begins to grow in their hearts and lives; (2) some receive the word with joy, but when the time of testing comes, they fall away; (3) in some, the immature plant of faith is choked by worries, riches, and pleasures of this world; (4) some hear the word, retain it, and produce a crop of faith and good works.

Sowing the seed of the Word would be very discouraging work if there were only three classes of listeners. But what keeps the farmer sowing, what keeps the proclaimer of God's Word sowing, is the fact that some seed does fall on soil that produces a wonderful crop. Jesus did not stop preaching because the response of so many of his listeners was superficial and unfruitful. Jesus kept on preaching because he knew that only by sowing the seed of the Word would a fruitful crop finally come forth. The faithful men and women who followed Jesus during his earthly ministry were the firstfruits of a much greater crop that was to follow. By God's grace, you and I are included in that number.

A lamp on a stand

¹⁶"No one lights a lamp and hides it in a jar or puts it under a bed. Instead, he puts it on a stand, so that those who come in can see the light. ¹⁷For there is nothing hidden that will not be disclosed, and nothing concealed that will not be known or brought out into the open. ¹⁸Therefore consider carefully how you listen. Whoever has will be given more; whoever does not have, even what he thinks he has will be taken from him."

From what Jesus said about his reason for speaking in parables (8:10), one might conclude that he is not really interested in people understanding the Word. This is certainly a false conclusion, as Jesus plainly indicates with his saying about the lamp on a stand. The Word of God is like a burning lamp. No one lights a lamp and then hides it under a jar or puts it under a bed. Rather, one puts the lamp on a stand so that those who come in can see the light. This saying is repeated in 11:33.

So it is with the Word of God. It is meant to give people light. The followers of Jesus must be serious about letting the light of the Word shine. They should not think of hiding the Word or keeping it just for themselves.

Verse 17 is repeated in 12:2 and helps to explain the statement Jesus made that "the knowledge of the secrets of the kingdom of God has been given" to the disciples (8:10). This knowledge was given to the disciples during his earthly ministry. Jesus told them some things that he did not tell to the crowds. But ultimately the apostles shared this knowledge in their preaching and writing. All the secrets that Jesus revealed to the disciples have been brought out into the open. The apostles did not keep some secret teachings for themselves that are yet to be revealed.

Because of their responsibility in making the Word known, Jesus urges the disciples once more to listen carefully. To this admonition is attached a promise found again in 19:26. Jesus promises that the more one has of the Word, the more one will receive; on the other hand, the person who does not have the Word will lose even what he thinks he has. The disciple has a great responsibility for listening to the Word for his own sake and for the sake of those to whom he will make it known.

Jesus' mother and brothers

¹⁹Now Jesus' mother and brothers came to see him, but they were not able to get near him because of the crowd. ²⁰Someone told him, "Your mother and brothers are standing outside, wanting to see you."

²¹He replied, "My mother and brothers are those who hear God's word and put it into practice."

This story of the visit of Mary and her sons to see Jesus probably did not take place on the occasion when Jesus told the parable of the sower. From verse 20 it appears that Jesus was inside a house crowded with people (much like the situation recorded in 5:18,19). Luke reports this incident at this point in his gospel because it stresses again the importance of hearing the Word of God.

Some commentators, especially those Roman Catholics who continue to believe that Mary was a virgin all her life, interpret the word "brothers" as meaning "relatives." There are times when the Greek word can have this meaning, but the more likely interpretation is that Mary did have other children. Mark gives the names of four brothers of Jesus: James, Joseph, Judas, and Simon (6:3).

However, the point of this brief story is not any kind of blood relationship that Jesus had. Jesus is saying that there is a relationship that is greater than any earthly family tie. That relationship is based on hearing God's Word and putting it into practice. In 6:47,48 Jesus characterized such a person as one who built his house on the foundation of rock. Here the one who hears God's Word and puts it into practice is called "my mother and brothers" by Jesus. How important to be listeners and doers of the Word!

Jesus calms the storm

²²One day Jesus said to his disciples, "Let's go over to the other side of the lake." So they got into a boat and set out. ²³As they

sailed, he fell asleep. A squall came down on the lake, so that the boat was being swamped, and they were in great danger.

²⁴The disciples went and woke him, saying, "Master, Master, we're going to drown!"

He got up and rebuked the wind and the raging waters; the storm subsided, and all was calm. ²⁵"Where is your faith?" he asked his disciples.

In fear and amazement they asked one another, "Who is this? He commands even the winds and the water, and they obey him."

Luke introduces the story of the calming of the storm with the words "one day." From Mark 4:35 we learn that it was the same day on which Jesus had told the parable of the sower. Luke does not so much connect this story with the preceding teaching as with the following story, the healing of the demon-possessed man. Crossing the Sea of Galilee took Jesus into gentile territory, where he will be confronted by a pagan man.

As Jesus and his disciples cross the sea, Jesus falls asleep. Suddenly, a squall comes up (something rather common on the Sea of Galilee). The Greek words here are very picturesque: "an intensive sucking of wind." One thinks of a tornado. This description helps us appreciate the terror of the disciples as they see their boat being swamped.

Fearing the worst, they wake Jesus. The master gets up and rebukes the wind and raging waters; the storm subsides, and all is calm. A miracle! Up to this point in Luke's gospel, he has reported only miracles that show the power of Jesus over the ills of people. Here is a miracle that reveals a power controlling even the forces of nature.

The disciples are amazed that even the winds and the water obey when Jesus commands. The word "obey" is formed from a Greek verb that includes the word *hear*. What human beings don't do so well, the winds and water did: they listened to Jesus when he spoke. Nature knows her Lord!

The fear of the disciples, as understandable as we find it, shows the small size of their faith. They are still learning about the almighty power that Jesus possesses. They are still asking "Who is this?" Only gradually will the complete answer to that question come to them.

The healing of a demon-possessed man

²⁶They sailed to the region of the Gerasenes, which is across the lake from Galilee. ²⁷When Jesus stepped ashore, he was met by a demon-possessed man from the town. For a long time this man had not worn clothes or lived in a house, but had lived in the tombs. ²⁸When he saw Jesus, he cried out and fell at his feet, shouting at the top of his voice, "What do you want with me, Jesus, Son of the Most High God? I beg you, don't torture me!" ²⁹For Jesus had commanded the evil spirit to come out of the man. Many times it had seized him, and though he was chained hand and foot and kept under guard, he had broken his chains and had been driven by the demon into solitary places.

³⁰Jesus asked him, "What is your name?"

"Legion," he replied, because many demons had gone into him. ³¹And they begged him repeatedly not to order them to go into the Abyss.

³²A large herd of pigs was feeding there on the hillside. The demons begged Jesus to let them go into them, and he gave them permission. ³³When the demons came out of the man, they went into the pigs, and the herd rushed down the steep bank into the lake and was drowned.

³⁴When those tending the pigs saw what had happened, they ran off and reported this in the town and countryside, ³⁵and the people went out to see what had happened. When they came to Jesus, they found the man from whom the demons had gone out, sitting at Jesus' feet, dressed and in his right mind; and they were afraid. ³⁶Those who had seen it told the people how the demon-possessed man had been cured. ³⁷Then all the people of the region of the Gerasenes asked Jesus to leave them, because they were overcome with fear. So he got into the boat and left.

³⁸The man from whom the demons had gone out begged to go with him, but Jesus sent him away, saying, ³⁹"Return home and tell how much God has done for you." So the man went away and told all over town how much Jesus had done for him.

The trip across the Sea of Galilee brought Jesus and his disciples to the region of the Gerasenes. The city of Gerasa (present-day Jerash) is located about 30 miles southeast of the Sea of Galilee. Another city named Gadara lies much closer to the sea, only about five miles away. This is the name given in Matthew 8:28 (and found in the KJV translation of Luke). Another name, Gergesenes, which appears in some early Greek manuscripts of the New Testament, perhaps comes from the name of the village Kersa situated on the east shore of the lake. These various names all refer to the same general region, so the story obviously takes place very close to the lake (see verse 33).

This was an area in which many Gentiles lived. The fact that herds of pigs were being tended indicates this. The demon-possessed man may be characterized by the term *pagan*. Here Jesus goes into heathen territory, away from the synagogues of the Jews, away from the people of Israel and their land. He brings his healing power to a pagan.

The man who meets Jesus is in terrible shape; he is unclothed and has been living in tombs (perhaps caves). People had tried chaining him up and keeping him under guard, but when seized by the evil spirit, he broke the chains and escaped into solitary places. Because he is under the control of an evil spiritual power, he recognizes Jesus (see 4:33,34). He answers the question of the disciples from the previous story: Jesus is the Son of the Most High God. The evil spirits know they deserve damnation, eternal torture in the abyss of hell (see Revelation 20:1-3).

When Jesus asks the man's name, he replies, "Legion." In the time of Caesar Augustus, a Roman legion numbered six thousand soldiers. The man is using the term in a general sense, referring to the great number of demons who had gone into him. This legion of devils begged Jesus not to order them off to hell. Instead, they request permission of Jesus to enter into the herd of pigs grazing on the hillside. (Mark 5:13 reports that there were about two thousand pigs.) Jesus gave them this permission, which in turn caused the herd to rush down the steep bank into the abyss of the sea and drown. This is a kind of foretaste of the lake of fire into which Satan will ultimately be cast (Revelation 20:10). The water from which the disciples had escaped by the power of Jesus becomes the final resting place for this herd of demonized pigs. Jesus shows his power over the devil even in pagan territory.

We need to note this man's total helplessness against the demons. He is powerless to save himself. He is completely controlled by the power of evil. In this condition only Jesus can rescue him. This is a vivid picture of our spiritual condition by nature, under the power of Satan. Thank God that Christ has rescued us from this dreadful power by his life of obedience and his death and resurrection.

Some have suggested that this story shows Jesus as being cruel to animals. One can hardly draw this conclusion considering the fact that the demons are the ones who suggest entering into the pigs and who bring about their death. The permission that Jesus grants serves as an object lesson concerning the destructive power of the devil. What matters to Jesus is the salvation of lost sinners. We need to interpret the destruction of the pigs in this light.

The people of the region of the Gerasenes, when they heard the report of what had happened to the pigs and saw the man dressed and in his right mind, asked Jesus to leave their country. This is a rather surprising request to make of a person who is obviously very powerful and who could potentially do much good for them. Luke twice notes the reason that lays behind their request: they were afraid. The same Greek word is used in 5:26 and 7:16, where the NIV translates it as "filled with awe." It's the same feeling that Peter had when he beheld the large catch of fish. Sinful man is filled with terror when confronted with the holy God. This is the fear that these gentile people felt. The good that Christ brought to the demon-possessed man is matched by the judgment that came upon the demons. It is this judgment that the sinner fears. Only in the cross is this fear taken away.

Jesus answers their request: he leaves the same way he had come. The man from whom the demons had gone out begged to go along. He wants to become a follower. But Jesus has other work for this man: he must be a witness. Even before Jesus sent out his own apostles as witnesses, he sends out this man who has such a wonderful story of salvation to tell. Here is a converted pagan who is ready to share what he has experienced because he has learned to know Christ as his Savior.

A dead girl and a sick woman

⁴⁰**Now when Jesus returned, a crowd welcomed him, for they were all expecting him. ⁴¹Then a man named Jairus, a ruler of the synagogue, came and fell at Jesus' feet, pleading with him to come to his house ⁴²because his only daughter, a girl of about twelve, was dying.**

As Jesus was on his way, the crowds almost crushed him. ⁴³And a woman was there who had been subject to bleeding for twelve years, but no one could heal her. ⁴⁴She came up behind him and touched the edge of his cloak, and immediately her bleeding stopped.

⁴⁵**"Who touched me?" Jesus asked.**

When they all denied it, Peter said, "Master, the people are crowding and pressing against you."

⁴⁶**But Jesus said, "Someone touched me; I know that power has gone out from me."**

⁴⁷**Then the woman, seeing that she could not go unnoticed, came trembling and fell at his feet. In the presence of all the people,**

she told why she had touched him and how she had been instantly healed. ⁴⁸Then he said to her, "Daughter, your faith has healed you. Go in peace."

⁴⁹While Jesus was still speaking, someone came from the house of Jairus, the synagogue ruler. "Your daughter is dead," he said. "Don't bother the teacher any more."

⁵⁰Hearing this, Jesus said to Jairus, "Don't be afraid; just believe, and she will be healed."

⁵¹When he arrived at the house of Jairus, he did not let anyone go in with him except Peter, John and James, and the child's father and mother. ⁵²Meanwhile, all the people were wailing and mourning for her. "Stop wailing," Jesus said. "She is not dead but asleep."

⁵³They laughed at him, knowing that she was dead. ⁵⁴But he took her by the hand and said, "My child, get up!" ⁵⁵Her spirit returned, and at once she stood up. Then Jesus told them to give her something to eat. ⁵⁶Her parents were astonished, but he ordered them not to tell anyone what had happened.

Luke does not tell us to which city Jesus returned after his trip across the Sea of Galilee. It is tempting to imagine that he returned to Capernaum. This would connect Jairus, a ruler of the synagogue, with the building constructed by the centurion whose servant Jesus had healed (7:5). In any case, Jairus must have had some personal acquaintance with Jesus and Jesus' ability to heal. This knowledge impelled him to fall on the ground before Jesus and beg Jesus to come to his house where his only daughter was critically ill. The fact that the name of Jairus is recorded may indicate that he was a well-known person in the early church.

There is a marked contrast between Jairus and the man we met in the last story. Jairus is a Jew, learned in the ways of the law and synagogue life. He has a home where he lived with his wife and daughter. But in the case of both men, they are in trouble and only Jesus is able to help. Jesus went to the demonized pagan man to bring help; Jairus comes to Jesus and appeals for help.

As Jesus is making his way to the home of Jairus, the crowds press around him. Several times previously, Luke has mentioned the press of the crowds (5:18,19; 8:19). In both cases, someone who was seeking Jesus was prevented from getting to him. In this story, the crowds serve as cover for a woman who seems too ashamed to request help from Jesus. This woman had been subject to menstrual bleeding for 12 years. Her medical problem began the same year the dying girl was born. This woman had sought a cure from the physicians of the time but to no avail. Now she touched the edge of Jesus' cloak, hoping to be healed (in 6:19 we heard of others who tried to touch Jesus because they knew of his power to heal). Immediately, her bleeding stopped. She was well again.

Jesus was at once aware that someone had received healing by touching him. He says, "I know that power has gone out from me." This is the power of the Spirit (4:14), the power of the Lord to heal (5:17). This is power that cannot be used up. The statement of Jesus that power had gone out from him is an example of God speaking in language that we humans can understand. His purpose in making this statement is to draw out the woman who had touched him and to deepen her spiritual understanding.

Seeing that she could not go unnoticed, this trembling woman fell at the feet of Jesus, and in the presence of the crowd, she told her story. It was obviously not easy for her to talk about something that had so deeply troubled her these many years, something that she had kept hidden from others as best as she could. Now she is put in a position where she must open up and tell all. Jesus wants to correct a wrong notion about this healing—as if the mechanical touching of a powerful person can bring about a cure.

Jesus said to the woman in the hearing of the crowd, "Daughter, your faith has healed you. Go in peace." This woman had faith in the healing power of Jesus. Faith saves!

Meanwhile, ahead at the home of Jairus, something tragic had taken place. Before the divine healer could arrive, the 12-year-old had died. Jairus is given the news: "Your daughter is dead. Don't bother the teacher any more." At this point, Jairus may have felt upset because of the interruption that had taken place preventing Jesus from arriving before his daughter died.

Jesus at once speaks a reassuring word to the devastated father: "Don't be afraid; just believe, and she will be healed." The NIV translation "healed" does not do justice to the Greek word that is used, a word that is often translated as "saved." That's what Jesus is saying: even people who have died will be kept safe; only have faith.

Upon arriving at the house, Jesus stopped the wailing and mourning. His statement that the girl was not dead but only asleep brought laughter. This is evidence for the fact that here was truly a raising from the dead and not just a case of rousing someone from a deep coma.

Jesus permitted only the child's father and mother plus the disciples Peter, James, and John to go into the house. Peter, James, and John were mentioned together when they were called to follow Jesus (5:8-11). They will be with him on the Mount of Transfiguration (9:28) and in the Garden of Gethsemane. Now they witness the raising of this girl from the dead.

At the command of Jesus, the girl stands up. Jesus asks that she be given something to eat as a demonstration that she is truly alive (see 24:41-43). This is the second instance of raising someone from the dead reported by Luke. In 7:11-17 an only son is restored to his widowed mother; here an only daughter is restored to Jairus and his wife.

What joy Jesus brings into the lives of people! Such is the power of the Lord of life.

Why does Jesus order the astonished parents not to tell anyone what had happened? It may not be possible for us to fully understand his reason for this. We must note a couple of things. In the previous story, Jesus sent the man in gentile territory home to tell how much God had done for him (8:39). And in the next story, Jesus sends out the apostles to preach the kingdom of God (9:2). In the case of the girl raised from the dead, it is as if Jesus is saying, "Don't tell people anything. Let them draw their own conclusions. They can see for themselves that she lives." For anyone who really wanted to see, the power of Jesus was obvious. There was no need of further testimony in that town.

Jesus sends out the Twelve

9 **When Jesus had called the Twelve together, he gave them power and authority to drive out all demons and to cure diseases, ²and he sent them out to preach the kingdom of God and to heal the sick. ³He told them: "Take nothing for the journey—no staff, no bag, no bread, no money, no extra tunic. ⁴Whatever house you enter, stay there until you leave that town. ⁵If people do not welcome you, shake the dust off your feet when you leave their town, as a testimony against them." ⁶So they set out and went from village to village, preaching the gospel and healing people everywhere.**

⁷Now Herod the tetrarch heard about all that was going on. And he was perplexed, because some were saying that John had been raised from the dead, ⁸others that Elijah had appeared, and still others that one of the prophets of long ago had come back to life. ⁹But Herod said, "I beheaded John. Who, then, is this I hear such things about?" And he tried to see him.

The previous chapter of Luke's gospel began with the information that the twelve apostles and a number of women accompanied Jesus as he made a preaching tour "from one town and village to another, proclaiming the good news of the kingdom of God" (verse 1). Now in this ninth chapter, Luke tells us that it is time for the apostles to be sent out on their own to preach the gospel and heal. All this was part of their training for a ministry that would continue long after the ascension of Christ into heaven.

Again and again we have heard of the power and authority that Jesus possessed as God's anointed Servant. Jesus now confers power and authority upon the Twelve to drive out demons and cure diseases. The book of Acts gives a number of examples of how they continued to use this healing power in the early church.

Jesus wants them to travel light, like soldiers living off the land. They are to take no staff, bag (knapsack), bread, money, or extra clothes. The prohibition of the staff here (permitted in Mark 6:8) may mean a spare in case the one normally carried by walkers is broken or lost (see also Matthew 10:10). Room and board will be provided in hospitable homes in each town. And if there is no welcome, Jesus tells the apostles to "shake the dust off your feet when you leave their town," to get rid of anything that belongs to that town which might still cling to them. The Twelve had left everything to follow Jesus (5:11); now they were getting a taste of what this really meant. It was a lesson in casting all care on the Lord.

While the apostles were on their preaching tour, Luke inserts a note about the perplexity of Herod Antipas, tetrarch of Galilee and Perea. The wife of Cuza, manager of Herod's household, was giving support to the popular Galilean preacher and healer (8:3). Herod's question is one that others were also asking: Who is this? Some were saying that Jesus is John the Baptist raised from the dead or Elijah or one of the other Old Testament prophets come back to life. Herod remembers well that he had beheaded John (the story is found in Mark 6:17-29) and is sure that this is not a case of the dead returning. But he finds no answer to his question and tries to see Jesus. His wish will be granted when Pilate sends Jesus to Herod for trial (23:8). Herod's curiosity about Jesus does not lead to faith.

Jesus feeds the five thousand

¹⁰**When the apostles returned, they reported to Jesus what they had done. Then he took them with him and they withdrew by themselves to a town called Bethsaida, ¹¹but the crowds learned about it and followed him. He welcomed them and spoke to them about the kingdom of God, and healed those who needed healing.**

¹²**Late in the afternoon the Twelve came to him and said, "Send the crowd away so they can go to the surrounding villages and countryside and find food and lodging, because we are in a remote place here."**

¹³**He replied, "You give them something to eat."**

They answered, "We have only five loaves of bread and two fish—unless we go and buy food for all this crowd." ¹⁴(About five thousand men were there.)

But he said to his disciples, "Have them sit down in groups of about fifty each." ¹⁵The disciples did so, and everybody sat down. ¹⁶Taking the five loaves and the two fish and looking up to heaven, he gave thanks and broke them. Then he gave them to the disciples to set before the people. ¹⁷They all ate and were satisfied, and the disciples picked up twelve basketfuls of broken pieces that were left over.

Herod had asked the question, Who is this? The answer to that question dominates the series of stories that follow in this key chapter of Luke's gospel: the feeding of the five thousand, Peter's confession of Christ, the first and second prediction of Christ's suffering and death, the transfiguration, and the beginning of the journey to Jerusalem. All help to answer the question of the identity of Jesus.

The apostles returned from their first preaching tour and reported to Jesus what they had done. But their training is far from completed. The next great lesson will be taught in a lonely place near the town of Bethsaida. In 10:13 Bethsaida is one of the places that Jesus especially singles out for judgment because of its refusal to repent despite being witness to miracles. Bethsaida means "house of hunting or fishing" and lies on the northeast shore of the Sea of Galilee. The apostles Philip, Peter, and Andrew had come from this town (John 1:44). That Jesus was not in the town but only in the vicinity of Bethsaida is indicated by verse 12.

The withdrawal of Jesus with his disciples into a remote place was to escape the crowds. But this did not happen; the crowds followed and were welcomed by Jesus, who spoke to them about the kingdom of God and did works of healing. The apostles were learning that it was difficult to get away from people who are looking for help.

As the day wore on, the Twelve become increasingly uneasy as to how this crowd was going to be fed and housed. Having just returned from a trip where this was a concern for themselves, they know the predicament of this large crowd. They suggest a solution to Jesus: send the crowd away. Jesus counters with the directive "You give them something to eat." The apostles are forced by Jesus to take the initiative in providing bread.

On their trip they had taken no bread (9:3), but here they do have on hand five loaves and two fish—just enough for their little group but hardly sufficient for five thousand men and their families.

Jesus now takes charge just as he had done at the wedding in Cana when wine was lacking (John 2:1-11). The disciples are told to seat the people in groups of 50 (perhaps to make the distribution more orderly and so that no one would be missed). Then Jesus took the five loaves and two fish, looked to heaven, gave thanks, and broke them. Then he gave them to the disciples for distribution. (The early church saw in this entire action a symbol of the Lord's Supper, which Jesus later instituted; the words describing what Jesus did are very similar to the words of institution.)

This entire episode appears to the crowd to be something altogether ordinary. They all eat, are satisfied, and go on their way. There is no audience reaction, no recognition that a miracle has occurred. Like the master of the banquet at the wedding in Cana, the crowd did not realize where the food had come from.

But the disciples knew! This was a miracle for the disciples, one of the secrets of the kingdom (8:10). Each had a basket full of leftovers to testify to the supernatural feeding from five loaves and two fish. What Jesus refused to do for himself when tempted by the devil, he did for the crowd as a learning experience for his disciples. In a literal way they learned the truth of Mary's words: "He has filled the hungry with good things" (1:53). They would be privileged to feed the nations with the bread of life, a resource that would satisfy and never be exhausted. The Lord provides.

This is the only miracle from the Galilean ministry of Jesus that is recorded by all four of the evangelists. It is obviously an important event because of the magnitude of the crowd and the theological importance that Jesus attaches to the feeding in a subsequent sermon recorded in John 6:25-71. The crowd continues to desire earthly bread, supposing that this is the purpose for Christ's ministry. Jesus declares that he is the bread of life and promises eternal life to those who eat this bread.

Peter's confession of Christ

¹⁸Once when Jesus was praying in private and his disciples were with him, he asked them, "Who do the crowds say I am?"

¹⁹They replied, "Some say John the Baptist; others say Elijah; and still others, that one of the prophets of long ago has come back to life."

²⁰"But what about you?" he asked. "Who do you say I am?"

Peter answered, "The Christ of God."

²¹Jesus strictly warned them not to tell this to anyone. ²²And he said, "The Son of Man must suffer many things and be rejected by the elders, chief priests and teachers of the law, and he must be killed and on the third day be raised to life."

²³Then he said to them all: "If anyone would come after me, he must deny himself and take up his cross daily and follow me. ²⁴For whoever wants to save his life will lose it, but whoever loses his life for me will save it. ²⁵What good is it for a man to gain the whole world, and yet lose or forfeit his very self? ²⁶If anyone is ashamed of me and my words, the Son of Man will be ashamed of him when he comes in his glory and in the glory of the Father and of the holy angels. ²⁷I tell you the truth, some who are standing here will not taste death before they see the kingdom of God."

"Who is this?" was the question asked by the disciples after Jesus had calmed the sea (8:25) and echoed by Herod when he heard of the works Jesus was doing (9:9). Jesus now puts this question to the disciples, asking first who the crowds take him to be and then their own evaluation. It is likewise a question for people to answer today: Just who is Jesus?

We've heard much about the crowds who swarmed around Jesus wherever he went. But when Jesus asks this question of his identity, he is very much alone with his disciples to the north of the Sea of Galilee near Caesarea Philippi (Mark 8:27). For Jesus it is a time of prayer and meditation, a time also to make a startling revelation to his disciples.

In answer to Jesus' question, the disciples reported a variety of opinions held by the crowd, all of them incorrect. It is Peter as spokesman for the group who responds to the request of Jesus for a personal confession. He correctly identifies Jesus as the Christ of God. For the reader of Luke's gospel, there is no surprise in this identification. The name Christ was used by the angel in the birth announcement to the shepherds, and the demons had given Jesus that title (4:41). But now for the first time we hear the word "Christ" on the lips of a human being.

This title, Christ, was in great danger of being misunderstood. It was a common opinion that the role of the promised Christ (Messiah) was to establish an earthly Jewish kingdom. Hence the prohibition issued by Jesus warning the disciples to tell no one of his true identity. For, as he soon reveals to them, his true role as Christ is to suffer and die on the cross.

This is the first of three predictions that Jesus makes concerning his death and resurrection. He refers to himself as the Son of Man to emphasize his true human nature. Luke reports no reaction from the disciples to this prediction, but from Mark 8:31-33 we learn that Peter led the protests against such an ending to the life of Jesus.

Luke gets right at the implications that the message of the cross has for the followers of Jesus. Following Jesus means self-denial. It means the sacrifice of one's own will for the sake of Christ. "Cross" here does not refer to the afflictions and troubles that commonly come in life to Christians and non-Christians alike. Rather, a believer taking up the cross means to accept whatever suffering might result from a sincere commitment to Christ and his kingdom. For many of the disciples, their confession of Christ would mean death.

Jesus makes it plain, however, that a life bent on personal survival is a life lost whereas a life lost for his sake is a life saved. Gaining the whole world by forfeiting life is not worth the price. "Life" here means more than what is only physical. Jesus is talking about life in a double sense: earthly and eternal. He makes a direct connection between a person's denial of him in this earthly life with what will happen on the day of judgment: the Son of Man will be ashamed of the person who is ashamed of Jesus and his words.

For the disciples this talk about suffering and death sounded strange and foreboding. Up to this point, Jesus had been tremendously successful in drawing appreciative crowds. But now there is the disclosure of the cross. This same chapter will find Jesus "resolutely set out for Jerusalem" (verse 51).

Yet the end is not the cross; the end is the kingdom of God. The end is victory and glory. Jesus concludes his talk with a beautiful promise: "I tell you the truth, some who are standing here will not taste death before they see the kingdom of God." Seeing the kingdom of God can mean many things. It can mean eternal life or the second coming of Christ. But because of the way Jesus here speaks of disciples who will not taste death before they see the kingdom of God, we need to think of the glorious unveiling of God's kingdom after the resurrection of Jesus as reported in the book of Acts. Peter and many other disciples who did take up the cross and follow Jesus saw the fulfillment of this promise. It is a fulfillment that we continue to behold today as we witness the spread of the message of Christ's cross to all nations. This is the kind of kingdom over which Christ is ruler, the kind of kingdom he won by his death and resurrection.

The transfiguration

²⁸About eight days after Jesus said this, he took Peter, John and James with him and went up onto a mountain to pray. ²⁹As he was praying, the appearance of his face changed, and his clothes became as bright as a flash of lightning. ³⁰Two men, Moses and

Elijah, ³¹**appeared in glorious splendor, talking with Jesus. They spoke about his departure, which he was about to bring to fulfillment at Jerusalem. ³²Peter and his companions were very sleepy, but when they became fully awake, they saw his glory and the two men standing with him. ³³As the men were leaving Jesus, Peter said to him, "Master, it is good for us to be here. Let us put up three shelters—one for you, one for Moses and one for Elijah." (He did not know what he was saying.)**

³⁴**While he was speaking, a cloud appeared and enveloped them, and they were afraid as they entered the cloud. ³⁵A voice came from the cloud, saying, "This is my Son, whom I have chosen; listen to him." ³⁶When the voice had spoken, they found that Jesus was alone. The disciples kept this to themselves, and told no one at that time what they had seen.**

Peter had correctly identified Jesus as the Christ of God. Yet calling Jesus by this title fell short of expressing his true nature. About eight days after Peter's confession, an event occurs that provides the heavenly Father's answer to the question, Who is this?

Jesus takes Peter, John, and James along as he goes up onto a mountain to pray. As Jesus prayed, his face and clothing suddenly changed. He is transfigured and appears in heavenly glory. Two famous Old Testament persons, long dead, appear with him. Moses, the giver of the law at Mount Sinai, had been privileged to enjoy intimate fellowship with the Lord (Exodus 33:12-23). Elijah had been taken by a whirlwind into heaven without dying (2 Kings 2:11-18). According to Jewish thought, these two men were expected to return at the end of the world.

Moses had spoken of a prophet who was to come: "The LORD your God will raise up for you a prophet like me from among your own brothers. You must listen to him" (Deuteronomy 18:15). Many recognized that Jesus was indeed a prophet. There were also ways in which Jesus, along with John the Baptist, had fulfilled the role of a returning Elijah. But neither of these identifications matches what was given here at the transfiguration by God himself.

The conversation among these three glorified saints on the mountain concerned the very subject Jesus had presented so recently to his disciples: his departure. The Greek word here is *exodus*. Moses had been the leader of the exodus that had brought Israel out of the slavery of Egypt to the freedom of the Promised Land. Jesus is the leader of the new exodus from the slavery of sin into the promised land of heaven. His own departure would take place in Jerusalem, an exodus by way of the cross to heavenly glory.

Peter and his companions only gradually become fully awake and aware of what is going on. (Did the transfiguration take place at night?) It is only when Moses and Elijah are about to leave that Peter attempts to perpetuate this vision of glory. His proposal that three shelters, or booths, be put up reveals his lack of understanding as to what he is seeing. Here is a vision that cannot be contained in earthly tents.

Peter is still speaking when the mountain is suddenly enveloped by a cloud (like Mount Sinai of old) and another voice is heard. At the baptism of Jesus, the heavenly voice addressed him directly: "You are my Son, whom I love; with you I am well pleased" (3:22). The three disciples had not heard those words. Now this identification is repeated for their sakes: "This is my Son, whom I have chosen; listen to him." Jesus is more than some prophet like Moses to whom people are bidden to listen; Jesus is God's own Son, and the words he speaks therefore take on added significance. He himself is the Word of God, the final and complete revelation of God's will for the world.

As quickly as the vision had come, so quickly it is gone. So also Moses and Elijah, the representatives of the Old Testament, vanish. The disciples are left alone with

Jesus. It was a thrilling but frightening experience, one which they did not share with others until after Jesus had risen from the dead (Mark 9:9). It was then that they began to understand what they had seen—a foretaste of the resurrection, a foretaste of heaven. Here is God's answer to the question about Jesus: "This is my Son."

The healing of a boy with an evil spirit

³⁷**The next day, when they came down from the mountain, a large crowd met him. ³⁸A man in the crowd called out, "Teacher, I beg you to look at my son, for he is my only child. ³⁹A spirit seizes him and he suddenly screams; it throws him into convulsions so that he foams at the mouth. It scarcely ever leaves him and is destroying him. ⁴⁰I begged your disciples to drive it out, but they could not."**

⁴¹**"O unbelieving and perverse generation," Jesus replied, "how long shall I stay with you and put up with you? Bring your son here."**

⁴²**Even while the boy was coming, the demon threw him to the ground in a convulsion. But Jesus rebuked the evil spirit, healed the boy and gave him back to his father. ⁴³And they were all amazed at the greatness of God.**

While everyone was marveling at all that Jesus did, he said to his disciples, ⁴⁴"Listen carefully to what I am about to tell you: The Son of Man is going to be betrayed into the hands of men." ⁴⁵But they did not understand what this meant. It was hidden from them, so that they did not grasp it, and they were afraid to ask him about it.

Down from the mount of glory, Jesus comes to face the suffering of this world caused by sin. From out of a large crowd steps a man begging for help. He describes his child's condition, characterized by symptoms similar to what we call epilepsy. The father had brought the afflicted child to Jesus' disciples (while Jesus was on the mountain), but they were of no help.

The words of Jesus in verse 41 are directed to all those present: the crowd, the father, and the disciples. The crowd is always ready to marvel at wonders done by Jesus but manifests no real faith; the father admits the weakness of his faith, as Mark reports (9:24); the disciples, by their inability to cast out the demon, show a lack of faith in the power and authority given to them by Jesus (9:1). Jesus is clearly irritated by this unbelieving and perverse generation. The burden of the cross he carries for the sins of the world, including the sin of unbelief, presses hard upon him.

Yet his compassion does not fail. He invites the father to bring his son. At that very moment, the lad is seized by another convulsion. The evil spirit knows that his control over this child has come to an end. Jesus rebukes the demon, heals the boy, and gives him back to his father. Once more, the greatness of God is manifested.

Luke makes a very close connection between this story and the second prediction Jesus makes of his passion. It is almost as if Jesus has his mind on other things while healing the boy. He is thinking of how as the only Son of his Father, he must be afflicted by all the powers of Satan and hell.

When Jesus was transfigured, the heavenly Father had given the command "This is my Son . . . ; listen to him." Jesus introduces his statement that the Son of Man will be betrayed into the hands of men with that very admonition to his disciples: "Listen carefully to what I am about to tell you." But what Jesus had to tell them was more than they could fathom. Betrayal and the cross did not fit into their thinking. For now, it was hidden from them. Jesus had said earlier, "There is nothing hidden that will not be disclosed, and nothing concealed that will not be known or brought out into the open" (8:17). Soon enough they would come to know the meaning of the cross.

A hint is given that Jesus was ready to help the disciples understand. But they are afraid to ask. Perhaps such subjects—suffering, rejection, death—were simply too painful to talk about. It was strange talk coming from one who obviously was filled with such almighty power. Here is the mystery of the cross.

Who will be the greatest?

⁴⁶An argument started among the disciples as to which of them would be the greatest. ⁴⁷Jesus, knowing their thoughts, took a little child and had him stand beside him. ⁴⁸Then he said to them, "Whoever welcomes this little child in my name welcomes me; and whoever welcomes me welcomes the one who sent me. For he who is least among you all—he is the greatest."

⁴⁹"Master," said John, "we saw a man driving out demons in your name and we tried to stop him, because he is not one of us."

⁵⁰"Do not stop him," Jesus said, "for whoever is not against you is for you."

If proof is needed that Jesus included his own disciples in characterizing his generation as perverse (9:41), one finds it in the argument that breaks out among them on the subject of "which of them would be the greatest." The question seems not to be about present greatness but rather greatness in the coming kingdom that Jesus, as the Messiah, would establish. How little the disciples understood when Jesus spoke of suffering and the cross! This argument about greatness will be repeated at the Last Supper (22:24-27).

Jesus had just healed a child afflicted by an evil spirit. Now he takes just such a little child, the smallest and weakest member of human society, and identifies himself with this child. He tells his disciples, "When you welcome this child, you welcome me; when you welcome me, you welcome my Father, who sent me." Again Jesus is answering the question of his identity. But becoming a child is not only for Jesus; it is also for the disciples, if they truly want to be the greatest.

The apostle John, one of those who had been on the Mount of Transfiguration, calls another matter to the attention of Jesus. John reports that the disciples had tried to stop a man from driving out demons in the name of Jesus. The disciples reasoned that the man should not be doing this because "he is not one of us." He was not among the group of close followers of Jesus. Jesus does not commend this action of the disciples but rather urges accepting help in the battle against demons from wherever it comes: "Whoever is not against you is for you." The disciples themselves had been notably unsuccessful in driving out a demon recently (9:40).

Both of these incidents suggest the ever-present danger of rivalry among believers. There is no room for arguments about greatness among the followers of Christ. And criticism of those who are not of one's fellowship needs to be tempered with an appreciation for what good they accomplish.

Service on the way to Jerusalem

Jesus urges people to get ready for the coming kingdom— Samaritan opposition

⁵¹As the time approached for him to be taken up to heaven, Jesus resolutely set out for Jerusalem. ⁵²And he sent messengers on ahead, who went into a Samaritan village to get things ready for him; ⁵³but the people there did not welcome him, because he was heading for Jerusalem. ⁵⁴When the disciples James and John saw this, they asked, "Lord, do you want us to call fire down from heaven to destroy them?" ⁵⁵But Jesus turned and rebuked them, ⁵⁶and they went to another village.

Already on the Mount of Transfiguration, Moses and Elijah had spoken with Jesus about the coming climactic events at Jerusalem (9:31). From now on, that city will be the central focus of Luke's gospel. In verse 51 we are told that "Jesus resolutely set out for Jerusalem." Luke later speaks of Jesus going through the towns and villages "as he made his way to Jerusalem" (13:22). In 17:11 Jesus is said to be "on his way to Jerusalem." Finally his triumphant entry will be reported in 19:28-38. Jerusalem is the city of destiny; here Jesus will die on the cross, rise on the third day, and ascend into heaven. With the ascension those climactic events will be completed.

To reach Jerusalem, Jesus proposes to journey through Samaritan territory. The province of Samaria lay between Galilee and Judea. It was inhabited by people who had been brought in by the Assyrians eight centuries earlier. They retained remnants of the Old Testament faith but differed from the Jews in some essential beliefs. Over the years an intense hatred had developed between the Samaritans and the Jews. The messengers whom Jesus sent ahead to prepare his way got a very hostile reception.

When the disciples James and John, the "Sons of Thunder" (Mark 3:17), saw this, they were prepared to imitate the actions of Elijah (2 Kings 1:9-12) and call down fire from heaven to destroy the opposition. The rebuke they received from Jesus was intended to teach the lesson that discipleship does not consist of zealous punishment of those who reject the gospel. Once more we see how much the disciples still had to learn. The journey to Jerusalem would provide many opportunities for further training in service.

The cost of following Jesus

⁵⁷**As they were walking along the road, a man said to him, "I will follow you wherever you go."**

⁵⁸**Jesus replied, "Foxes have holes and birds of the air have nests, but the Son of Man has no place to lay his head."**

The man at the plow

⁵⁹He said to another man, "Follow me."

But the man replied, "Lord, first let me go and bury my father."

⁶⁰Jesus said to him, "Let the dead bury their own dead, but you go and proclaim the kingdom of God."

⁶¹Still another said, "I will follow you, Lord; but first let me go back and say good-by to my family."

⁶²Jesus replied, "No one who puts his hand to the plow and looks back is fit for service in the kingdom of God."

"Jesus resolutely set out for Jerusalem" (9:51). He walks along the road with conviction and determination; he is unwavering in pursuit of his goal. Along the way Jesus is met by some who wish to join his band of followers. The first comes as a volunteer promising to "follow you wherever you go." It is a bold promise. In response Jesus points out that to be one of his followers means joining company with one who has less than even foxes and birds: "The Son of Man has no place to lay his head." Are you ready to give up house and home for my sake? Count the cost.

In another case Jesus invites a man to follow. The man seems to be willing, if Jesus first permits him to fulfill a sacred family obligation: "Let me go and bury my father." Jesus is not ready to give him that permission. To go and proclaim the kingdom of God must have top priority. Someone else (Jesus suggests the spiritually dead) will take care of the man's family obligations. Following Jesus will result in conflicting loyalties.

Finally another would-be follower wants only to go back and say good-by to his family before falling in behind Jesus. Elijah had permitted Elisha that favor (1 Kings 19:19-21). Jesus, however, wants no looking back. No one is fit for service in the kingdom of God who looks back. One plowing in the field must keep looking ahead. So also the followers of Jesus.

These are hard sayings. They dare not be interpreted in isolation from the rest of Scripture, especially the commandment so often repeated by Jesus: "Love one another." In these statements Jesus is obviously making a strong statement to get across the point he wants to make for all who would follow him: you will need to be ready to make sacrifices. To be a follower of Jesus means to be ready to reorder the priorities of this earthly life.

Jesus sends out the 72 disciples

10 After this the Lord appointed seventy-two others and sent them two by two ahead of him to every town and place where he was about to go. ²He told them, "The harvest is plentiful, but the workers are few. Ask the Lord of the harvest, therefore, to send out workers into his harvest field. ³Go! I am sending you out like lambs among wolves. ⁴Do not take a purse or bag or sandals; and do not greet anyone on the road.

⁵"When you enter a house, first say, 'Peace to this house.' ⁶If a man of peace is there, your peace will rest on him; if not, it will return to you. ⁷Stay in that house, eating and drinking whatever they give you, for the worker deserves his wages. Do not move around from house to house.

⁸"When you enter a town and are welcomed, eat what is set before you. ⁹Heal the sick who are there and tell them, 'The kingdom of God is near you.' ¹⁰But when you enter a town and are not welcomed, go into its streets and say, ¹¹'Even the dust of your town that sticks to our feet we wipe off against you. Yet be sure of this: The kingdom of God is near.' ¹²I tell you, it will be more bearable on that day for Sodom than for that town.

¹³"Woe to you, Korazin! Woe to you, Bethsaida! For if the miracles that were performed in you had been performed in Tyre and Sidon, they would have repented long ago, sitting in sackcloth and ashes. ¹⁴But it will be more bearable for Tyre and Sidon at the judgment than for you. ¹⁵And you, Capernaum, will you be lifted up to the skies? No, you will go down to the depths.

¹⁶"He who listens to you listens to me; he who rejects you rejects me; but he who rejects me rejects him who sent me."

¹⁷The seventy-two returned with joy and said, "Lord, even the demons submit to us in your name."

¹⁸He replied, "I saw Satan fall like lightning from heaven. ¹⁹I have given you authority to trample on snakes and scorpions and to overcome all the power of the enemy; nothing will harm you. ²⁰However, do not rejoice that the spirits submit to you, but rejoice that your names are written in heaven."

²¹At that time Jesus, full of joy through the Holy Spirit, said, "I praise you, Father, Lord of heaven and earth, because you have hidden these things from the wise and learned, and revealed them to little children. Yes, Father, for this was your good pleasure.

²²"All things have been committed to me by my Father. No one knows who the Son is except the Father, and no one knows who the Father is except the Son and those to whom the Son chooses to reveal him."

²³Then he turned to his disciples and said privately, "Blessed are the eyes that see what you see. ²⁴For I tell you that many prophets and kings wanted to see what you see but did not see it, and to hear what you hear but did not hear it."

As Jesus made his way to Jerusalem, it became increasingly obvious that a vast number of people were prospects for the kingdom of God. Samaria was an entirely new mission field. However, workers to proclaim God's message were few. Jesus makes a comparison with the harvesting of ripe grain. No matter how plentiful the harvest, the crop will be small if the workers are scarce.

To be a harvester for God's kingdom was difficult work. Jesus had laid strict demands on those who would follow (9:57-62). Proclaiming the kingdom of God called for dedication and commitment that, unfortunately, too few people had. Yet there were some ready for this task of harvesting. We are told that the Lord appointed 72 men and sent them out two by two into the towns through which he would be passing. Some of the Greek manuscripts have

70 as the number appointed (which accounts for the figure in the KJV). Whichever was the original number, these appointees were *in addition to* the apostles. The work of harvesting was not limited to just the Twelve. It was too big a job. In fact, the first assignment Jesus gives these new recruits is to pray for the owner of the harvest, God himself, to provide more workers.

Jesus makes no guarantees to the 72 disciples that they are in for an easy time. There will be spiritual and physical dangers; they are bidden to travel light; they were not to spend time on the road in casual talk since their task is urgent. Jesus' instructions are very similar to those he gave to the twelve apostles when he had sent them out previously (9:1-6).

In some homes and towns the 72 disciples would find a ready welcome. They were to accept room and board with graciousness. However, other towns would not have the welcome mat out. The action of wiping off the dust that sticks to one's feet was a symbol of God's coming judgment against those who refuse the message of grace. Yet whether welcomed or not, the workers were to announce that the kingdom of God was near in the person of Jesus.

The thought that some towns would reject the message of God's kingdom provokes Jesus to speak out against such ingratitude and lack of repentance. Sodom was the city destroyed by burning sulfur because of its wickedness (Genesis 19:24). Yet even Sodom will be judged less severely than those cities that closed their hearts to Jesus and his messengers.

Words of woe are spoken against Korazin, Bethsaida, and Capernaum. The site of Korazin, recently excavated, is near the Sea of Galilee. Jesus performed the miracle of the feeding of the five thousand near Bethsaida (9:10). He had done many mighty works in Capernaum (4:31). Jesus did no preaching or miracles in Tyre or Sidon, Canaanite (gentile) cities lying on the Mediterranean coast. He condemns the Jewish cities for their failure to repent; in fact they compare most unfavorably with the gentile cities. Far from being lifted up to the skies for being the scene of the activities of the Son of God, Capernaum will go down into the depths. The Greek word for "depths" is hades, the abode of the dead.

Jesus is deeply hurt by the failure of his ministry in the Galilean cities. There was no real change of heart, no readiness to receive his gracious message of salvation. Few were ready to take up the cross and follow. He tells the 72 disciples that they are his personal representatives and can expect the same mixed response. Jesus comes in the words of his messengers. The response to the messengers is a response to Jesus and to the Father who sent him.

The 72 disciples returned from their mission and reported exuberantly that even demons submitted when the name of Jesus was invoked. They were not used to wielding such power. Jesus shares in their rejoicing and tells of a vision he had of Satan falling from heaven. This fall is compared to that of a lightning strike descending from the skies. It is a vision of the ultimate judgment of Satan and all his demons.

When Jesus speaks of the authority given to the missioners "to trample on snakes and scorpions," we can apply this to the devil and his brood (see Genesis 3:1). John the Baptist had addressed some in the crowds coming for baptism as a "brood of vipers" (3:7). To imagine that Christ today gives his followers immunity from snake bites on the basis of this and other passages of Scripture is to miss the main point. The believer's chief enemy is not some member of the animal kingdom but the devil himself.

Yet Jesus seeks to temper the enthusiasm of these returning messengers that was focused upon the works they had accomplished. What matters more than any power they had over the evil powers is the fact that their names are written in heaven. Jesus had seen the fall of Satan from heaven; his disciples are promised a place in heaven, thereby gaining what Satan had forfeited by his rebellion.

The triumphant return of the 72 disciples and the vision of Satan's fall from heaven fills Jesus with great joy. Moved by the Holy Spirit, he praises his heavenly Father for the revelation of salvation that "little children" have seen. "Little children" is a term Jesus commonly uses when speaking of his followers. They are contrasted with the wise and learned, from whom this revelation has been hidden. The spiritual blindness of the vast majority of Jesus' contemporaries, especially the wise and learned, is evident. It was the Father's will to make known to little children the way of salvation, which is in Christ.

This revelation is mediated through Jesus himself. The Father did not give some immediate or direct revelation to the disciples. They learned to know the secrets of salvation through Jesus himself. Jesus is the Word of God. Revelation today also is through the Word of Jesus; one dare not look for any other way of knowing the divine secrets. The wise and learned may still seek other ways of knowing divine things, but such mysteries remain hidden to them because of their refusal to become listeners of Jesus.

Earlier Jesus had pronounced "woes" on some of the cities of Galilee that had refused to listen to him. Now addressing his disciples, he balances this by speaking a beatitude: "Blessed are the eyes that see what you see." The disciples were blessed because of what they saw and heard, the fulfillment of the Old Testament promises, things that prophets like Isaiah and kings like David were not privileged to see or hear. Believers today are also blessed. With the eyes of faith we have been privileged to see what Christ has done for us; we can hear the revelation he speaks to us. With the 72 disciples, we can rejoice that our names are written in heaven.

The parable of the good Samaritan

²⁵On one occasion an expert in the law stood up to test Jesus. "Teacher," he asked, "what must I do to inherit eternal life?"

²⁶"What is written in the Law?" he replied. "How do you read it?"

²⁷He answered: "'Love the Lord your God with all your heart and with all your soul and with all your strength and with all your mind'; and, 'Love your neighbor as yourself.'"

²⁸"You have answered correctly," Jesus replied. "Do this and you will live."

²⁹But he wanted to justify himself, so he asked Jesus, "And who is my neighbor?"

³⁰In reply Jesus said: "A man was going down from Jerusalem to Jericho, when he fell into the hands of robbers. They stripped him of his clothes, beat him and went away, leaving him half dead. ³¹A priest happened to be going down the same road, and when he saw the man, he passed by on the other side. ³²So too, a Levite, when he came to the place and saw him, passed by on the other side. ³³But a Samaritan, as he traveled, came where the man was; and when he saw him, he took pity on him. ³⁴He went to him and bandaged his wounds, pouring on oil and wine. Then he put the man on his own donkey, took him to an inn and took care of him. ³⁵The next day he took out two silver coins and gave them to the innkeeper. 'Look after him,' he said, 'and when I return, I will reimburse you for any extra expense you may have.'

³⁶"Which of these three do you think was a neighbor to the man who fell into the hands of robbers?"

³⁷The expert in the law replied, "The one who had mercy on him."

Jesus told him, "Go and do likewise."

The expert in the law who stands up to put Jesus to the test is a representative of the "wise and learned" from whom the things of God remain hidden (10:21). He demonstrates his knowledge of the Old Testament Scriptures by quoting Deuteronomy 6:5 concerning love to God and Leviticus 19:18 about love for one's neighbor. He gives the correct answer; Jesus then directs him to do the law, to put it into practice (see 8:21).

Jesus has made this law expert look foolish. He feels the need to "justify himself" for asking a question that had such a simple answer, one he himself easily supplied. So the lawyer asks a further question, seeking to demonstrate that loving your neighbor as yourself does call for a legal definition of the term *neighbor*. Generally among the Jews, the "neighbor" was defined as a fellow countryman, one of the same race.

The story that Jesus tells overturns such an understanding of the word *neighbor*. Jesus says that three men came upon the bloodied body of one who had been robbed and abandoned for dead. Of these three, a priest and a Levite (temple assistant) both saw the man but did not stop to help. Both of these men represented respectable and religiously honorable positions, the kind the lawyer no doubt would have been eager to include among his neighbors. The third who came by was a Samaritan (see the commentary on 9:52,53). Such people were mistrusted and despised by Jews. However, it is this foreigner who cared for the stricken Jew, and he did so in a manner which far surpassed ordinary obligation. This Samaritan, whom the lawyer would probably have excluded from his definition of a neighbor, shows himself as the one who fulfilled the command to love one another, in this case even an enemy.

The expert in the law had asked, "Who is my neighbor?" In the parable that Jesus tells, this question is answered. But

Jesus goes a step further with the question he now puts to the lawyer: "Which of these three do you think was a neighbor . . . ?" For Jesus, the real question is not Who is my neighbor? but How does one prove oneself to be a neighbor to others? Being a neighbor is more important than legally defining the term *neighbor*. Jesus makes this hated Samaritan a model for true neighborliness. The Samaritan is one of the "little children" to whom the hidden wisdom of God has been revealed. He sees beyond the racial divisions of this world to the will of God, which bids us to love our neighbor regardless of whom that neighbor might be.

This is a parable which shatters the values of the Jewish religion as practiced by the experts of the law and the Pharisees. The priest and Levite are pictured in a bad light; the Samaritan outcast becomes the example of love. The early church saw in the good Samaritan none other than Christ himself. No one else so radically fulfilled the commandment to love. Faith in Jesus is the way to eternal life, a faith that shows its life by love for God and neighbor.

At the home of Martha and Mary

38As Jesus and his disciples were on their way, he came to a village where a woman named Martha opened her home to him. 39She had a sister called Mary, who sat at the Lord's feet listening to what he said. 40But Martha was distracted by all the preparations that had to be made. She came to him and asked, "Lord, don't you care that my sister has left me to do the work by myself? Tell her to help me!"

41"Martha, Martha," the Lord answered, "you are worried and upset about many things, 42but only one thing is needed. Mary has chosen what is better, and it will not be taken away from her."

When Jesus sent out the 72 men, he told them that they would find food and drink in homes along the way.

Jesus and his disciples often must have had the same experience. The invitation Martha extended to Jesus is an example of such a welcome along the way.

One can understand why Martha is very busy making meal preparations, particularly if the invitation included Jesus' disciples also. Meanwhile, her sister Mary is sitting at the Lord's feet doing nothing but listening. Martha becomes irritated and asks the Lord to put Mary to work helping her. Jesus does not agree with Martha's assessment of the problem. It is Martha who has the problem and not Mary. "Mary has chosen what is better," says Jesus, "and it will not be taken away from her." Martha is distracted with many things; Mary is satisfied with the one thing needful.

Is this the same Martha and Mary who lived with their brother Lazarus in the village of Bethany near Jerusalem? (John 11:1) If so, Luke either reports this story out of chronological order (in Luke's account, Jesus arrives at Bethany in 19:29), or these sisters previously lived in a different village. It is more likely that Luke reports this story here as a contrast to the parable of the good Samaritan.

The good Samaritan is an example of active doing; Mary is an example of quiet listening. Martha is very busy serving her neighbor, but what she is doing is not so essential as what Mary is doing. A service that bypasses the Word is one that will never have lasting character. The example of Mary correctly shows that hearing God's Word must be our first priority.

Jesus' teaching on prayer

11 One day Jesus was praying in a certain place. When he finished, one of his disciples said to him, "Lord, teach us to pray, just as John taught his disciples."

²**He said to them, "When you pray, say:**

" 'Father,
hallowed be your name,
your kingdom come.
³Give us each day our daily bread.
⁴Forgive us our sins,
for we also forgive everyone who sins against us.
And lead us not into temptation.' "

⁵Then he said to them, "Suppose one of you has a friend, and he goes to him at midnight and says, 'Friend, lend me three loaves of bread, ⁶because a friend of mine on a journey has come to me, and I have nothing to set before him.'

⁷"Then the one inside answers, 'Don't bother me. The door is already locked, and my children are with me in bed. I can't get up and give you anything.' ⁸I tell you, though he will not get up and give him the bread because he is his friend, yet because of the man's boldness he will get up and give him as much as he needs.

⁹"So I say to you: Ask and it will be given to you; seek and you will find; knock and the door will be opened to you. ¹⁰For everyone who asks receives; he who seeks finds; and to him who knocks, the door will be opened.

¹¹"Which of you fathers, if your son asks for a fish, will give him a snake instead? ¹²Or if he asks for an egg, will give him a scorpion? ¹³If you then, though you are evil, know how to give good gifts to your children, how much more will your Father in heaven give the Holy Spirit to those who ask him!"

Prayer is one of the essential ingredients for fueling a life that will be busy doing the will of God. Jesus recognized this fact and spent much time in prayer (3:21; 6:12; 9:28). As this new chapter in Luke's gospel begins, we are once more told that Jesus was praying. He was a very busy person but never so busy that he did not find time for prayer.

Jesus' disciples observed the very active prayer life of their master. Now comes a request from one of them: "Lord, teach us to pray, just as John taught his disciples." In 5:33 we heard that not only did John teach his disciples to pray, but so did the Pharisees. The criticism was leveled at Jesus that he and his disciples seemed to spend more time eating and drinking.

It is somewhat surprising to us that this request for instruction in prayer should come only now in Luke's gospel. Jesus had previously sent out the twelve apostles and the 72 disciples on preaching tours. He gave them power over the demons and the ability to heal diseases. But why is there not a word encouraging prayer?

A possible answer is to suggest that what Luke here records actually took place much earlier in the ministry of Jesus. It is reported at this point in the gospel to form a continuation of the previous story in which Jesus commends Mary for her attention to the Word of God. The life of the disciples also needs to include persistent prayer.

The pattern, or outline, for prayer that Jesus gives to his disciples has come to be known as the Lord's Prayer. We find a slightly longer version of this prayer in Matthew 6:9-13, part of the Sermon on the Mount.

In 10:21 we heard Jesus speaking in prayer to his Father. Jesus instructs his disciples to address God with that same precious name. It is a great privilege granted us by Jesus to speak as children would to our dear Father in heaven. This is a form of address that neither John nor the Pharisees dared teach their disciples to use.

The first two sentences of the Lord's Prayer fit closely together. The request is expressed that the Father would bring it to pass that his name be hallowed and his kingdom come. In John 12:28 Jesus is asking for the same thing: "Father, glorify your name!" To speak of God's name is just another way of referring to God himself. In Ezekiel 36:23 the Lord said to Israel, "I will show the holiness of my great name, which has been profaned among the nations." God is treated with contempt by so many. When God acts in history, he brings himself glory and makes his name holy. Believers glorify God's name because of his works of creation, redemption, and sanctification. At the end of the world, "every tongue [will] confess that Jesus Christ is Lord, to the glory of God the Father" (Philippians 2:11). In the Lord's Prayer we pray for the time when God's name will be hallowed and the promise of his kingdom will reach complete fulfillment.

In the final three petitions Jesus teaches his disciples to pray for blessings that they need as they live out their lives on this earth while waiting for the end. There is need for daily bread; there is need of forgiveness; there is need for divine help against the temptations that will come. The most critical of these temptations is the danger of falling from faith and losing the eternal reward. Our plea for the Father's forgiveness includes an expression of our readiness to pass on forgiveness to everyone who sins against us.

This prayer has become very familiar to Christians through repeated use. From earliest times, these words have been incorporated into the worship orders of the church. The prayer Jesus taught his disciples serves as an outline and pattern for all prayer.

Following the Lord's Prayer, Jesus tells a parable about a person who goes at midnight to a friend requesting three loaves of bread to feed a guest who had arrived unexpectedly. The friend at first refuses the request because his entire household is settled in for the night behind locked doors. But persistence proves a greater motive than friendship for his finally providing the bread requested. The point Jesus makes with this parable is that persistence in prayer pays off. If a human friend is moved to respond by persistent requests, how much more likely it is that our heavenly Father will respond when we come to him again and again with our needs. Our asking, seeking, and knocking will not be in vain.

What the heavenly Father grants in response to our persistent prayer will be good for us. Again using a comparison, Jesus points out that an earthly father will not give what is harmful to his son. How much more should we trust our heavenly Father to give us good gifts. One of these good gifts is the Holy Spirit. In answer to our prayers, our Father will always give what is best for us.

Jesus and Beelzebub

¹⁴**Jesus was driving out a demon that was mute. When the demon left, the man who had been mute spoke, and the crowd was amazed. ¹⁵But some of them said, "By Beelzebub, the prince of demons, he is driving out demons." ¹⁶Others tested him by asking for a sign from heaven.**

¹⁷**Jesus knew their thoughts and said to them: "Any kingdom divided against itself will be ruined, and a house divided against itself will fall. ¹⁸If Satan is divided against himself, how can his kingdom stand? I say this because you claim that I drive out demons by Beelzebub. ¹⁹Now if I drive out demons by Beelzebub, by whom do your followers drive them out? So then, they will be your judges. ²⁰But if I drive out demons by the finger of God, then the kingdom of God has come to you.**

²¹**"When a strong man, fully armed, guards his own house, his possessions are safe. ²²But when someone stronger attacks and overpowers him, he takes away the armor in which the man trusted and divides up the spoils.**

²³**"He who is not with me is against me, and he who does not gather with me, scatters.**

²⁴**"When an evil spirit comes out of a man, it goes through arid places seeking rest and does not find it. Then it says, 'I will return to the house I left.' ²⁵When it arrives, it finds the house swept clean and put in order. ²⁶Then it goes and takes seven other spirits more**

wicked than itself, and they go in and live there. And the final condition of that man is worse than the first."

²⁷As Jesus was saying these things, a woman in the crowd called out, "Blessed is the mother who gave you birth and nursed you."

²⁸He replied, "Blessed rather are those who hear the word of God and obey it."

The previous section on prayer concluded with a reference to the gift of the Holy Spirit. Time and again, Jesus demonstrated that he was filled with the Spirit. However, his opponents attributed his amazing ability to cast out demons and to heal illnesses to a different spirit, the spirit of Beelzebub. This was a popular term for the devil based on the name of the Philistine idol Baal-Zebub (2 Kings 1:2). As laughable as it might seem to us, this would make Jesus a partner with Satan in frustrating God's purposes.

Jesus answers by pointing out how totally illogical this charge is. Human history testifies to the folly of civil war. Satan is not so foolish as to supply Jesus with the power to cast out demons! Furthermore, Jesus makes reference to the fact that exorcisms (casting out of demons) were actions which followers of the Pharisees claimed to be able to do. "Are they also in league with Beelzebub? Let them render a decision with respect to the charge you bring against me."

Human beings sometimes do accomplish works that appear to be miraculous. The magicians of Pharaoh, with "their secret arts," were able to duplicate some of the acts of Moses and Aaron in Egypt (Exodus 7:22). But, ultimately, when confronted with more and more miracles, these magicians said to Pharaoh: "This is the finger of God" (Exodus 8:19). Describing miracles as being worked by God's finger emphasizes the greatness of his power. Now Jesus uses this same expression, admonishing his opponents to recognize that his miracles are worked by God and are not black magic.

The devil is certainly a strong and powerful being. He does all he can to guard his possessions, the people whom he controls. When Jesus wrests these helpless victims out of the hands of the devil, it shows that Jesus is the stronger one.

In verse 23 Jesus issues a challenge to his listeners. One has to take sides in the struggle between Jesus and Satan. Those who don't stand with Jesus are on the side of the enemy; those who don't work with Jesus in gathering people into God's kingdom are guilty of scattering. To link Christ and Satan as coworkers is not only foolish; it is blasphemy, and it hinders the work of the kingdom.

Jesus did much good in driving out evil spirits from many a person's life. Once healed, such a person has the responsibility of making sure that the devil isn't given the opportunity to get back in. The demon goes searching for a resting place (see 8:32), and if none is found, it may come right back along with seven other spirits and reoccupy its former quarters. Jesus is warning against leaving one's life empty, of living in a vacuum. Only the heart filled with the Holy Spirit is fortified against the assaults of Satan.

The opponents of Jesus may have attributed his wonderful power to the working of Beelzebub, but a woman in the crowd listening to Jesus has other ideas. She rather blesses the mother who gave him birth and nursed him. Was his mother perhaps a goddess? wonders the woman. Jesus had earlier identified his mother and brothers as those who "hear God's word and put it into practice" (8:21). He repeats the same thought now, expressing himself in the form of a beatitude: those who hear God's Word and obey it are blessed. They are fortified against the evil one.

The sign of Jonah

**²⁹As the crowds increased, Jesus said, "This is a wicked genera-
tion. It asks for a miraculous sign, but none will be given it except
the sign of Jonah. ³⁰For as Jonah was a sign to the Ninevites, so also
will the Son of Man be to this generation. ³¹The Queen of the South
will rise at the judgment with the men of this generation and condemn them; for she came from the ends of the earth to listen to
Solomon's wisdom, and now one greater than Solomon is here.
³²The men of Nineveh will stand up at the judgment with this generation and condemn it; for they repented at the preaching of Jonah,
and now one greater than Jonah is here.**

We have heard the response of Jesus to those in the
crowd who charged that he drove out a demon by the
power of Beelzebub. There were others who asked for
some special sign which would authenticate that he really
was from God. The miracles were not convincing proof for
them; they were looking for something even more spectacular. Jesus characterizes his generation as wicked because
of this demand for a sign. He will only give them the sign
of Jonah.

Jonah was the Old Testament prophet called by the
Lord to preach repentance to the gentile city of Nineveh.
Jonah fled from that assignment by taking a ship in the
opposite direction. Cast overboard from the ship during a
storm, Jonah was carried inside a great fish for three days
and three nights before being deposited on land again.
Then he went and preached to Nineveh, and as a result,
that great city repented.

Luke omits the words found in Matthew 12:40 which
specify that the sign of Jonah is the resurrection of Jesus
on the third day. The sign of Jonah also includes the fact
that the people of Nineveh repented due to the preaching
of Jonah. This is something that the contemporaries of
Jesus failed to do (see 7:31-34). At the last judgment, the

gentile Ninevites will condemn Jesus' countrymen. So will the gentile Queen of the South (Sheba) who came to listen to the wisdom of King Solomon (1 Kings 10:1-10,13). Jesus is greater than both Solomon and Jonah, but his own generation rejects the blessedness of hearing and obeying his Word (11:28). They fail to follow the example of Mary (10:39), Nineveh, and the Queen of Sheba.

The lamp of the body

[33]"No one lights a lamp and puts it in a place where it will be hidden, or under a bowl. Instead he puts it on its stand, so that those who come in may see the light. [34]Your eye is the lamp of your body. When your eyes are good, your whole body also is full of light. But when they are bad, your body also is full of darkness. [35]See to it, then, that the light within you is not darkness. [36]Therefore, if your whole body is full of light, and no part of it dark, it will be completely lighted, as when the light of a lamp shines on you."

Earlier in this gospel, the light of a lamp was used by Jesus to illustrate the fact that the message of God cannot be hidden (8:16). Now Jesus uses this example of a lamp to say something about himself. The people of his generation were demanding a sign. No sign is needed because Jesus himself is like the light of a lamp. One only has to look to see that a lamp is burning. One only has to look at Jesus, his preaching and his works to see that he is of God. Jesus is for all to see.

Yet some don't see. The problem is not with the lighted lamp; the problem is bad eyes. Jesus speaks of the eye as being the lamp of the body. The eye lets light into the body; we would be in total darkness if we had no eyes. If we don't see well, then there is something wrong with our eyes. This can also be true in a spiritual sense. Those who don't see Jesus, the burning lamp, continue in darkness (John 3:19,20).

The light that comes into the body through the eyes is there for the benefit of the entire body. When with the eye of faith one sees Jesus, the true light, this seeing will be reflected in bodily actions, in practicing the Word. Then the light that is Christ will also make the Christian a light burning in this dark world (Matthew 5:14-16).

Six woes

[37]When Jesus had finished speaking, a Pharisee invited him to eat with him; so he went in and reclined at the table. [38]But the Pharisee, noticing that Jesus did not first wash before the meal, was surprised.

[39]Then the Lord said to him, "Now then, you Pharisees clean the outside of the cup and dish, but inside you are full of greed and wickedness. [40]You foolish people! Did not the one who made the outside make the inside also? [41]But give what is inside the dish to the poor, and everything will be clean for you.

[42]"Woe to you Pharisees, because you give God a tenth of your mint, rue and all other kinds of garden herbs, but you neglect justice and the love of God. You should have practiced the latter without leaving the former undone.

[43]"Woe to you Pharisees, because you love the most important seats in the synagogues and greetings in the marketplaces.

[44]"Woe to you, because you are like unmarked graves, which men walk over without knowing it."

[45]One of the experts in the law answered him, "Teacher, when you say these things, you insult us also."

[46]Jesus replied, "And you experts in the law, woe to you, because you load people down with burdens they can hardly carry, and you yourselves will not lift one finger to help them.

[47]"Woe to you, because you build tombs for the prophets, and it was your forefathers who killed them. [48]So you testify that you approve of what your forefathers did; they killed the prophets, and you build their tombs. [49]Because of this, God in his wisdom said, 'I will send them prophets and apostles, some of whom they will kill and others they will persecute.' [50]Therefore this generation will be held responsible for the blood of all the prophets that

has been shed since the beginning of the world, [51]from the blood of Abel to the blood of Zechariah, who was killed between the altar and the sanctuary. Yes, I tell you, this generation will be held responsible for it all.

[52]"Woe to you experts in the law, because you have taken away the key to knowledge. You yourselves have not entered, and you have hindered those who were entering."

[53]When Jesus left there, the Pharisees and the teachers of the law began to oppose him fiercely and to besiege him with questions, [54]waiting to catch him in something he might say.

John's gospel includes the story of how Jesus healed a man born blind (chapter 9). The Pharisees contest this miracle, questioning whether the man was ever really blind. They were not willing to admit that Jesus had opened the eyes of this man. At the conclusion of the story, Jesus makes a statement as to the reason for his coming into the world: "For judgment I have come into this world, so that the blind will see and those who see will become blind" (John 9:39). The Pharisees claimed to be able to see but were actually spiritually blind. As a result, Jesus tells them, "your guilt remains" (verse 41).

Jesus is the light of the world, the lamp for all to see. As religious leaders, the Pharisees and experts in the law claimed to have keen spiritual sight. But, in fact, they had eyes only for minute points of the law, totally overlooking the kind of practice of his Word that the Lord was looking for. Jesus catalogs the guilt of the Pharisees and the lawyers, condemning them in a series of six woes. The occasion for this denunciation was another invitation from a Pharisee for dinner (see 7:36). We might suppose that one reason for this invitation was a desire to catch Jesus in some fault, something to tarnish that image of a brightly burning lamp.

The Pharisee found what he was looking for when he noted that Jesus had not washed his hands before eating.

In Mark 7:3 we are told that "the Pharisees and all the Jews do not eat unless they give their hands a ceremonial washing, holding to the tradition of the elders." They believed that unwashed hands would bring ritual defilement upon the food that had been blessed by prayer.

Jesus responds to the Pharisee's shocked surprise by faulting that sect for their attention to external cleanliness while neglecting the inside, the heart. In the case of the Pharisees, that inside is "full of greed and wickedness." Jesus challenges them to give alms to the poor; such a loving action would clean up both the outside and the inside. It would make ritual washing of hands unnecessary.

Continuing on the subject of the sins of the Pharisees and the experts in the law, Jesus six times utters the words "woe to you." This expression of judgment was used previously in 6:24-26. These woes are in contrast to the beatitude spoken by Jesus in 11:28. Though on the surface the Pharisees seem to be very religious, they do not truly hear the Word of God and obey it. They therefore receive these words of woe.

The first woe denounces the wrong priorities of the Pharisees. They are fastidious about making sure that God gets a tenth of the tiny seeds of their garden herbs like mint and rue, but justice and the love of God are neglected. Jesus is not criticizing tithing; he rather faults the Pharisees for forgetting words like those spoken by the prophet Micah: "What does the LORD require of you? To act justly and to love mercy and to walk humbly with your God" (6:8).

Next Jesus castigates the Pharisees for their showy pride. They love the most important seats in the synagogue and the habit of being the first ones greeted in the marketplace. The third woe has reference to the practice of carefully marking the graves of the dead lest a person be defiled and made unclean by walking on them. The Pharisees are walking graves, and people do not realize what evil is really within them and what contamination comes from them. One should not read these woes of Jesus as condemning each individual Pharisee but rather as a judgment upon their theological system, which produces such spiritual attitudes.

One of the experts in the law interrupts Jesus with the comment "Teacher, when you say these things, you insult us also." We have met these experts in the law (lawyers) several times previously in Luke's gospel (see 5:17). They may have been a specific group among the Pharisees who were specialists in the study and teaching of the law. When Jesus levels woes against the whole body of the Pharisees, he is thereby including also the smaller, professional class of law experts. At least one of them does not think this is being fair.

Jesus knew what he was talking about and now specifically utters a like number of woes against the experts in the law. In the first of these, he condemns them for burdening people with so many different laws that the common person can't begin to keep all the religious laws straight, let alone practice them. For example, the law experts had carefully determined that 39 classes of work were forbidden on the Sabbath. And what is even worse, the lawyers weren't even lifting a finger to keep the laws themselves.

The fifth woe in this series denounces the law experts for their attitude toward prophets. It is true that many fine tombs were being built to honor the memory of the prophets. But Jesus observes that the present generation is really no better than the forefathers who killed the prophets. Building tombs in no way makes up for the failure to listen to the words of the prophets (including John the Baptist and Jesus). The Old Testament fathers killed the prophet Zechariah son of Jehoiada in the court-yard of the temple (2 Chronicles 24:20-22). God sends New Testament prophets and apostles knowing that they will suffer a similar fate because of the hostility of the religious leaders of Jesus' generation.

The final woe addresses a failure that is the most seri-ous of all: "You have taken away the key to knowledge. You yourselves have not entered, and you have hindered those who were entering." The key to knowledge is God's plan of salvation through Christ. The law experts rejected Jesus, and by their attitude they kept others from entering into the kingdom of God. This is their greatest sin.

Back in 6:11 Luke tells us that the Pharisees "were furi-ous and began to discuss with one another what they might do to Jesus." As Jesus makes his journey to Jerusalem and continues to speak out against the sins of the Pharisees and experts of the law, that opposition grows more fierce. It becomes increasingly obvious that Jesus is making a journey which will lead to the cross.

Warnings and encouragements

12 **Meanwhile, when a crowd of many thousands had gath-ered, so that they were trampling on one another, Jesus began to speak first to his disciples, saying: "Be on your guard against the yeast of the Pharisees, which is hypocrisy. ²There is nothing concealed that will not be disclosed, or hidden that will not be made known. ³What you have said in the dark will be heard in the daylight, and what you have whispered in the ear in the inner rooms will be proclaimed from the roofs.**

⁴"I tell you, my friends, do not be afraid of those who kill the body and after that can do no more. ⁵But I will show you whom you should fear: Fear him who, after the killing of the body, has

power to throw you into hell. Yes, I tell you, fear him. ⁶Are not five sparrows sold for two pennies? Yet not one of them is forgotten by God. ⁷Indeed, the very hairs of your head are all numbered. Don't be afraid; you are worth more than many sparrows.

⁸"I tell you, whoever acknowledges me before men, the Son of Man will also acknowledge him before the angels of God. ⁹But he who disowns me before men will be disowned before the angels of God. ¹⁰And everyone who speaks a word against the Son of Man will be forgiven, but anyone who blasphemes against the Holy Spirit will not be forgiven.

¹¹"When you are brought before synagogues, rulers and authorities, do not worry about how you will defend yourselves or what you will say, ¹²for the Holy Spirit will teach you at that time what you should say."

Jesus had spoken out without fear against the Pharisees and experts in the law. By doing this, Jesus knew that he was risking his very life. The descendants of those who had killed prophets in the past would not hesitate to kill prophets themselves in the present. And what was true for Jesus is also true for his disciples. The bold witness risks persecution and death.

This fact dare not keep the disciples from bearing witness to Jesus. There are so many who need to hear. In 11:29 Luke notes that "the crowds increased." Now a crowd of many thousands presses in upon Jesus. Here is impressive evidence of the need for fearless witnesses.

The danger for the disciple is to follow the course of the Pharisees. They appear to be genuinely religious, but this is pretense; there is spiritual deadness within. This hypocrisy is like yeast, which permeates the entire loaf. One will not function well as a disciple and witness of Christ if he is not genuine.

To back up this warning against hypocrisy, Jesus again quotes a saying that was used earlier (8:17). Hypocrisy can only be hidden for so long; it will be disclosed in the end.

The disciples are challenged to speak what Jesus had made known to them in his private teaching; they are urged to proclaim from the housetops what during the earthly ministry of Jesus they had only whispered to one another in closed rooms. The disciples put this kind of bold witness into practice beginning with Pentecost.

If the disciples are to confess their faith despite persecution, Jesus knows that they will need encouragement. They are reminded that the most other human beings can do to them is kill the body; on the other hand, God is able not only to kill the body but to throw it into hell. The word "hell" is a translation of the Greek word *gehenna*. This was the name given to a valley just south of Jerusalem that served as a rubbish dump and where fires often burned. The name became a symbol for the place of eternal torment after death.

Jesus is contrasting hollow fear (to be afraid of men) with true fear (awe and respect for the Almighty). To fear God is also to trust him who cares about the little sparrows and knows the number of hairs on one's head. Nothing will happen to the fearless witness without the permission of the heavenly Father.

The disciple who is tempted to disown his master should take into account the eternal consequences: the Son of Man will disown him on the day of judgment with the angels of God as witnesses. On the other hand, the disciple who courageously witnesses faith in Jesus will be acknowledged on that day. Here is added incentive to be fearless.

Verse 10 might better be included with 11 and 12 as a new paragraph rather than being joined with verses 8 and 9. Jesus is here speaking about a possible response that the witness of the disciples might elicit. As the Son of Man, Jesus was spoken against many times during his earthly ministry. There is the possibility of forgiveness for such hostile words against Christ. But people who blasphemed against the Holy Spirit, who would speak through the disciples, would not be forgiven. Such people who persistently and stubbornly refuse the message of the gospel as proclaimed by the representatives of Christ (see Acts 7:51) have no hope of salvation.

This section closes with the assurance to the disciples that when they are brought before religious or secular authorities, the Holy Spirit will lead them in what they should say. We have several examples of this in the book of Acts (4:8; 6:10). Human inarticulateness will give way to the strength and eloquence that comes from God's Spirit. Here is the final encouragement to speak up for Jesus despite opposition and persecution.

The parable of the rich fool

¹³Someone in the crowd said to him, "Teacher, tell my brother to divide the inheritance with me."

¹⁴Jesus replied, "Man, who appointed me a judge or an arbiter between you?" ¹⁵Then he said to them, "Watch out! Be on your guard against all kinds of greed; a man's life does not consist in the abundance of his possessions."

¹⁶And he told them this parable: "The ground of a certain rich man produced a good crop. ¹⁷He thought to himself, 'What shall I do? I have no place to store my crops.'

¹⁸"Then he said, 'This is what I'll do. I will tear down my barns and build bigger ones, and there I will store all my grain and my goods. ¹⁹And I'll say to myself, "You have plenty of good things laid up for many years. Take life easy; eat, drink and be merry."'

²⁰"But God said to him, 'You fool! This very night your life will be demanded from you. Then who will get what you have prepared for yourself?'

²¹"This is how it will be with anyone who stores up things for himself but is not rich toward God."

There are any number of obstacles which may keep a disciple from being a faithful witness to Jesus. A most serious temptation is to become attached to worldly possessions. Jesus has the opportunity to warn against greed and covetousness when someone from the crowd makes this request of him: "Teacher, tell my brother to divide the inheritance with me." In chapter 15 Jesus will tell a parable in which a son makes that same request of his father.

Jesus refuses to be drawn into this dispute between brothers, just as he did not intervene when Martha wanted his support to get her sister's help. Rather, Jesus uses this request to warn against the underlying problem: greed. So easily people imagine that the worth of life is measured by the abundance of possessions. One of Jesus' charges against the Pharisees was their greed (11:39). Disciples need to be especially on guard against this sin.

To illustrate the point he is making, Jesus tells a parable. The rich man had an abundance of possessions. No doubt his neighbors considered him to be very successful in life. His barns quickly became too small to hold all the grain his fields produced. Larger ones were built. He had no worries about the future as he looked forward to a retirement filled with leisure and good times.

But the rich man had not taken God and his judgment into consideration. Far from being wise and resourceful, this man was an utter fool. Like the Pharisees who busied themselves with externals, proving that they were fools (11:40), so this man was ill prepared when God's summons came. For the sake of earthly gain, he had forfeited his life (9:25).

Jesus is not condemning riches here; he is rather condemning a wrong attitude toward riches that hold them as the most important thing in life. He is warning against greed and the failure to use riches properly. He had urged the Pharisees to "give what is inside the dish to the poor" (11:41). This is one way of being rich toward God. The theme of viewing life in terms of God's coming judgment is one that runs through the following portions of Luke's gospel.

Do not worry

²²**Then Jesus said to his disciples: "Therefore I tell you, do not worry about your life, what you will eat; or about your body, what you will wear. ²³Life is more than food, and the body more than clothes. ²⁴Consider the ravens: They do not sow or reap, they have no storeroom or barn; yet God feeds them. And how much more valuable you are than birds! ²⁵Who of you by worrying can add a single hour to his life? ²⁶Since you cannot do this very little thing, why do you worry about the rest?**

²⁷**"Consider how the lilies grow. They do not labor or spin. Yet I tell you, not even Solomon in all his splendor was dressed like one of these. ²⁸If that is how God clothes the grass of the field, which is here today, and tomorrow is thrown into the fire, how much more will he clothe you, O you of little faith! ²⁹And do not set your heart on what you will eat or drink; do not worry about it. ³⁰For the pagan world runs after all such things, and your Father knows that you need them. ³¹But seek his kingdom, and these things will be given to you as well.**

³²**"Do not be afraid, little flock, for your Father has been pleased to give you the kingdom. ³³Sell your possessions and give to the poor. Provide purses for yourselves that will not wear out, a treasure in heaven that will not be exhausted, where no thief comes near and no moth destroys. ³⁴For where your treasure is, there your heart will be also.**

The rich man in the parable is an example of someone whose barns and storehouses were filled to the brim and yet was not truly prepared for the future. The very opposite of the rich man is the raven. This scavenger is satisfied with leftovers and would not think of storing up food for the future. In ancient times ravens were regarded as careless creatures that even failed to return to their nests. But in

Psalm 147:9 we learn that God provides food "for the young ravens when they call."

Not the rich man but the raven is held up by Jesus for his disciples to imitate. In addition, Jesus directs attention to lilies and the grass of the field. The word translated here as "lilies" may refer to any of the colorful flowers that dot the Palestinian hillsides. Jesus declares that their beauty surpasses that of King Solomon. Even the grass that clothes the fields has a certain beauty, yet that grass is here today and gone tomorrow, commonly used as fuel to heat an oven.

When Jesus sent out the twelve apostles and the 72 disciples, he told them to take no food along. They were to eat in homes along the way. Such a day-to-day existence might easily cause one to wonder where the next meal would be coming from. Jesus, however, urges his disciples, "Do not worry." Life is more than just eating and drinking. In rejecting the devil's first temptation, Jesus said much the same: "Man does not live on bread alone" (4:4). Worrying about anything and everything will not add a single hour to a person's life.

The attitude that Jesus looks for in his disciples is one of faith and trust in the heavenly Father. This is the very opposite of the pagan world, which runs after food, drink, and clothing for fear of not having enough. Jesus gives his followers the comforting assurance: "Your Father knows that you need them." The disciples had been taught to pray, "Give us each day our daily bread" (11:3). God's answer to this prayer is really all that a disciple needs to live in this world.

Rather than setting one's heart "on what you will eat or drink," Jesus urges, "Seek his kingdom, and these things will be given to you as well." Once again, as so often, it is a question of right priorities. The Pharisees had their priorities messed up, so did Martha and the rich man. Later we will hear Jesus declare, "You cannot serve both God and Money" (16:13). Right priorities are essential for the disciples of Jesus.

The kingdom is ever central in the thinking of Jesus. In this world, opposed by mighty forces, the little flock of believers may forget the kingdom and be afraid. Jesus seeks to allay such fears with the reminder "Your Father has been pleased to give you the kingdom." This is the kingdom that the disciple must ever seek.

One who has the promise of this kingdom will be much less concerned with the possessions of this world. In fact, Jesus advises, "Sell your possessions and give to the poor." The treasure that really matters, the treasure that no one or nothing can take away, is stored in heaven. And if one's treasure is safely deposited in heaven, then heaven will be the center of one's thoughts and desires. This will be a remedy for worry and fear.

Throughout the ages, Christians have asked just how literally these words of Jesus are to be understood. Saint Francis of Assisi gave away all possessions including his clothing and lived a life of total poverty. Is this what Jesus wants every Christian to do? Hardly. We need to read these words of Jesus in the context of God's total revelation. Jesus is saying something here that every disciple must hear and hear often. Jesus says it in a way that is bold, that catches our attention. Disciples of Jesus need to distance themselves from the attitude of the world that glorifies this earthly life and its possessions. The disciple needs to always remember that the end is coming. The first priority in life always must be to seek God's kingdom. This is to listen to what Jesus is saying.

Watchfulness

[35]"Be dressed ready for service and keep your lamps burning, [36]like men waiting for their master to return from a wedding banquet, so that when he comes and knocks they can immediately open the door for him. [37]It will be good for those servants whose master finds them watching when he comes. I tell you the truth, he will dress himself to serve, will have them recline at the table and will come and wait on them. [38]It will be good for those servants whose master finds them ready, even if he comes in the second or third watch of the night. [39]But understand this: If the owner of the house had known at what hour the thief was coming, he would not have let his house be broken into. [40]You also must be ready, because the Son of Man will come at an hour when you do not expect him."

[41]Peter asked, "Lord, are you telling this parable to us, or to everyone?"

[42]The Lord answered, "Who then is the faithful and wise manager, whom the master puts in charge of his servants to give them their food allowance at the proper time? [43]It will be good for that servant whom the master finds doing so when he returns. [44]I tell you the truth, he will put him in charge of all his possessions. [45]But suppose the servant says to himself, 'My master is taking a long time in coming,' and he then begins to beat the menservants and maidservants and to eat and drink and get drunk. [46]The master of that servant will come on a day when he does not expect him and at an hour he is not aware of. He will cut him to pieces and assign him a place with the unbelievers.

[47]"That servant who knows his master's will and does not get ready or does not do what his master wants will be beaten with many blows. [48]But the one who does not know and does things deserving punishment will be beaten with few blows. From everyone who has been given much, much will be demanded; and from the one who has been entrusted with much, much more will be asked.

When Jesus was transfigured, the subject of conversation was his departure, or exodus, at Jerusalem (9:31).

Shortly thereafter, Jesus resolutely set out for Jerusalem with his disciples; on the way, he taught them many things. A truth the disciples needed to learn was the fact that the same Jesus who would depart from Jerusalem was coming again. As servants of the Lord, the disciples were expected to be watchful and to carry out their responsibilities with faithfulness.

Jesus compares his coming again with that of a master who had left home to attend a wedding banquet. The servants are to be dressed, ready for service with lamps burning, waiting for their master's knock on the door. The NIV translation "be dressed ready for service" is an interpretation of the Greek expression "let your loins be girded" (see the KJV). At the time of the exodus out of Egypt, the Lord told the Israelites to have "your cloak tucked into your belt," ready for travel (Exodus 12:11). Servants are ready to serve when their long robes are tucked into a belt around the waist. That's the state of watchfulness Jesus expects of his servants.

Such watchful servants will be rewarded. In the parable told by Jesus, this reward takes the form of sitting at a banquet and being served by the master (one is reminded of how Jesus washed the disciples' feet at the Last Supper). Here is a role reversal, with the master putting on the apron and waiting on his servants.

One problem for waiting servants is the fact that they do not know the time of their master's return. It might be in the second watch (9–12 P.M.); it might be in the third (12–3 A.M.). To emphasize the uncertainty of the time of the master's return, Jesus introduces a different illustration. It is the example of a homeowner who has no way of knowing when a thief might come in the night to rob him. Saint Paul uses this same illustration when writing to the Thessalonians:

"You know very well that the day of the Lord will come like a thief in the night" (1 Thessalonians 5:2). The Son of Man will come at an hour when he is not expected.

In speaking of the coming of the Son of Man, Jesus is referring first of all to his return at the end of the world. When that will be, no one knows. And those who attempt to calculate such things are defying the will of God, who does not choose to reveal this date to us. What is true of the end of the world is to some extent also true of the end of our earthly lives, as the rich fool discovered. The servants of Christ must be ready, watchful at all times for their master's return.

The question Peter asks prompts Jesus to say more about what is expected especially of leaders in the church. He introduces another example, this time of a manager (steward) who has been given charge of his fellow servants by his master. He has the responsibility of distributing the food allowance and, in general, of managing the household wisely in the absence of his master. If this manager fulfills his duties faithfully, then the master will reward him with greater authority and responsibility.

A manager may, however, suppose that the return of his master is a long way off and exploit his power and authority. He begins to beat his fellow servants, both men and women; he spends his time in feasting and drunkenness. When the master of that manager returns suddenly and unexpectedly, the punishment will be severe. Jesus says that the master "will cut him to pieces and assign him a place with the unbelievers." This violent form of punishment might not have been out of character for the times in which Jesus lived. Like Peter and the apostles, leaders in the church receive a stern warning here that the authority given them by the master dare not be abused.

Servants must be watchful and faithful. Yet not all are punished alike when they fail to carry out their duties. Those who know the master's will very well but fail to carry out what he wants will be beaten with many blows. However, the unfaithful servant who is not well informed of his master's desires will receive only a few blows. The reason Jesus gives for this variation in punishment results from an unequal distribution of talents and opportunities: the more one has been given, the more will be expected.

Peter had asked if Jesus was talking just to the disciples or to everyone. Certainly, the words of Jesus are meant for everyone. But, obviously, Jesus is directing them especially to his own closest followers. They had been given much. Much would be expected of them in watchfulness and faithfulness. Today also, some Christians receive greater gifts and responsibilities. Jesus looks for them to set an example of watchfulness and faithfulness. And if they fail, they can expect the greater punishment. This punishment may not refer so much to eternity as to the consequences a disgraced leader of the church experiences in this earthly life.

Not peace but division

⁴⁹"I have come to bring fire on the earth, and how I wish it were already kindled! ⁵⁰But I have a baptism to undergo, and how distressed I am until it is completed! ⁵¹Do you think I came to bring peace on earth? No, I tell you, but division. ⁵²From now on there will be five in one family divided against each other, three against two and two against three. ⁵³They will be divided, father against son and son against father, mother against daughter and daughter against mother, mother-in-law against daughter-in-law and daughter-in-law against mother-in-law."

Jesus was expecting much of his followers in the way of faithfulness to their calling. But no disciple has such a demanding role to fulfill as does his master. Of no one is so much expected than of Jesus. After speaking of what he looks for from his servants, Jesus speaks of his own mission in this world. One catches a glimpse of a soul deeply distressed.

Jesus' mission included bringing fire on the earth. John the Baptist had said of Jesus that "he will baptize you with the Holy Spirit and with fire" (3:16). James and John were ready to call down the fire of judgment on the Samaritan village that would not welcome Jesus (9:54). The rebuke they received makes it plain that the time for fiery judgment had not yet come. But the day of fire will come. The master will return. Jesus' wish that the fire "were already kindled" suggests that he would like to get it over with since it is so dreadful to contemplate.

But before the fire of judgment will fall on the earth, Jesus himself must undergo a fiery judgment, which he refers to as his baptism. To compare baptism with death may reflect the great flood, when water brought God's judgment upon the whole world. Saint Paul picks up on this connection when he writes in Romans 6:4, "We were therefore buried with [Christ] through baptism into death." The baptism that Jesus must undergo is distressing because all the fiery judgment of hell is heaped upon him as punishment for the sins of the world.

As Jesus made his way to Jerusalem to undergo this baptism, it was becoming increasingly clear that many were not ready to accept his message of salvation. The angels had sung of the peace which the birth of the Savior would bring to the earth. God wants peace for the world, but human beings refuse his offer of reconciliation. Families were divided over Jesus and this will go on to the end. What Simeon had foretold, Jesus sees happening. It is all very painful to Jesus; he wishes that his mission were finished.

Interpreting the times

⁵⁴**He said to the crowd: "When you see a cloud rising in the west, immediately you say, 'It's going to rain,' and it does. ⁵⁵And when the south wind blows, you say, 'It's going to be hot,' and it is. ⁵⁶Hypocrites! You know how to interpret the appearance of the earth and the sky. How is it that you don't know how to interpret this present time?**

⁵⁷**"Why don't you judge for yourselves what is right? ⁵⁸As you are going with your adversary to the magistrate, try hard to be reconciled to him on the way, or he may drag you off to the judge, and the judge turn you over to the officer, and the officer throw you into prison. ⁵⁹I tell you, you will not get out until you have paid the last penny."**

The world is clearly moving toward God's final judgment. Yet so many fail to reckon with this fact. They are like the rich fool who was busy making money and unconcerned about his impending death.

Jesus tells the crowds following him on the way to Jerusalem that people are able to read the weather signs but fail to read the signs of the times. They are meteorologically sensitive but religiously stupid. Many show a wisdom in earthly matters, like business and weather, but are blind and stubborn in spiritual things.

In applying the word "hypocrites" to the crowd, Jesus hints at a common trait found among people—they act as if they don't know any better. It is not as if people are unable to see the end coming. They are rather unwilling to face this fact and to make the necessary changes in their lives.

But there is still time to escape. Jesus uses an illustration to make this plain to the crowds. In human affairs if someone brings a complaint against a person, an attempt is usually made to settle the problem before the accused ends up in jail. Jesus is probably referring to a case of failure to pay an outstanding debt. One might be able to get off by paying a lesser amount to satisfy the adversary. But once in prison, the debt must be paid to the last penny.

People should be as discerning about settling their debts with God as they are when it comes to worldly accounts. But unfortunately, as with interpreting the signs of the times, people don't use wisdom in making sure that they will escape the eternal prison. Jesus wonders why people are so dense, so unwilling to take the opportunities given them to repent before it is too late. It is another example of human foolishness.

Repent or perish

13 Now there were some present at that time who told Jesus about the Galileans whose blood Pilate had mixed with their sacrifices. ²Jesus answered, "Do you think that these Galileans were worse sinners than all the other Galileans because they suffered this way? ³I tell you, no! But unless you repent, you too will all perish. ⁴Or those eighteen who died when the tower in Siloam fell on them—do you think they were more guilty than all the others living in Jerusalem? ⁵I tell you, no! But unless you repent, you too will all perish."

⁶Then he told this parable: "A man had a fig tree, planted in his vineyard, and he went to look for fruit on it, but did not find any. ⁷So he said to the man who took care of the vineyard, 'For three years now I've been coming to look for fruit on this fig tree and haven't found any. Cut it down! Why should it use up the soil?'

⁸"'Sir,' the man replied, 'leave it alone for one more year, and I'll dig around it and fertilize it. ⁹If it bears fruit next year, fine! If not, then cut it down.'"

Jesus had been critical of the crowd following him for their inability to interpret "this present time" (12:56). One senses that some in the crowd respond to this criticism by telling Jesus of the Galileans murdered by Pilate to suggest that they were aware of how God does indeed punish sinners. They are not as dense as Jesus makes them out to be.

Jesus is compelled to correctly interpret this event for the crowd. Very likely there was a group of pilgrims from Galilee making sacrifices at the temple in Jerusalem when the soldiers of Pilate struck. But only a few of the worshipers were killed. Jesus questions the crowd as to whether those individuals who suffered death were worse sinners than the others who were not killed. Jesus rejects this conclusion.

He goes on to cite another example of tragic death. Eighteen people were killed when the tower of Siloam fell on them. This tower was located near the pool of Siloam in the southeast corner of Jerusalem. Jesus asks if these 18 were more guilty than others living in Jerusalem at the time. Once again he rejects this conclusion. Jesus breaks the connection between these tragic deaths and punishment for sin. We must not interpret unusual earthly suffering and death as a specific punishment for some sin that an individual has committed, unless there is proof.

Jesus provides the proper interpretation of these two events: "Unless you repent, you too will all perish." Brutal murders, shocking accidents, death in whatever form—all are sermons of God's law: the soul that sins will die. Death is one way God calls people to repentance, lest they perish eternally. Some falsely conclude that if nothing really bad happens to them in life, it is a sign that they have been living good lives. Jesus is teaching that not only certain very wicked people need to repent but repentance is necessary for everyone.

The murders by Pilate are a foreshadowing of the death of Jesus Christ. There were many in his generation who falsely interpreted his death on the cross as a sign of his own guilt. We know that such was not the case at all. Jesus was altogether innocent of any sin. His death was for the sins of the world, which were laid on him.

The woman who had an infirmity for 18 years

The parable told by Jesus about the fig tree brings out the truth that God gives people time to repent. God is very patient, not willing that any should perish but that all would come to repentance (2 Peter 3:9). However, the delay in judgment should not cause people to put off repentance. The time will finally come when the unfruitful tree is cut down. The opportunity for repentance does finally come to an end.

A crippled woman healed on the Sabbath

¹⁰**On a Sabbath Jesus was teaching in one of the synagogues,** ¹¹**and a woman was there who had been crippled by a spirit for eighteen years. She was bent over and could not straighten up at all.** ¹²**When Jesus saw her, he called her forward and said to her, "Woman, you are set free from your infirmity."** ¹³**Then he put his hands on her, and immediately she straightened up and praised God.**

¹⁴**Indignant because Jesus had healed on the Sabbath, the synagogue ruler said to the people, "There are six days for work. So come and be healed on those days, not on the Sabbath."**

¹⁵**The Lord answered him, "You hypocrites! Doesn't each of you on the Sabbath untie his ox or donkey from the stall and lead it out to give it water?** ¹⁶**Then should not this woman, a daughter of Abraham, whom Satan has kept bound for eighteen long years, be set free on the Sabbath day from what bound her?"**

¹⁷**When he said this, all his opponents were humiliated, but the people were delighted with all the wonderful things he was doing.**

Jesus used his journey to Jerusalem as a time for teaching. That will be brought out clearly in 13:22: "Jesus went through the towns and villages, teaching as he made his way to Jerusalem." Most of this teaching took place out in the open. But on occasion, Jesus did go into the Jewish synagogues for this purpose. The present mention of Jesus teaching in the synagogue is the last that we have in Luke's gospel.

Jesus taught not only by word of mouth; he taught by his actions. That is particularly true in the present instance. In the synagogue there was a woman who had been crippled for 18 years. Her body was stiffly bent, and she enjoyed little freedom of movement. Jesus observed her pitiful condition and set her free from her infirmity with a touch of his hands. What a joy it was for this woman to be able to stand tall and straight after 18 years!

The ruler of the synagogue, however, was indignant because the healing was accomplished on the Sabbath. We are reminded of similar criticism that came from the Pharisees when Jesus had healed a man with a shriveled hand on the Sabbath (6:6-11). The ruler of the synagogue does not address Jesus directly but rather makes his comments to the people, instructing them about what he considers an unlawful action on the Sabbath.

Jesus responds by calling his critics "hypocrites." He had used that word back in 12:56 to characterize the crowd's unwillingness to interpret the signs of the times. It is appropriate here to describe people who will loose an animal on the Sabbath and lead it to water but who find fault with loosing a fellow Israelite from bondage imposed by Satan. Jesus sees people here whose priorities are terribly out of order.

The ruler of the synagogue would not have agreed, but he himself is one who needs to repent. Repentance is not only for wrong deeds; repentance is necessary for false attitudes. The ruler demonstrates a wrong understanding of the purpose of the Old Testament Sabbath. Rather than binding people with intolerable restrictions, the Sabbath was to be a day of freedom, freedom from toil to celebrate God's goodness. For this woman whom Jesus healed, it had become exactly that, a day of freedom and salvation. The perfect Sabbath will be the rest we enjoy in heaven, free from all sin and sickness.

The parables of the mustard seed and yeast

¹⁸Then Jesus asked, "What is the kingdom of God like? What shall I compare it to? ¹⁹It is like a mustard seed, which a man took and planted in his garden. It grew and became a tree, and the birds of the air perched in its branches."

²⁰Again he asked, "What shall I compare the kingdom of God to? ²¹It is like yeast that a woman took and mixed into a large amount of flour until it worked all through the dough."

The parables of the mustard seed and the yeast conclude this first portion of the journey of Jesus to Jerusalem. Luke does not give us a literal travelogue of this journey; rather, he describes a spiritual journey. It is a learning experience for the disciples who follow Jesus on the way to the cross.

This first portion of the journey to Jerusalem has been titled "Jesus urges people to get ready for the coming kingdom." Though that kingdom is far from obvious to those walking with Jesus, they are given the assurance that the kingdom will most certainly come. The growth of the small mustard seed and the hidden power of the yeast to work in flour both demonstrate this ultimate truth. The journey of Jesus and the disciples will end in triumph. These two parables sound that note of triumph.

The mustard plant was a garden herb with a minute seed (see 17:6, where the seed is used again as an example of something small). Jewish literature describes such a small seed growing to the height of a fig tree. Such will be the spectacular fulfillment of God's kingdom. In the other parable, the yeast works in a large amount of flour (one-half bushel?). A small amount of yeast is powerful enough to cause that large mass of dough to rise. So powerful is God's kingdom at work in the world.

The crowds in Jesus' day were delighted with the wonderful things he was doing. And well they might be, since where Jesus is, there is the kingdom of God. That kingdom comes to us in God's Word and sacrament. It will have its glorious fulfillment when Jesus comes again at the end of time.

Jesus reveals some surprises as to who will inherit the kingdom

The narrow door

²²Then Jesus went through the towns and villages, teaching as he made his way to Jerusalem. ²³Someone asked him, "Lord, are only a few people going to be saved?"

He said to them, ²⁴"Make every effort to enter through the narrow door, because many, I tell you, will try to enter and will not be able to. ²⁵Once the owner of the house gets up and closes the door, you will stand outside knocking and pleading, 'Sir, open the door for us.'

"But he will answer, 'I don't know you or where you come from.'

²⁶"Then you will say, 'We ate and drank with you, and you taught in our streets.'

²⁷"But he will reply, 'I don't know you or where you come from. Away from me, all you evildoers!'

²⁸"There will be weeping there, and gnashing of teeth, when you see Abraham, Isaac and Jacob and all the prophets in the kingdom of God, but you yourselves thrown out. ²⁹People will come from east and west and north and south, and will take their places at the feast in the kingdom of God. ³⁰Indeed there are those who are last who will be first, and first who will be last."

Luke tells us in 9:51 that "Jesus resolutely set out for Jerusalem." In the present section the fact is noted that Jesus is making his way to Jerusalem. In 17:11 we will read that "on his way to Jerusalem, Jesus traveled along the border between Samaria and Galilee." The border between those two provinces is a long way from Jerusalem. This journey to Jerusalem is hardly in a straight line; it is rather a spiritual pilgrimage interrupted by much teaching and several miracles. But there can be no doubt as to the ultimate goal. Jerusalem will finally be reached. This is the city where the salvation of the world will be accomplished.

A question about salvation often discussed by Jewish teachers is now put to Jesus: "Are only a few people going to be saved?" Some of the rabbis taught that all Israelites would have a share in the world to come. Jesus answers the question in quite a different way.

Several of the parables of Jesus compare salvation to a great feast, or banquet, given by a king. That is also the picture he uses here. Entrance into the banquet hall is by a door. The first thing Jesus says about that door is that it is narrow. A narrow door prevents great crowds of people from entering all at once. Entrance into the banquet is gained by going through the door one at a time. That narrow door is a symbol for Jesus himself. One enters the banquet hall by way of Jesus. Jesus urges his hearers to "make every effort to enter." A Greek word is used in the original text which suggests a contest or struggle to enter. The struggle is not against other people but rather against our own sinful flesh and the temptations of the devil.

Jesus has something else to say about that door. The time will come when the owner of the house is going to close that door. There will be some who come knocking on the locked door demanding entry. But just knowing the owner of the house will not cause him to open. Jesus is obviously picturing himself as the owner since the people speak of his teaching in their streets. Just as the time will come when the unfruitful tree will be cut down (13:9), so also the time will come in each individual's life and in the history of the world when the entrance to salvation will be closed. The message is plain: don't delay but strive to enter now.

Finally, we have a description of the people sitting at the banquet tables. As is to be expected, Abraham, Isaac, Jacob, and the prophets are there. But then comes a surprise: many of Jesus' contemporaries will find themselves on the outside looking in. Weeping and grinding of teeth will express their disappointment and shock. They will see that other people from all over the world will be sitting in their places at the banquet of salvation. Those who first had the opportunity to respond to Christ's preaching will find themselves left out; those at the very ends of the earth who heard the gospel message last will find themselves honored with choice seating at the heavenly banquet.

Jesus does not really answer the question that he was asked. Rather, he is saying to all who will listen, "Just be sure that you are going to be saved."

Jesus' sorrow for Jerusalem

[31]At that time some Pharisees came to Jesus and said to him, "Leave this place and go somewhere else. Herod wants to kill you."

[32]He replied, "Go tell that fox, 'I will drive out demons and heal people today and tomorrow, and on the third day I will reach my goal.' [33]In any case, I must keep going today and tomorrow and the next day—for surely no prophet can die outside Jerusalem!

[34]"O Jerusalem, Jerusalem, you who kill the prophets and stone those sent to you, how often I have longed to gather your children together, as a hen gathers her chicks under her wings, but you were not willing! [35]Look, your house is left to you desolate. I tell you, you will not see me again until you say, 'Blessed is he who comes in the name of the Lord.'"

Herod Antipas was the ruler over the provinces of Galilee and Perea (an area east of the Jordan River). The advice of the Pharisees that Jesus "leave this place" would indicate that Jesus was still traveling through one of these two provinces. Why some of the Pharisees would come to Jesus with this warning has been interpreted various ways. Perhaps the advice was with the evil intent of speeding Jesus on to Jerusalem, where he would meet with death. Or perhaps some of the Pharisees were sympathetic with Jesus and wanted to spare him from meeting the fate of John the Baptist, whom Herod had beheaded.

In any case, Jesus does not heed the warning. Rather, he sends the Pharisees back to Herod with the message that he will continue his work as Servant of the Lord till he reaches his goal. Jesus calls Herod a "fox." This term was used by Jewish rabbis as an epithet for a crafty or sly person. Perhaps Herod had sent the Pharisees to Jesus with this warning to get Jesus out of his territory, even though earlier we are told that Herod tried to see Jesus (9:9).

But Herod will not determine the outcome of Jesus' life. Jesus knows that he will die where true prophets have died before: in Jerusalem (11:47-51). Jesus is speaking figuratively when he refers to his goal as being reached on the third day. Christian readers of this gospel cannot see this as anything but a reference to his resurrection on the third day.

How sad that Jesus should die in Jerusalem! He dearly wanted to gather the inhabitants of that sacred city under his protecting care. But speaking directly to the city, Jesus utters those sad words: "You were not willing." The "house" that Jesus says "is left . . . desolate" may refer to the spiritual bankruptcy of the temple and its worship. Or perhaps it is a veiled hint of the coming destruction of the city by the Romans.

Jesus closes his message to Jerusalem with words quoted from Psalm 118:26, words used by the Jews as part of their liturgy on great festival days. The disciples would shout these very words when Jesus entered the city of Jerusalem as the humble King on Palm Sunday (19:38). In a more far reaching sense, they refer to the final advent when all the world will recognize Jesus as the one who comes in the name of the Lord not as Savior but as judge.

Matthew records nearly identical words spoken by Jesus to Jerusalem when he had already entered that city (23:37-39). Luke perhaps has recorded these words of Jesus at this point in his gospel because they are so fitting. Jesus does not literally stand before the city, but Jerusalem is his goal, and he speaks as one who sees that city standing clearly before him.

Jesus at a Pharisee's house

14 **One Sabbath, when Jesus went to eat in the house of a prominent Pharisee, he was being carefully watched. ²There in front of him was a man suffering from dropsy. ³Jesus asked the Pharisees and experts in the law, "Is it lawful to heal on the Sabbath or not?" ⁴But they remained silent. So taking hold of the man, he healed him and sent him away.**

⁵Then he asked them, "If one of you has a son or an ox that falls into a well on the Sabbath day, will you not immediately pull him out?" ⁶And they had nothing to say.

⁷When he noticed how the guests picked the places of honor at the table, he told them this parable: ⁸"When someone invites you to a wedding feast, do not take the place of honor, for a person more distinguished than you may have been invited. ⁹If so, the host who invited both of you will come and say to you, 'Give this man your seat.' Then, humiliated, you will have to take the least important place. ¹⁰But when you are invited, take the lowest place, so that when your host comes, he will say to you, 'Friend, move up to a better place.' Then you will be honored in the presence of all your fellow guests. ¹¹For everyone who exalts himself will be humbled, and he who humbles himself will be exalted."

¹²**Then Jesus said to his host, "When you give a luncheon or dinner, do not invite your friends, your brothers or relatives, or your rich neighbors; if you do, they may invite you back and so you will be repaid. ¹³But when you give a banquet, invite the poor, the crippled, the lame, the blind, ¹⁴and you will be blessed. Although they cannot repay you, you will be repaid at the resurrection of the righteous."**

In 13:22-30 Jesus compared salvation to eating a feast in a banquet hall that one enters through a narrow door. After the door was locked by the owner, some came knocking, seeking to gain entrance. They said, "We ate and drank with you, and you taught in our streets." The present story is an example of people who might talk like that. Jesus is again invited to the home of a Pharisee for a festive Sabbath meal (see 7:36-50 and 11:37-54 for previous meals with Pharisees).

As Jesus is reclining at the table, he finds himself face-to-face with a man suffering from dropsy. This is an affliction that causes an abnormal accumulation of fluids in connective tissues and cavities of the body, with symptoms of swelling and defective circulation. It is usually a sign of more serious medical problems.

Before helping this diseased man, Jesus asks a question of the Pharisees and experts in the law who were present at the meal: "Is it lawful to heal on the Sabbath or not?" In the case of the crippled woman healed in the synagogue on the Sabbath, Jesus did not ask before he acted (13:10-17). But in 6:6-11 we have a story in which Jesus asks a similar question about what is lawful on the Sabbath.

The query of Jesus elicits an uneasy silence. A study of Jewish religious teaching reveals that there was disagreement as to the proper answer. In one law book it is written, "Let no one assist a beast in giving birth on the Sabbath day.

Even if it drops [its newborn] into a cistern or into a pit, one is not to raise it up on the Sabbath." But other teachers said that needed assistance should be given even on the Sabbath to animals who required it.

When the religious authorities present at the meal refused to answer Jesus' question, he went ahead and healed the man with dropsy. The follow-up question asked by Jesus implies that actions speak louder than words. No matter what the law experts might teach in theory, in actual practice they would help a child or an animal that falls into a well on the Sabbath Day. This proves that healing on the Sabbath is lawful even if that healing could have been put off to another day. Again, there is only silence from Jesus' critics. Their very silence speaks volumes.

While sitting at the meal, Jesus tells three parables. The first is prompted by the practice of the invited guests to pick the places of honor at the table. Jesus tells a story about a person invited to a wedding banquet who chooses a place of honor. The host is forced to ask this person to move to a place away from the head table to make room for a more distinguished guest. Just as some of Jesus' contemporaries are replaced at the feast of salvation by people from far-away lands (13:28-30), so here humiliation comes to a proud person who is demoted. Jesus suggests the proper course of action: start out sitting in the lowest place. All the guests will take note when the host asks such a person to take a better place. The general rule stated by Jesus in verse 11 will be repeated at the conclusion of the parable of the Pharisee and the tax collector (18:14). Jesus is hoping that even if the Pharisees won't heed his admonition, at least his disciples will learn to practice humility.

The second parable is directed to Jesus' host. It concerns the guest list for such festive banquets as the one to which Jesus had been invited. Four categories of people who should not be included on the guest list are balanced by four categories of guests who should be invited. What Jesus suggests is the very opposite of common practice. The people in the first four categories are likely to return the favor to the host; those in the second category could not. But what a host does not enjoy on earth as repayment for generosity will be enjoyed at the banquet of salvation. God himself is the model of one who invites all classes of people to his great supper of salvation (14:21).

The parable of the great banquet

¹⁵**When one of those at the table with him heard this, he said to Jesus, "Blessed is the man who will eat at the feast in the kingdom of God."**

¹⁶**Jesus replied: "A certain man was preparing a great banquet and invited many guests. ¹⁷At the time of the banquet he sent his servant to tell those who had been invited, 'Come, for everything is now ready.'**

¹⁸**"But they all alike began to make excuses. The first said, 'I have just bought a field, and I must go and see it. Please excuse me.'**

¹⁹**"Another said, 'I have just bought five yoke of oxen, and I'm on my way to try them out. Please excuse me.'**

²⁰**"Still another said, 'I just got married, so I can't come.'**

²¹**"The servant came back and reported this to his master. Then the owner of the house became angry and ordered his servant, 'Go out quickly into the streets and alleys of the town and bring in the poor, the crippled, the blind and the lame.'**

²²**"'Sir,' the servant said, 'what you ordered has been done, but there is still room.'**

²³**"Then the master told his servant, 'Go out to the roads and country lanes and make them come in, so that my house will be full. ²⁴I tell you, not one of those men who were invited will get a taste of my banquet.'"**

Earlier, a question had been put to Jesus: "Lord, are only a few people going to be saved?" (13:23). In his answer,

Jesus did not enter into the numbers game. Rather, he urged all his listeners to strive to enter the banquet hall by the narrow door. He also told his audience that there will be some surprises among those seated at the feast of salvation. Jesus continues to carry out that thought in this third parable told at the dinner given by the Pharisee.

The parable of the great banquet is prompted by a remark made by one of Jesus' table companions: "Blessed is the man who will eat at the feast in the kingdom of God." This beatitude reminds one of a number of earlier such pronouncements by Jesus and others (6:20-22; 11:27,28). It is very similar to the words of Revelation 19:9: "Blessed are those who are invited to the wedding supper of the Lamb!"

Yet it becomes obvious from the parable which Jesus tells that not everyone really regards God's salvation banquet as something so wonderful. A man who prepared a great banquet made provisions for many guests. Invitations had gone out. When all is ready, the host sends out his servant to bid the invited guests to come and eat.

But, surprisingly, the servant is met with a barrage of excuses. Three samples are given as characteristic of the many that are made. The first two put property and possession above partaking in the banquet of salvation. The claims of money take precedence (16:13). In businesslike fashion, they politely ask to be excused from coming.

The third excuse involves family responsibilities. The one just married is somewhat like the disciple who could not follow Jesus since he was obliged to bury his dead father (9:59). This rejection is less courteous than the first two. This man considers family matters more important than accepting the invitation. Thus he misses out on God's banquet.

In this parable's servant we see none other than Jesus Christ, who has come to invite his contemporaries to enter the narrow door to the feast of the kingdom of God. The call to repentance and faith is greeted with hostility and criticism by the prominent. The Servant of the Lord is deeply disappointed in this reception (13:34).

The host is angered by such rejection of his kind invitation. He has made preparations for many and is determined to fill the hall. He sends his servant out again to go into the streets and alleys of the town and bring in the poor, the crippled, the blind, and the lame. Note that these are the very same categories of people whom Jesus previously had urged his dinner host to invite (14:13). These are people living nearby in the same town, but people who know nothing about being invited to great banquets. This is the kind of people who responded positively to the preaching of Jesus.

But still there is room for more. So for a third time, the servant is sent out. He is to go to people in rural areas, into the country lanes and roads not often traveled. The host tells his servant to "make them come in, so that my house will be full." Here is a marvelous picture of people streaming into the banquet hall from the far corners of the earth. Those who were first invited have missed their chance; the door is locked and they will not taste of the banquet. They refused to hear the preaching of Jesus and find themselves excluded.

No one can enter God's kingdom without an invitation. The good news is that God has made all things ready and extends his invitation to all. Those who remain outside, refusing his gracious offer, have only themselves to blame. People cannot save themselves, but they can damn themselves.

This parable supplies a partial answer to the original question as to whether only a few people are going to be saved. It is an answer that emphasizes the abundance of God's love for sinners. But it is an answer that also warns of the danger of rejecting God's gracious invitation.

The cost of being a disciple

²⁵**Large crowds were traveling with Jesus, and turning to them he said:** ²⁶**"If anyone comes to me and does not hate his father and mother, his wife and children, his brothers and sisters—yes, even his own life—he cannot be my disciple.** ²⁷**And anyone who does not carry his cross and follow me cannot be my disciple.**

²⁸**"Suppose one of you wants to build a tower. Will he not first sit down and estimate the cost to see if he has enough money to complete it?** ²⁹**For if he lays the foundation and is not able to finish it, everyone who sees it will ridicule him,** ³⁰**saying, 'This fellow began to build and was not able to finish.'**

³¹**"Or suppose a king is about to go to war against another king. Will he not first sit down and consider whether he is able with ten thousand men to oppose the one coming against him with twenty thousand?** ³²**If he is not able, he will send a delegation while the other is still a long way off and will ask for terms of peace.** ³³**In the same way, any of you who does not give up everything he has cannot be my disciple.**

³⁴**"Salt is good, but if it loses its saltiness, how can it be made salty again?** ³⁵**It is fit neither for the soil nor for the manure pile; it is thrown out.**

"He who has ears to hear, let him hear."

Jesus is finished with his table talk and is back on the road again, followed (as always it seems) by large crowds. They have not lost their curiosity and anticipate the next miracle with enthusiasm. The words they now hear from the mouth of Jesus are meant to cool some of the shallow ardor the crowds so often displayed.

Jesus sets forth three conditions for following. First, there must be a willingness to leave behind family ties including the tie to oneself. The word "hate" sounds harsh to our ears, so much at odds with the earlier command to love even one's enemy (6:27). Jesus means to shock his listeners with this word, to make them realize that nothing dare come before him in the life of the disciple.

The second condition is to carry the cross. What this means is explained in the commentary on 9:18-27. The third condition for following is the willingness to give up all earthly possessions. This is the demand that the rich ruler will not able to fulfill (18:22,23). These three conditions must be set alongside of those given in 9:57-62.

Jesus adds to these conditions three illustrations. The first is about a man who plans to build a tower. The builder will make sure that he has enough money to finish the job before even starting. Otherwise, he will be a laughingstock to his neighbors.

And no king thinks of starting a war without having a big enough army to finish the job. If he finds himself on the short end of things, his best course of action is to plead for peace.

Finally, Jesus uses the illustration of salt that loses all its taste. Such salt becomes totally worthless, not good for use even on a manure pile.

There needs to be mature, prior self-examination before joining the crowd of pilgrims surging after Jesus on the road to the cross. Being a follower calls for renouncing family, self, and possessions. Unless this happens, the follower will be like a builder who can't finish his tower or a king who can't win his war. When the going gets tough, lukewarm allegiance to Jesus will grow cold. Halfhearted commitment won't do.

The closing admonition to hear was sounded previously at the end of the parable of the sower whose seed fell into four kinds of soil (8:8). Fruitful hearing of the Word is choked by the trials and temptations of this world, by both its hardships and pleasures. The follower of Jesus needs to listen to everything Jesus has to say, not only what one wants to hear. It means hearing him tell us about the great supper of salvation and God's gracious invitation to all. It means hearing him describe the narrow door of entry into the banquet hall.

The parable of the lost sheep

15 Now the tax collectors and "sinners" were all gathering around to hear him. ²But the Pharisees and the teachers of the law muttered, "This man welcomes sinners and eats with them."

³Then Jesus told them this parable: ⁴"Suppose one of you has a hundred sheep and loses one of them. Does he not leave the ninety-nine in the open country and go after the lost sheep until he finds it? ⁵And when he finds it, he joyfully puts it on his shoulders ⁶and goes home. Then he calls his friends and neighbors together and says, 'Rejoice with me; I have found my lost sheep.' ⁷I tell you that in the same way there will be more rejoicing in heaven over one sinner who repents than over ninety-nine righteous persons who do not need to repent.

The previous section of Luke's gospel had the cost of being a disciple as its subject. It concluded with Jesus' admonition: "He who has ears to hear, let him hear." This new chapter tells us who did gather to hear: tax collectors and sinners. And not only did they listen to Jesus—they were even welcomed to eat with him!

The word "sinner" may refer to people who were especially immoral and wicked; it may, however, refer simply to people who were not strict about fulfilling all the varied requirements of the ceremonial law. They were "sinners" in the eyes of the Pharisees because of their neglectful attitude toward religion. Tax collectors are one striking example of such sinners.

The question of eating with tax collectors and sinners was raised previously in 5:30 after Jesus had called Levi to become one of his followers. The Pharisees and teachers of the law again mutter about the table companions with whom Jesus fellowships. A Jewish commentary on Exodus 18:1 says, "Let not a man associate with the wicked, not even to bring him to the law." Jesus is going totally against this rabbinic advice.

In answer to the criticism, Jesus tells three parables. All three have to do with joy over finding what was lost. First, a shepherd rejoices over finding the one lost sheep out of a hundred; next, a woman rejoices to find the one coin she had lost out of ten; finally, a father who has two sons gives a joyous banquet to celebrate the return of the one who had been lost.

Chapter 15 has been called "the lost and found chapter." It has also been called the heart of the third gospel. This chapter introduces a larger unit, running through 19:27, that presents a series of stories about outcasts. We will hear Jesus say, "The Son of Man came to seek and to save what was lost" (19:10). The lost find in Jesus a Savior; the proud and self-righteous find in him a judge.

For a shepherd to have a flock of one hundred sheep was quite normal. It also marked him as being moderately rich. That such a shepherd would leave his flock in open country in search of one lost sheep seems a bit unrealistic. Likewise unrealistic is the conduct of the father when his lost son returns home. Both point to a love for the lost that goes beyond anything human; it is a divine love which seeks the lost.

The description Jesus gives of the shepherd joyfully returning home carrying the lost sheep on his shoulders is heartwarming. He bids his friends to come and celebrate with him the recovery of one lost sheep. There is no mention at all of the 99 sheep out there in the open country. All attention is focused upon the lost sheep that was found. Jesus says that the same is true in heaven: there is more rejoicing over the lost sinner who repents than over the 99 righteous people who do not need to repent.

The suggestion that some people don't need to repent sounds like heresy to us. Jesus had said to the crowds, "Unless you repent, you too will all perish" (13:5). We need to understand the statement of Jesus as a criticism of the

Pharisees who thought they were so righteous that they did not need to repent. Jesus is saying to them, "God is not rejoicing over you and your attitude; God is rejoicing over the lost sinner who repents."

In the parable there is an invitation by the shepherd for his friends to share in the joy of finding the lost. The question needs to be asked, Are we able to share in God's joy over the repenting sinner? This was something we will find that the older brother could not do. It was something that the Pharisees and law experts could not do. But the angels of God take part in his joyful celebration.

The parable of the lost coin

8"Or suppose a woman has ten silver coins and loses one. Does she not light a lamp, sweep the house and search carefully until she finds it? 9And when she finds it, she calls her friends and neighbors together and says, 'Rejoice with me; I have found my lost coin.' 10In the same way, I tell you, there is rejoicing in the presence of the angels of God over one sinner who repents."

This second lost-and-found parable presents a contrast with the previous one. Here the subject is not a moderately rich shepherd but a poor woman. There might be some rich people who would not make much of an effort to seek a coin that was lost. But this woman diligently seeks until she finds it.

The word "coin" here is a translation of the word *drachma,* the only time this particular Greek silver coin is mentioned in the Bible. Much more common is the Roman denarius. Both were worth about the same: a day's wages of a hired hand. This peasant woman lived in a house only dimly lit with small windows and a low door. It would be hard to find the lost coin on the dirt floor. But she uses every possible means to recover what she had lost. To her the coin is very valuable.

That a poor woman should search so diligently for a lost coin does not surprise us. But that she should invite her friends and neighbors to join in celebrating her find is a bit much. It's the way in which Jesus stresses the divine joy over the repentance of a single sinner.

The parable of the lost son

¹¹Jesus continued: "There was a man who had two sons. ¹²The younger one said to his father, 'Father, give me my share of the estate.' So he divided his property between them.

¹³"Not long after that, the younger son got together all he had, set off for a distant country and there squandered his wealth in wild living. ¹⁴After he had spent everything, there was a severe famine in that whole country, and he began to be in need. ¹⁵So he went and hired himself out to a citizen of that country, who sent him to his fields to feed pigs. ¹⁶He longed to fill his stomach with the pods that the pigs were eating, but no one gave him anything.

¹⁷"When he came to his senses, he said, 'How many of my father's hired men have food to spare, and here I am starving to death! ¹⁸I will set out and go back to my father and say to him: Father, I have sinned against heaven and against you. ¹⁹I am no longer worthy to be called your son; make me like one of your hired men.' ²⁰So he got up and went to his father.

"But while he was still a long way off, his father saw him and was filled with compassion for him; he ran to his son, threw his arms around him and kissed him.

²¹"The son said to him, 'Father, I have sinned against heaven and against you. I am no longer worthy to be called your son.'

²²"But the father said to his servants, 'Quick! Bring the best robe and put it on him. Put a ring on his finger and sandals on his feet. ²³Bring the fattened calf and kill it. Let's have a feast and celebrate. ²⁴For this son of mine was dead and is alive again; he was lost and is found.' So they began to celebrate.

²⁵"Meanwhile, the older son was in the field. When he came near the house, he heard music and dancing. ²⁶So he called one

175

of the servants and asked him what was going on. ²⁷'Your brother has come,' he replied, 'and your father has killed the fattened calf because he has him back safe and sound.'

²⁸"The older brother became angry and refused to go in. So his father went out and pleaded with him. ²⁹But he answered his father, 'Look! All these years I've been slaving for you and never disobeyed your orders. Yet you never gave me even a young goat so I could celebrate with my friends. ³⁰But when this son of yours who has squandered your property with prostitutes comes home, you kill the fattened calf for him!'

³¹" 'My son,' the father said, 'you are always with me, and everything I have is yours. ³²But we had to celebrate and be glad, because this brother of yours was dead and is alive again; he was lost and is found.'"

The traditional title for this third parable is "The prodigal son." This title is found in 16th-century English Bibles and goes back to the Latin Vulgate. The NIV calls it "The parable of the lost son." Yet the central figure in this parable is not the son but the father. It has been suggested that a better title might be "The parable of the father's love."

The first two parables in this series raised a question: "Does he/she not . . . ?" But the action of this father is so out of the ordinary that Jesus does not even dare to ask such a question in the case of the reception given to the returning son.

Here is a father more than human. Yet the son speaks of having "sinned against heaven and against you," distinguishing his earthly father from the heavenly Father. This father is not so otherworldly that he is unable to serve as a model for the listeners of this parable.

Whereas the first two parables dealt with a lost animal and a lost coin, what the father loses is his son. The portrayal of this son evokes negative feelings. He does live up to the designation "prodigal." He is recklessly wasteful. He can't wait until his father dies to get his share of the property, which he immediately converts to cash. He does not remain at home to care for his aging father but goes to a country far off where he lives among Gentiles. There he squanders his money in wild living. The older brother adds the detail that the money was spent with prostitutes.

The time comes, however, when the money is gone; famine grips the land, and the prodigal son is forced to work on a pig farm caring for unclean animals. The pigs ate pods from the carob tree. This tree is found all over the Mediterranean area. Its long pods contain a sweet pulp and indigestible seeds, and they were used as food for animals, sometimes even for humans.

The prodigal son has plenty of time to think as he toils at his dirty job. He compares his condition to the far better status enjoyed by the hired servants of his father. He resolves to go back to his father, confess his sin, admit his unworthiness as a son, and beg to work as a hired hand.

But even before he is able to make his confession, the waiting father spots his returning son on the road. He runs to his son and welcomes him with hugs and kisses. He loves the sinner even before that sinner makes his statement of repentance. He orders the best robe, a ring and sandals, and a feast. The fatted calf kept for special occasions is killed. The celebration begins at once. The dead son lives—the lost has been found.

The excesses of the prodigal son are matched by the excesses of the loving father. What the father does is amazing. He runs to meet his wayward son. He does not put him on probation or lecture him for his sins. He is bountiful in the welcome he gives to his son. These are not the normal actions of a human father. Here a portrayal of divine joy over a repenting sinner.

This joy is not at all shared by the older brother. We may feel a bit negative toward him but can surely understand why he might be upset. On returning from the field where he has been laboring faithfully in his father's service, he hears music and dancing (the Greek words used here are carried over into English: *symphony* and *chorus*). When the older brother hears the reason for this expensive party, he refused to enter the house. He stands outside fuming.

The loving father again comes into the picture. He pleads for his older son to take part in the joyful celebration. What the father hears is criticism of his love. The older son reminds his father of the years of dutiful service he has rendered. But his virtue was not rewarded even with a young goat for a fun time with his friends. Yet the vice of "this son of yours" (the older son does not call him "brother") is forgotten and a fatted calf is killed in his honor. There seems to be every reason for this older son's bitterness.

One cannot fail to see Jesus here drawing a portrait of the Pharisees and experts in the law. They were proud of the dutiful way in which they observed all of God's commands. They felt fully justified in criticizing Jesus for his fellowship with sinners and tax collectors. And they were not about to join in joyfully celebrating the repentance of a sinner.

The parable ends with one last attempt on the father's part to explain his actions. He speaks of the prodigal son as "this brother of yours" and repeats the reason for celebrating. Jesus does not tell us whether or not the older son was persuaded. The parable is open ended, inviting the listener to respond—do we participate in the joy?

This has been judged by some to be the greatest of Jesus' parables. It has often been interpreted in music, art, and drama. Who can fail to be moved by the boundless love and joy of this father who welcomes back his lost son? Such is the nature of our heavenly Father, as demonstrated by his one and only Son, Jesus Christ.

The parable of the shrewd manager

16 Jesus told his disciples: "There was a rich man whose manager was accused of wasting his possessions. ²So he called him in and asked him, 'What is this I hear about you? Give an account of your management, because you cannot be manager any longer.'

³"The manager said to himself, 'What shall I do now? My master is taking away my job. I'm not strong enough to dig, and I'm ashamed to beg—⁴I know what I'll do so that, when I lose my job here, people will welcome me into their houses.'

⁵"So he called in each one of his master's debtors. He asked the first, 'How much do you owe my master?'

⁶"'Eight hundred gallons of olive oil,' he replied.

"The manager told him, 'Take your bill, sit down quickly, and make it four hundred.'

⁷"Then he asked the second, 'And how much do you owe?'

"'A thousand bushels of wheat,' he replied.

"He told him, 'Take your bill and make it eight hundred.'

⁸"The master commended the dishonest manager because he had acted shrewdly. For the people of this world are more shrewd in dealing with their own kind than are the people of the light. ⁹I tell you, use worldly wealth to gain friends for yourselves, so that when it is gone, you will be welcomed into eternal dwellings.

¹⁰"Whoever can be trusted with very little can also be trusted with much, and whoever is dishonest with very little will also be dishonest with much. ¹¹So if you have not been trustworthy in handling worldly wealth, who will trust you with true riches? ¹²And if you have not been trustworthy with someone else's property, who will give you property of your own?

¹³"No servant can serve two masters. Either he will hate the one and love the other, or he will be devoted to the one and despise the other. You cannot serve both God and Money."

¹⁴The Pharisees, who loved money, heard all this and were sneering at Jesus. ¹⁵He said to them, "You are the ones who justify

yourselves in the eyes of men, but God knows your hearts. What is highly valued among men is detestable in God's sight.

¹⁶"The Law and the Prophets were proclaimed until John. Since that time, the good news of the kingdom of God is being preached, and everyone is forcing his way into it. ¹⁷It is easier for heaven and earth to disappear than for the least stroke of a pen to drop out of the Law.

¹⁸"Anyone who divorces his wife and marries another woman commits adultery, and the man who marries a divorced woman commits adultery.

Already in the previous chapter, Jesus had introduced the subject of money. There is the parable about the woman who searched diligently for a coin she had lost; the prodigal son is an example of one who is recklessly wasteful with money he had inherited. This 16th chapter of Luke's gospel continues to deal with the subject of money management.

We will find two major parables here; in both of them a rich man is introduced. In one the rich man is forced to fire his dishonest manager for wasting his possessions. In the other the rich man is guilty of selfish indulgence, unmindful of the needs of poor Lazarus. Both of these parables are an encouragement for disciples to make good use of their money.

The manager about to be fired takes steps to insure a decent future for himself. He directs those who owed his master money to reduce their large bills. One is halved, and the other is discounted by 20 percent. The rich man compliments his manager for the shrewd and prudent way in which he uses money (even though it's not his own) to guarantee a more secure future for himself. This manager is not too different from the prodigal son who was very free with money he had not earned.

The application of this parable by Jesus begins in the last sentence of verse 8. He picks up on the words of the rich man and comments that the people of this world are more shrewd in handling money than are his own followers, "the people of the light." Jesus would like to see his disciples use their money more wisely. He directs them to "use worldly wealth to gain friends for yourselves, so that . . . you will be welcomed into eternal dwellings."

The exact meaning of verse 9 has been the subject of much discussion. The translation of the NIV is not as literal as that of the KJV, which reads, "Make to yourselves friends of the mammon of unrighteousness; that, when ye fail, they may receive you into everlasting habitations." The word *mammon* is found in the Greek text and goes back to the same Hebrew root as that found in *amen*. It means "that in which one puts trust." It came to mean simply "money" or "possessions," the earthly things in which so many trust. It is called unrighteous, or worldly, in contrast to the true heavenly treasure.

The KJV has the words "when ye fail"; the NIV says "when it is gone." The Greek copies differ at this point. The KJV refers to the time of a person's death; the NIV refers to when the money runs out. When either happens, the person who has gained friends with money will have a secure future in heaven. The point is this: use money wisely to insure your earthly future. One wise use for money is giving to the poor (see 11:41 and 12:33,34). The giving of alms is a testimony to the reality of discipleship and self-denial.

Jesus continues with some additional applications based on this parable. There are contrasts between "very little" and "much," between "worldly wealth" and "true riches," between "someone else's property" and "property of your own." The worldly wealth that God might put into the hands of a person is really nothing in comparison to the true riches of heaven. The person who mismanages this worldly wealth by making it an object of trust or by using it in a selfish way is unfit to be given the heavenly treasure.

Jesus concludes with the familiar statement that no one can serve two masters: "You cannot serve both God and Money." The KJV again uses the term *mammon*. Worldly wealth is given by God to be used in his service. The master who gives the money must always be more important than the money he gives. When the money has priority over the master, then one has a classic case of mismanagement. That was true of the rich fool whose tragic end Jesus described in 12:16-21. It also will be true of the rich man described in the next section.

Though Jesus had been speaking to his disciples, the Pharisees were listening in and now sneer at what they hear. They looked at riches as being a sign of God's special favor. Riches were regarded as the reward for the good life. For that reason the Pharisees loved riches.

Jesus reproves them for their wrong attitude toward riches. They think to use their riches as a sign to other people that their teachings and life are pleasing to God. Jesus sees in riches just so much outward glitter that says nothing at all about the heart. People might put a high value on riches, but riches carry no impact at all with God. God is concerned with the right management of riches in a way that brings glory to him and shows love to those in need.

With verses 16 to 18, the subject seems to change briefly. Perhaps Jesus is replying to some remark made by one of the Pharisees that he has no right to talk about what is "detestable in God's sight" in view of the lax way in which he seems to regard some of the laws (6:1-5). Jesus observes that from the Old Testament period up to the time of John, the Law and the Prophets were proclaimed. In the New Testament period, people are eagerly listening to the good news and seeking to enter into the kingdom. Some people might think that the law has no more validity in this New Testament period. Jesus declares that he has not come to relax the law one little bit. In 16:31 Moses (the Law) and the Prophets are declared to be sufficient for salvation.

As one example of the seriousness with which he regards the law, Jesus refers to the question of divorce. Many of the Pharisees made it very easy for a man to divorce his wife. One Jewish teacher of the law said that a wife could be divorced if she spoiled a dish of food, if she spun in the street, if she talked to a strange man, or if she raised her voice so as to be heard next door.

The law against adultery was strictly observed. But this law could be circumvented by a man who divorced his wife and married the woman he desired. Wives became nothing more than possessions to be disposed of at will. Jesus shows his concern for the sanctity of marriage and for the rights of women by declaring that it was adultery for a husband to divorce his wife and marry another; likewise, the Sixth Commandment was broken also when a man married a divorced woman. Jesus was certainly not guilty of relaxing the law. He set much higher standards for his disciples than did the Pharisees.

The rich man and Lazarus

¹⁹"There was a rich man who was dressed in purple and fine linen and lived in luxury every day. ²⁰At his gate was laid a beggar named Lazarus, covered with sores ²¹and longing to eat what fell from the rich man's table. Even the dogs came and licked his sores.

²²"The time came when the beggar died and the angels carried him to Abraham's side. The rich man also died and was buried. ²³In hell, where he was in torment, he looked up and saw Abraham far away, with Lazarus by his side. ²⁴So he called to him, 'Father Abraham, have pity on me and send Lazarus to dip the tip of his finger in water and cool my tongue, because I am in agony in this fire.'

183

Lazarus at the rich man's door

²⁵"But Abraham replied, 'Son, remember that in your lifetime you received your good things, while Lazarus received bad things, but now he is comforted here and you are in agony. ²⁶And besides all this, between us and you a great chasm has been fixed, so that those who want to go from here to you cannot, nor can anyone cross over from there to us.'

²⁷"He answered, 'Then I beg you, father, send Lazarus to my father's house, ²⁸for I have five brothers. Let him warn them, so that they will not also come to this place of torment.'

²⁹"Abraham replied, 'They have Moses and the Prophets; let them listen to them.'

³⁰"'No, father Abraham,' he said, 'but if someone from the dead goes to them, they will repent.'

³¹"He said to him, 'If they do not listen to Moses and the Prophets, they will not be convinced even if someone rises from the dead.'"

The rich man whom Jesus introduces in this parable is not too different from the one portrayed in 12:16-21. That man planned to "take life easy; eat, drink and be merry." He never got the chance. The rich man in the present parable gets that chance, but the end result remains the same when his time comes to die.

The name Dives is sometimes given to this rich man. That word comes from the Latin translation of the opening verses, "Homo quidern erat *dives*," and simply means "rich." The rich man is a person without a name. But the poor man has a name: Lazarus ("God has helped"). This was also the name of the brother of Mary and Martha whom Jesus would raise from the dead (John 11:44).

The condition of Lazarus reminds us of the prodigal son when he found himself starving to death in a faraway country. The very same words are used by Jesus to describe their extreme hunger: "longing to eat" (see 15:16). We are not told that this poor man was even permitted to eat the scraps from the table of the rich man. In his weakness he is unable to drive away the dogs who lick his sores, adding to his misery.

But no act of kindness comes from the rich man to help this poor beggar. He is not "rich toward God" (12:21). He does not make himself clean by giving to the poor (11:41). Far from selling his possessions to give to the poor, he does not even give his leftovers. He has no thought of preparing a purse in heaven that will not wear out (12:33). The rich man did not use worldly wealth to gain friends so that when he died, he would be welcomed into eternal dwellings (16:9).

When death comes to Lazarus and the rich man, they experience a great reversal of fortune. Mary had sung of a God who "has filled the hungry with good things but has sent the rich away empty" (1:53). Jesus pronounced those blessed "who hunger now, for you will be satisfied"; on the other hand, he said "woe to you who are well fed now, for you will go hungry" (6:21,25). These statements are vividly illustrated by the situation in which Lazarus and the rich man find themselves in the afterlife. The poor man finds himself at the banquet table of salvation, reclining next to Abraham. His counterpart would welcome even a taste of cool water. The rich man soon learns from Abraham that there is no hope for a visit from blessed Lazarus to bring him relief.

The thoughts of the rich man turn to his five brothers who still live on the earth. He suggests to Abraham that a visit from the dead by Lazarus might knock some sense into their heads. Abraham replies that they have Moses and the Prophets and should listen to them. "Moses and the Prophets" refers to the Old Testament Scriptures. The rich man pleads his case by arguing that only a resurrection from the dead will bring his brothers to repentance. Abraham rejects this argument. If the Word of God does not convince, neither will a resurrection from the dead. Later in

Jesus' ministry, a Lazarus would rise from the dead, but the result would be a deepening of the animosity against Jesus (John 11:46-53). And the resurrection of Jesus himself did not bring about mass conversions.

The details of this parable dare not be pressed to discover exactly what heaven and hell will be like. This is a story told by Jesus to make a point. Perhaps we might better say that he is making two points. The first simply emphasizes something Jesus has repeatedly been stressing: wisely use the money that God puts into your hands. One wise use of income is to give to the poor.

The second point of this parable is to emphasize the sufficiency of the Word of God to bring about repentance and a changed life. Jesus was accused by the Pharisees of relaxing the law of God. Jesus rejects the charge (16:17). With this parable he again affirms the importance of proclaiming the entire Word of God, both law and gospel, for the conversion of sinners.

Sin, faith, duty

17 Jesus said to his disciples: "Things that cause people to sin are bound to come, but woe to that person through whom they come. ²It would be better for him to be thrown into the sea with a millstone tied around his neck than for him to cause one of these little ones to sin. ³So watch yourselves.

"If your brother sins, rebuke him, and if he repents, forgive him. ⁴If he sins against you seven times in a day, and seven times comes back to you and says, 'I repent,' forgive him."

⁵The apostles said to the Lord, "Increase our faith!"

⁶He replied, "If you have faith as small as a mustard seed, you can say to this mulberry tree, 'Be uprooted and planted in the sea,' and it will obey you.

⁷"Suppose one of you had a servant plowing or looking after the sheep. Would he say to the servant when he comes in from the field, 'Come along now and sit down to eat'? ⁸Would he not rather

say, 'Prepare my supper, get yourself ready and wait on me while I eat and drink; after that you may eat and drink'? ⁹Would he thank the servant because he did what he was told to do? ¹⁰So you also, when you have done everything you were told to do, should say, 'We are unworthy servants; we have only done our duty.'"

The specific subject of money management is left behind as we enter the 17th chapter of Luke's gospel. Jesus will pick up the topic of riches several more times as he continues his journey to Jerusalem.

The NIV titles this section "Sin, faith, duty." We have here four sayings of Jesus that set forth various aspects of discipleship. These sayings focus on two questions: (1) What are disciples of Jesus called to do? (2) Are disciples able to do these things?

The subject of the first two sayings is sin: the seriousness of sin and the way in which a disciple should deal with those who sin. Things that cause people to sin are bound to occur, but this fact should not promote the idea that sin is not serious. The anger of Jesus blazes against the person who causes "little ones" to sin. The term "little ones" is used for any Christian, though we might think especially of a Christian new to the faith or not so far along in knowledge. Jesus pronounces a woe against the person who leads the innocent into sin and declares that a violent death would have been better for that person than to face God's wrath. He means this warning for his disciples: "So watch yourselves."

It inevitably happens that a disciple will become aware of a fellow Christian who is sinning. Rather than harboring bad feelings against the brother or speaking to someone else about the sin, Jesus tells his disciples to "rebuke" the sinner. The word "rebuke" carries the idea of a frank but gentle admonition: politely tell him what he has done wrong. If this rebuke leads to repentance on the part of the sinner, then he should be forgiven. This is not only true of sins in general but specifically of sins "against you." Jesus calls on the disciple to practice such forgiveness seven times a day if necessary. The number seven is not meant to be taken literally but rather suggests any number of times. Though sin is serious and should not be taken lightly, this is not reason to withhold forgiveness from the repenting sinner.

The statements of Jesus about sin prompt the apostles to request of Jesus, "Increase our faith." This is something they must have prayed for often. But here they realize how difficult it is to deal correctly with the sinning brother. They need Jesus' help to fulfill what he has given them to do.

The answer Jesus gives his apostles suggests that they should not use lack of faith as an excuse for not dealing correctly with the sinning brother. He indicates that even with a little faith, great things can be done. If you are responding in faith to God's forgiveness, then you will be able to forgive. Use the little faith you have.

Finally, Jesus tells a parable that begins in the same way as the one he told about the shepherd who lost one of his sheep: "Suppose one of you . . ." (15:3). It's Jesus' way of saying, Just imagine this. The parable asks whether a master would excuse a servant who had worked all day in the fields from making his supper. Or would he thank his servant for doing what he was told to do? Jesus makes the application that the disciples should not look for any special praise or commendation for only doing their duty.

Jesus makes quite a different point in the parable he told in 12:35-37. In that story the returning master rewards his waiting servants by himself assuming the role of a servant. Each parable has its own meaning and purpose. One must take into account all of Scripture to correctly understand the individual parts.

This parable is meant to discourage disciples from thinking more highly of themselves in comparison to others who perhaps do less or are caught in serious sins. When all is said and done, every disciple is an unworthy servant in need of God's grace and forgiveness. So the second phase of Jesus' journey to Jerusalem with his disciples ends with this note of their unworthiness for service in the kingdom.

Jesus wants people to be aware that the work of the kingdom is going on right now

Ten healed of leprosy

¹¹Now on his way to Jerusalem, Jesus traveled along the border between Samaria and Galilee. ¹²As he was going into a village, ten men who had leprosy met him. They stood at a distance ¹³and called out in a loud voice, "Jesus, Master, have pity on us!"

¹⁴When he saw them, he said, "Go, show yourselves to the priests." And as they went, they were cleansed.

¹⁵One of them, when he saw he was healed, came back, praising God in a loud voice. ¹⁶He threw himself at Jesus' feet and thanked him—and he was a Samaritan.

¹⁷Jesus asked, "Were not all ten cleansed? Where are the other nine? ¹⁸Was no one found to return and give praise to God except this foreigner?" ¹⁹Then he said to him, "Rise and go; your faith has made you well."

With this section the third phase of Jesus' journey to Jerusalem begins. There will be a quickening of the pace as Luke includes additional geographical notes. Jesus will again predict his death in Jerusalem (18:31-33). Two stories happening in Jericho, just 18 miles from Jerusalem, will be recorded. Jesus will tell a parable when he was "near Jerusalem" (19:11), and finally the city of destiny will be reached, and he will enter in triumph (19:28-38).

The information that "Jesus traveled along the border between Samaria and Galilee" poses a bit of a problem.

As was mentioned in the commentary on 13:22, the border between Samaria and Galilee is a long way from Jerusalem. If Jesus set out already in 9:51 to go up to Jerusalem, he has made little progress. This suggests that the journey may not so much be thought of as a literal trip (though it was that) but as a spiritual pilgrimage. Possibly the reference to "Galilee" in this section includes the province of Perea, east of the Jordan River, over which Herod Antipas also ruled. In that case, Jesus would be much closer to Jerusalem when he healed the ten lepers.

Jesus had healed a single leper near the beginning of his Galilean ministry (5:12-16). Now ten lepers come to him asking for mercy (the NIV translates it as "pity"). In the case of the single leper, Jesus first healed him and then sent him to the priests to verify the cure. Here Jesus sends them off to the priests, and they are cleansed enroute.

Of the ten, only one returns to Jesus to say thanks and give praise to God. Now the reader learns that this one of the ten lepers was a Samaritan. The assumption is that the other nine were Jews. Though Jews and Samaritans usually had no fellowship, misery loves company. Jesus commends this "foreigner" for his act of worship and asks in disappointment about the other nine.

At the start of the journey to Jerusalem, Jesus and his disciples came to a Samaritan village that refused to welcome him. James and John were rebuked by Jesus when they wanted to call down fire to destroy that village (9:51-55). Jesus had told a parable starring a Samaritan (10:30-35). Here this Samaritan leper manifests his faith. The disciples are learning that response to the message of the gospel breaks down racial barriers. People from the far corners of the earth will sit down at the banquet of salvation.

The coming of the kingdom of God

²⁰Once, having been asked by the Pharisees when the kingdom of God would come, Jesus replied, "The kingdom of God does not come with your careful observation, ²¹nor will people say, 'Here it is,' or 'There it is,' because the kingdom of God is within you."

²²Then he said to his disciples, "The time is coming when you will long to see one of the days of the Son of Man, but you will not see it. ²³Men will tell you, 'There he is!' or 'Here he is!' Do not go running off after them. ²⁴For the Son of Man in his day will be like the lightning, which flashes and lights up the sky from one end to the other. ²⁵But first he must suffer many things and be rejected by this generation.

²⁶"Just as it was in the days of Noah, so also will it be in the days of the Son of Man. ²⁷People were eating, drinking, marrying and being given in marriage up to the day Noah entered the ark. Then the flood came and destroyed them all.

²⁸"It was the same in the days of Lot. People were eating and drinking, buying and selling, planting and building. ²⁹But the day Lot left Sodom, fire and sulfur rained down from heaven and destroyed them all.

³⁰"It will be just like this on the day the Son of Man is revealed. ³¹On that day no one who is on the roof of his house, with his goods inside, should go down to get them. Likewise, no one in the field should go back for anything. ³²Remember Lot's wife! ³³Whoever tries to keep his life will lose it, and whoever loses his life will preserve it. ³⁴I tell you, on that night two people will be in one bed; one will be taken and the other left. ³⁵Two women will be grinding grain together; one will be taken and the other left."

³⁷"Where, Lord?" they asked.

He replied, "Where there is a dead body, there the vultures will gather."

This section begins with the Pharisees asking "when the kingdom of God would come" and closes with the disciples of Jesus asking "where" the Son of Man will be revealed when he comes again. Then as now, many people seek to calculate the when and where of Christ's second coming.

Some in the days of the early church taught that Jesus had returned in a way not recognized by the average person. That same teaching has been put forth in modern times. But the words of Jesus recorded here warn Christians against being timekeepers of God's kingdom; rather, we should be prepared for whenever and wherever it comes.

The question asked by the Pharisees is similar to the one that the disciples of Jesus will ask him at the time of his ascension: "Lord, are you at this time going to restore the kingdom to Israel?" (Acts 1:6) The journey to Jerusalem may have prompted the Pharisee's question. With his answer Jesus wants to bring out the truth that one should not be looking into the future for the kingdom of God. The entire ministry of Jesus should have shown to all his contemporaries that the kingdom of God was already among them. "The kingdom of God has come to you" (11:20). The NIV translation of "within you" here is not the best in view of the fact that Jesus is speaking to the Pharisees. We would prefer the translation given in the footnote: "The kingdom of God is among you." The healing of the ten lepers demonstrated that truth.

In the instruction concerning the future coming of the Son of Man, Jesus makes six points: (1) that day won't come as soon as they wish; (2) that day will be known to all and not happen in secret; (3) there must first come a time of suffering; (4) that day will catch many people unprepared; (5) the end will be in a moment; (6) family and friends will be separated by the final judgment. After arriving in Jerusalem, Jesus will speak further about the end of the world (chapter 21).

This mention of suffering presents another brief glimpse of what Jesus must undergo in Jerusalem (see 9:22,44 for earlier predictions; another will come in 18:31-33).

The disciples, as well as the Jews in general, were totally unprepared for a suffering Messiah but rather expected a conquering hero.

In the midst of talking about the end, Jesus urges his disciples to be ready to give up their lives for his sake. He had said the same after hearing Peter's confession of him as the Christ (Messiah) of God (9:24). Not only would Jesus have to suffer before the final day, but so would the disciples.

Jesus compares the day of the Son of Man to the days of Noah and Lot. The people before the flood were not at all responsive to the preaching of Noah and went about their normal activities with no thought of the coming judgment. So also the wicked inhabitants of Sodom and Gomorrah were totally unprepared for the fiery destruction of those cities in the days of Lot. The same will be true on the day when the Son of Man comes again.

The word "taken" used by Jesus in verses 34 and 35 has caused some Bible readers to think that there will be a "rapture" before the final day, that some people will literally be taken into heaven while others are left to continue to live on this earth. The use of the word "taken" is related to the examples of Noah and Lot, who were taken to safety from the place of destruction. But this happened at the same time when those who were left met destruction. There will be no rapture. The believer will be taken to the safety of heaven on the Last Day.

The disciples show that they really haven't been listening very well when they ask the question "Where?" Jesus had warned against people who propose a *where* by saying "Here he is" or "There he is." When and where are not important. Jesus' reply to the disciples' question is given in the form of a proverb. He is saying, "Birds of prey circling in the sky give clear evidence to everyone of the presence of a dead body; the *where* of the Son of Man will be just as obvious to everyone on the Last Day. You need not ask that question."

The when and where of the coming of the Son of Man is not something we Christians today should concern ourselves with. What matters is that we are aware that this day will come and are prepared.

Between verses 35 and 37, some ancient manuscripts include another verse: "Two men will be in the field; one will be taken and the other left." This verse occurs in Matthew 24:40 and was also inserted in Luke's gospel by some translations.

The parable of the persistent widow

18 Then Jesus told his disciples a parable to show them that they should always pray and not give up. ²He said: "In a certain town there was a judge who neither feared God nor cared about men. ³And there was a widow in that town who kept coming to him with the plea, 'Grant me justice against my adversary.'

⁴"For some time he refused. But finally he said to himself, 'Even though I don't fear God or care about men, ⁵yet because this widow keeps bothering me, I will see that she gets justice, so that she won't eventually wear me out with her coming!'"

⁶And the Lord said, "Listen to what the unjust judge says. ⁷And will not God bring about justice for his chosen ones, who cry out to him day and night? Will he keep putting them off? ⁸I tell you, he will see that they get justice, and quickly. However, when the Son of Man comes, will he find faith on the earth?"

Jesus had told his disciples that "the time is coming when you will long to see one of the days of the Son of Man, but you will not see it" (17:22). He speaks of the suffering that is coming for himself and urges them to be ready to give up their lives (17:33). Difficult times are coming, and the followers of Jesus may suppose that God is not being just, because of the persecutions he permits them to endure. Jesus tells his disciples a short parable to encourage them to continue praying for justice with the assurance that their persistent prayer will be heard by the righteous judge.

In the parable, a wicked judge unfit for office refuses at first to listen to the pleas of a poor widow for justice against an adversary who is giving her trouble. The only weapon she has is her persistence. She bothers the judge until he takes action to see that justice is done in her case. His reason for acting is stated literally in the Greek: "Lest by coming she in the end gives me a black eye." He uses a term borrowed from boxing. He can't take the constant pounding of her petitions any longer. This parable is similar to that of the persistent friend (11:5-8).

Jesus leads from this story to the application: if an unjust judge will finally act as a result of persistent prayer, how much more quickly will God bring about justice for his chosen ones if only they keep on praying to him. "He will see that they get justice, and quickly." The disciples are urged to keep praying in the midst of the sufferings they endure. God will see to it that justice is done.

The question that Jesus asks in verse 8 suggests that the disciples need to pray especially for a strong faith. The delay of the end and the suffering that must be endured will be a real test of faith. The mention of the coming of the Son of Man takes the reader back to the previous section, which raised the question of when this would happen. The *when* is not important; what matters is that faith is found. Each individual is called upon to answer Jesus' question, "When the Son of Man comes, will he find faith on the earth?" The implication seems to be that faith will be hard to find.

The parable of the Pharisee and the tax collector

⁹To some who were confident of their own righteousness and looked down on everybody else, Jesus told this parable: ¹⁰"Two men

went up to the temple to pray, one a Pharisee and the other a tax collector. ¹¹The Pharisee stood up and prayed about himself: 'God, I thank you that I am not like all other men—robbers, evildoers, adulterers—or even like this tax collector. ¹²I fast twice a week and give a tenth of all I get.'

¹³"But the tax collector stood at a distance. He would not even look up to heaven, but beat his breast and said, 'God, have mercy on me, a sinner.'

¹⁴"I tell you that this man, rather than the other, went home justified before God. For everyone who exalts himself will be humbled, and he who humbles himself will be exalted."

This is another parable about prayer, but it is quite different from the previous one. It also says something about God's kind of justice. Jesus directs it to some who were confident of their own righteousness and who looked down on everyone else. Though it is not said, this characterization fits the Pharisees who sought to "justify" themselves in the eyes of men (16:15).

The usual time for prayer in the temple was 9 A.M. and 3 P.M. The Pharisee moved far to the front, in the court of Israel near the Holy Place. His is not really a prayer at all but simply bragging about himself, his righteousness and moral superiority over others. He specifically mentions "this tax collector." The Pharisees fasted on Monday and Thursday; the law required only one day of fasting a year (Leviticus 16:29). We previously heard how they tithed even their garden herbs (11:42). The Pharisee boasted of how much God needed him.

In striking contrast, the tax collector confessed how much he needed God. He stands as far back in the temple as possible and does not look up but beats his breast as a mark of repentance. His is a genuine prayer based on the words of David in Psalm 51: "God, have mercy on me, a sinner." His prayer has come down to us in the liturgy of the church as a perfect cry for God's help and grace.

Jesus renders his verdict: the tax collector, rather than the Pharisee, is justified before God. The words "righteousness," "evildoers," and "justified" all have the same Greek root. The Pharisee was confident that he was right and not as sinful as others were, but in God's judgment the tax collector was right. His was a righteousness based on confession of sinfulness and faith in God's mercy. This is the righteousness that counts for salvation. As so often is the case, God baffles human thinking and evaluation: God humbles the exalted and exalts the humble. This is God's kind of justice.

The little children and Jesus

15People were also bringing babies to Jesus to have him touch them. When the disciples saw this, they rebuked them. 16But Jesus called the children to him and said, "Let the little children come to me, and do not hinder them, for the kingdom of God belongs to such as these. 17I tell you the truth, anyone who will not receive the kingdom of God like a little child will never enter it."

The kingdom of God belongs to the Samaritan leper and the tax collector. It belongs also to babies. Jesus has already used a little child to teach his disciples a lesson about greatness (9:46-48). Here they learn about the kind of people who enter God's kingdom.

The touch of Jesus brought healing to a leper (5:12,13). People bringing babies to Jesus expected his touch to convey a blessing. The disciples thought that this was all a waste of Jesus' time and perhaps was quite senseless, but Jesus invites the little children to come to him. Mark 10:16 tells us that he took them in his arms and blessed them. Anyone who wishes to enter God's kingdom is told to receive it "like a little child." Like the sinful tax collector pleading for mercy, the person who desires to enter the kingdom must come in childlike weakness and take what God has to give.

This story has a traditional place in the service of infant baptism. Infant baptism is an excellent example of pure grace. There is nothing that the little babe brings to baptism except the status of sinner. God's grace works forgiveness and makes us fit for the kingdom of God.

The rich ruler

¹⁸A certain ruler asked him, "Good teacher, what must I do to inherit eternal life?"

¹⁹"Why do you call me good?" Jesus answered. "No one is good—except God alone. ²⁰You know the commandments: 'Do not commit adultery, do not murder, do not steal, do not give false testimony, honor your father and mother.'"

²¹"All these I have kept since I was a boy," he said.

²²When Jesus heard this, he said to him, "You still lack one thing. Sell everything you have and give to the poor, and you will have treasure in heaven. Then come, follow me."

²³When he heard this, he became very sad, because he was a man of great wealth. ²⁴Jesus looked at him and said, "How hard it is for the rich to enter the kingdom of God! ²⁵Indeed, it is easier for a camel to go through the eye of a needle than for a rich man to enter the kingdom of God."

²⁶Those who heard this asked, "Who then can be saved?"

²⁷Jesus replied, "What is impossible with men is possible with God."

²⁸Peter said to him, "We have left all we had to follow you!"

²⁹"I tell you the truth," Jesus said to them, "no one who has left home or wife or brothers or parents or children for the sake of the kingdom of God ³⁰will fail to receive many times as much in this age and, in the age to come, eternal life."

Several rich men have been the subject of parables told by Jesus. One was a farmer who stored up goods for himself but was not rich toward God (12:16-21). Another lived in luxury unmindful of the plight of poor Lazarus (16:19-31). In the present story a rich ruler comes to Jesus with a question. Perhaps he was a ruler of a synagogue (see 8:41) or possibly some sort of political leader. He questions Jesus as to what he must do to inherit eternal life. This same question was asked previously by an expert in the law (10:25). Inheriting eternal life is the same as receiving the kingdom of God. We have just heard that one must receive the kingdom of God like a little child. For the rich ruler that meant selling all his possessions, giving to the poor, and following Jesus.

The rich ruler addresses Jesus as "good teacher." Students of Jewish literature claim that teachers (rabbis) were never described with the adjective *good,* which was reserved for God alone. Some have wondered why Jesus rejects this title since he is the Son of God. No doubt Jesus finds this address out of place in his role as the Son of Man on the way to the cross. It is more flattery than true devotion. The rich ruler would have followed Jesus if he had truly believed in him as the Son of God.

Jesus directs the rich ruler to the commandments and hears from him the boast that he has kept them all since he was a boy. He wanted something more to do which would insure him of inheriting the kingdom. However, when Jesus gives him the double task of selling all for the sake of the poor (12:33) and then following Jesus, the rich ruler turns away in sadness. His riches obstruct his entrance into the kingdom. He did not recognize covetousness as a form of idolatry (Colossians 3:5). He served money rather than God (16:13). The cost of following Jesus was too great (9:57-62).

After the rich ruler had gone his own way, Jesus makes a comment about the difficulty rich people have in entering the kingdom of God. He says that a camel has an easier time of going through the eye of a needle than a rich person has of passing through the narrow door into the banquet hall of salvation. Some have tried to eliminate this startling hyperbole by claiming that Jesus is really talking about a small opening in a city wall when he speaks of the "eye of a needle." But that misses his point, which he clearly states in answer to Peter's question as to who can be saved: "What is impossible with men is possible with God." With childlike faith one must pray like the tax collector in the temple: "God, have mercy on me, a sinner." Salvation is all gift.

What the rich ruler would not do, Peter and other of the followers of Jesus had done (5:11). Jesus gives the assurance that such sacrifices for the sake of the kingdom will be rewarded many times over in this life and in the life to come. Rich people who are moved by the Spirit of God to use their wealth for the sake of those in need will find this statement of Jesus fulfilled in their lives.

Jesus again predicts his death

³¹Jesus took the Twelve aside and told them, "We are going up to Jerusalem, and everything that is written by the prophets about the Son of Man will be fulfilled. ³²He will be handed over to the Gentiles. They will mock him, insult him, spit on him, flog him and kill him. ³³On the third day he will rise again."

³⁴The disciples did not understand any of this. Its meaning was hidden from them, and they did not know what he was talking about.

Three times previously Jesus had told his disciples of his impending suffering and death (9:22; 9:44; 17:25). But in none of these predictions did he tell them that this was going to take place in the holy city of Jerusalem. There is a hint of the place of his death in 13:33, but now for the first time the disciples are plainly told why Jesus had "resolutely set out for Jerusalem" (9:51). The next story will find the band of travelers in the city of Jericho, quite near the goal of their journey.

What is also new to this prediction is the fact that the death of Jesus will fulfill what is written in the prophets.

Jesus has in mind especially Isaiah chapter 53. The disciples also hear for the first time that Jesus will be handed over to the Gentiles; his own people will ask the foreign governor Pontius Pilate to pronounce the sentence of death.

The disciples are totally unprepared to accept this chain of events. They hear the words Jesus speaks but do not understand. The meaning is hidden. Only after his resurrection did Jesus open "their minds so they could understand the Scriptures" (24:45). At this point in his ministry, he is content to allow the disciples to remain in their ignorance.

A blind beggar receives his sight

35As Jesus approached Jericho, a blind man was sitting by the roadside begging. 36When he heard the crowd going by, he asked what was happening. 37They told him, "Jesus of Nazareth is passing by."

38He called out, "Jesus, Son of David, have mercy on me!"

39Those who led the way rebuked him and told him to be quiet, but he shouted all the more, "Son of David, have mercy on me!"

40Jesus stopped and ordered the man to be brought to him. When he came near, Jesus asked him, 41"What do you want me to do for you?"

"Lord, I want to see," he replied.

42Jesus said to him, "Receive your sight; your faith has healed you." 43Immediately he received his sight and followed Jesus, praising God. When all the people saw it, they also praised God.

The old city of Jericho had been rebuilt by Herod the Great on a new site. Located 820 feet below sea level, its tropical climate turned this place into a luxurious pleasure town especially during the winter months. Jericho was a military city and customs center for taxes. It was located on the main road leading westward to Jerusalem and commanded a ford across the Jordan River.

Luke tells us that as Jesus approached Jericho, a blind man was sitting by the roadside begging. Matthew writes about two blind men whom Jesus met on leaving the city (Matthew 20:29-34). Mark's gospel speaks of one blind man named Bartimaeus waiting for Jesus as he left the city (Mark 10:46-52). Unless Jesus healed several blind people near Jericho, the differences in these accounts are best explained by supposing that Jesus healed two blind men while he was between the old city of Jericho and the new one built by Herod. Luke mentions only one of the two who was sitting near the entrance to the new city.

In response to the blind man's question, the crowd tells him that "Jesus of Nazareth is passing by." The mention of Nazareth alerts us to the fact that this Galilean is now in Judean country, quite far from home. The blind man has another name for Jesus, calling him "Son of David." The angel Gabriel had told Mary that her son would be given "the throne of his father David" (1:32). But no person to this point in Luke's gospel had addressed Jesus with the title "Son of David." It is found in Jewish literature as a term for the Messiah.

Despite the rebuke of the crowd, the blind man continued to cry out for mercy. He takes his place alongside the ten lepers (17:13) in turning to Jesus for help. And he is not disappointed. The healing of the blind man is the fourth miracle recorded by Luke on the journey of Jesus to Jerusalem. This blind man had faith in Jesus whereas many who could see physically remained spiritually blind. This man became a follower, something that the rich ruler was not able to do.

Zacchaeus the tax collector

19 **Jesus entered Jericho and was passing through. ²A man was there by the name of Zacchaeus; he was a chief tax**

collector and was wealthy. ³He wanted to see who Jesus was, but being a short man he could not, because of the crowd. ⁴So he ran ahead and climbed a sycamore-fig tree to see him, since Jesus was coming that way.

⁵When Jesus reached the spot, he looked up and said to him, "Zacchaeus, come down immediately. I must stay at your house today." ⁶So he came down at once and welcomed him gladly.

⁷All the people saw this and began to mutter, "He has gone to be the guest of a 'sinner.'"

⁸But Zacchaeus stood up and said to the Lord, "Look, Lord! Here and now I give half of my possessions to the poor, and if I have cheated anybody out of anything, I will pay back four times the amount."

⁹Jesus said to him, "Today salvation has come to this house, because this man, too, is a son of Abraham. ¹⁰For the Son of Man came to seek and to save what was lost."

Rich people have not fared well in Luke's gospel to this point. Jesus tells several parables in which he portrays rich men who abused their wealth (12:16-21; 16:19-31). When a rich man turned away from discipleship, Jesus spoke of the great difficulty that those with riches had in entering the kingdom of God (18:24,25). Yet he added, "What is impossible with men is possible with God" (18:27). As Jesus passes through the city of Jericho, that possibility becomes an actuality. Luke presents a rich man who is a true son of Abraham, who was a rich man himself.

The name Zacchaeus comes from a word meaning "clean" or "innocent." He was the chief tax collector in Jericho, an important commerical city. He had to work closely with the Roman governor in his position. Over the years he had accumulated a great store of wealth. This wealth might easily have kept him from entering into the kingdom of God.

Zacchaeus had evidently heard about Jesus. Perhaps he was even acquainted with one of the followers of Jesus who had himself been a tax collector: Levi, also called

Matthew (5:27). Zacchaeus was a short man and could not see over the crowds surrounding Jesus. So he ran ahead and climbed a sycamore-fig tree. This tree belongs to the same family as the mulberry (see 17:6) and has no relation to the American sycamore. It produces figs (the Greek word for "figs" is *sykon*).

When Jesus reaches the spot where Zacchaeus is perched in the tree, he orders Zacchaeus down immediately. A divine necessity is laid upon Jesus that he stay in the house of Zacchaeus and dine with him. There is an old English poem which describes the haste of this little man in coming down that sycamore:

> Methinks I see, with what a busy haste
> Zacchaeus climbed the tree. But, oh, how fast,
> How full of speed, canst thou imagine, when
> Our Savior called, he powdered down again?
> Bird that was shot ne'er dropped so quick as he.

The crowd reaction to the entry of Jesus into the house of this "sinner" is highly predictable based on past performance (15:2). The people thought it despicable for a Jewish rabbi to set foot in the house of a tax collector. Yet for Zacchaeus the entry of Jesus was truly his day of salvation. He expresses his overwhelming joy at being accepted by Jesus by promising half of his possessions to the poor and a fourfold restitution for anyone whom he had cheated.

The final comment of Jesus emphasizes that he has come to seek and save the lost. The Pharisees and experts in the law regarded people like Zacchaeus as lost and beyond hope of salvation because of their occupations and cooperation with the hated Romans. Yet this man proved himself far more righteous than the Pharisees who loved money (16:14) and who failed to clean up their lives by giving to the poor (11:41). Zacchaeus is the model for the rich believer.

The parable of the ten minas

¹¹While they were listening to this, he went on to tell them a parable, because he was near Jerusalem and the people thought that the kingdom of God was going to appear at once. ¹²He said: "A man of noble birth went to a distant country to have himself appointed king and then to return. ¹³So he called ten of his servants and gave them ten minas. 'Put this money to work,' he said, 'until I come back.'

¹⁴"But his subjects hated him and sent a delegation after him to say, 'We don't want this man to be our king.'

¹⁵"He was made king, however, and returned home. Then he sent for the servants to whom he had given the money, in order to find out what they had gained with it.

¹⁶"The first one came and said, 'Sir, your mina has earned ten more.'

¹⁷" 'Well done, my good servant!' his master replied. 'Because you have been trustworthy in a very small matter, take charge of ten cities.'

¹⁸"The second came and said, 'Sir, your mina has earned five more.'

¹⁹"His master answered, 'You take charge of five cities.'

²⁰"Then another servant came and said, 'Sir, here is your mina; I have kept it laid away in a piece of cloth. ²¹I was afraid of you, because you are a hard man. You take out what you did not put in and reap what you did not sow.'

²²"His master replied, 'I will judge you by your own words, you wicked servant! You knew, did you, that I am a hard man, taking out what I did not put in, and reaping what I did not sow? ²³Why then didn't you put my money on deposit, so that when I came back, I could have collected it with interest?'

²⁴"Then he said to those standing by, 'Take his mina away from him and give it to the one who has ten minas.'

²⁵" 'Sir,' they said, 'he already has ten!'

²⁶"He replied, 'I tell you that to everyone who has, more will be given, but as for the one who has nothing, even what he has will be taken away. ²⁷But those enemies of mine who did not want me to be king over them—bring them here and kill them in front of me.'"

According to the Jewish historian Josephus, who lived near the time of Jesus, the distance between Jericho and Jerusalem was 150 stadia through "desert and rocky" country. A Roman stadium was slightly more than 600 feet. This makes the final leg of Jesus' journey about 18 miles, uphill all the way. There is no way of knowing how large a crowd was following. It was the spring season of the year, and the Jewish festival of the Passover would soon be celebrated.

The Passover festival stirred nationalistic sentiments since it celebrated Jewish independence from captivity in Egypt. The mood of the people walking along with Jesus was one of expectation: "The kingdom of God is going to appear very soon; we're marching with the king."

To cool their misplaced enthusiasm, Jesus tells a parable about a man of noble birth who went to a distant country to have himself appointed king. Before leaving, he gave one mina each to ten of his servants, instructing them to put the money to work. "Mina" comes from the Greek word *mna,* a coin valued at 1/60 of a talent and equivalent to about three months wages. In Matthew 25:14-30 a parable is recorded in which a man distributes talents to his servants, a much larger sum of money.

After this nobleman left home, some of his subjects sent a delegation to inform the distant authorities that they didn't want this man as their king. Such a thing actually happened when a delegation of Jews went to Rome to appear before Caesar Augustus opposing the appointment of a son of Herod the Great as their king. Perhaps Jesus had this incident in mind. In the present parable their protest had no effect. In fact, they end up being killed by the new king for opposing him. Jesus is no doubt thinking of those contemporaries of his who opposed his kingship. They will be condemned in the final judgment for rejecting him.

When the new king returns home, he summons his servants to find out what they have done with the minas he had given them. We have reports from three of the ten servants. The first earned ten more minas; the second, five more. Both are commended and put in charge of some of the king's cities.

However, one of the ten servants reports to the king that he had kept his mina "laid away in a piece of cloth." He knew the hard-driving personality of the new king and was afraid of losing his mina if he invested it with the bankers. The king condemns him, calling him a wicked servant. He orders that the returned mina be given to the servant who has ten. When questioned about this seeming unfairness, the king quotes a proverb which says that the person with much will get more and the person with nothing will lose even that. The same proverb was quoted by Jesus in 8:18, where he applied it to listening to the Word of God.

This parable is another of those dealing with the subject of proper stewardship. Two of the servants were good stewards; one did not put to use what he had received from his master. The disciples of Jesus needed to realize that the kingdom of God was not about to appear in the near future. As they wait for Jesus' return, they are to be busy using the resources that have been given to them. Like the servants that Jesus spoke of in 12:35-48, he wants them to carry out their responsibilities faithfully. The mina, which every disciple of Jesus has been given, must be none other than the gospel. Jesus wants them to invest that gospel treasure they have received so that it may produce much fruit.

PART THREE

The Servant at Work, Opening the Doors of the Kingdom: Suffering, Dying, Rising Again (19:28–24:53)

Jesus arrives in Jerusalem

The triumphal entry

²⁸After Jesus had said this, he went on ahead, going up to Jerusalem. ²⁹As he approached Bethphage and Bethany at the hill called the Mount of Olives, he sent two of his disciples, saying to them, ³⁰"Go to the village ahead of you, and as you enter it, you will find a colt tied there, which no one has ever ridden. Untie it and bring it here. ³¹If anyone asks you, 'Why are you untying it?' tell him, 'The Lord needs it.'"

³²Those who were sent ahead went and found it just as he had told them. ³³As they were untying the colt, its owners asked them, "Why are you untying the colt?"

³⁴They replied, "The Lord needs it."

³⁵They brought it to Jesus, threw their cloaks on the colt and put Jesus on it. ³⁶As he went along, people spread their cloaks on the road.

³⁷When he came near the place where the road goes down the Mount of Olives, the whole crowd of disciples began joyfully to praise God in loud voices for all the miracles they had seen:

³⁸"Blessed is the king who comes in the name of the Lord!"

"Peace in heaven and glory in the highest!"

³⁹Some of the Pharisees in the crowd said to Jesus, "Teacher, rebuke your disciples!"

⁴⁰"I tell you," he replied, "if they keep quiet, the stones will cry out."

⁴¹As he approached Jerusalem and saw the city, he wept over it ⁴²and said, "If you, even you, had only known on this day what would bring you peace—but now it is hidden from your eyes. ⁴³The days will come upon you when your enemies will build an embankment against you and encircle you and hem you in on every side. ⁴⁴They will dash you to the ground, you and the children within your walls. They will not leave one stone on another, because you did not recognize the time of God's coming to you."

As one approaches Jerusalem from the east, the road crosses over the Mount of Olives, which rises some three hundred feet above the city. Bethphage was a small village on the Mount of Olives, but its exact site is uncertain. Bethany is located on the eastern slope of the mount about three miles from Jerusalem. This is the village in which Jesus' friends Martha, Mary, and Lazarus lived. From John's gospel we learn that Jesus spent some time in Bethany at the home of Mary and Martha. Only recently he had raised Lazarus from the dead (John 11,12).

On the Sunday before the Passover festival, Jesus sets in motion an action that will result in a public demonstration in his behalf. He sends two disciples into Bethphage to bring him a colt on which no one has ever ridden. Perhaps Jesus had made a previous arrangement with the owners to use this colt when he needed it. The disciples bring the colt to Jesus and help him to mount.

The significance of what Jesus has done is immediately apparent to the people who are following. Jesus is consciously fulfilling the words of the prophet Zechariah: "Rejoice greatly, O Daughter of Zion! Shout, Daughter of Jerusalem! See, your king comes to you, righteous and having salvation, gentle and riding on a donkey, on a colt, the foal of a donkey" (Zechariah 9:9). Matthew and John quote this prophecy in telling the story of the triumphal entry into Jerusalem. The people spread cloaks on the road as a kind of royal carpet. John tells us that they carried palm branches (John 12:13), an action that gives this Sunday its special name in the Christian church year.

As the triumphal procession crosses over the ridge at the top of the Mount of Olives and begins the descent, the city of Jerusalem, with its beautiful temple, comes into full view. At last Jesus has reached the goal of his journey, which was first mentioned in 9:51. He comes not to establish an earthly kingdom; he comes not to bring this world to its end; rather, he is the King, the Messiah, who comes to die on the cross. With his death and resurrection, he will open the doors of the kingdom of God for all people.

As the royal procession moves forward, a whole crowd of disciples shouts in loud praise to God. Using words from Psalm 118, they honor this king who comes in the name of the Lord. The words of the people, "Peace in heaven and glory in the highest!" bear a resemblance to the song of the angels at the birth of Jesus (2:14). Such talk is too much for the Pharisees. Luke mentions them for the last time in his gospel as they advise Jesus to silence his disciples. In answer Jesus says that if the people keep quiet, then the stones will cry out.

Then, suddenly, the shouts of the people are stilled; only the sobbing of Jesus is heard, weeping over the city of Jerusalem. Previously, Luke had recorded words of Jesus spoken in sorrow about this sacred city which refused his ministry (13:34,35). Jesus was the bringer of peace, that peace of which the angels and the crowd of disciples had sung. But Jerusalem, like the Pharisees, was not looking for the peace that Jesus came to bring. As a result, they would experience not peace but dreadful war. The future is hidden to the inhabitants of this walled city, but Jesus knows what is to come.

The words of Jesus describe the Roman siege of Jerusalem that resulted in its capture in the year A.D. 70. Jesus' words that "they will not leave one stone on another" are an echo of his statement to the Pharisees: if the people are quiet, the stones will speak. The people of Jerusalem were not ready to speak words of praise in honor of the coming King. Since they would not speak, the fallen stones will speak God's word of judgment.

Jesus at the temple

⁴⁵Then he entered the temple area and began driving out those who were selling. ⁴⁶"It is written," he said to them, "'My house will be a house of prayer'; but you have made it 'a den of robbers.'"

⁴⁷Every day he was teaching at the temple. But the chief priests, the teachers of the law and the leaders among the people were trying to kill him. ⁴⁸Yet they could not find any way to do it, because all the people hung on his words.

When Jesus was 40 days old, Mary and Joseph had brought him to the temple to present him to the Lord (2:22). At age 12 Jesus was found by his mother in the temple courts among the teachers, listening to them and asking them questions (2:46). He told his mother that she should have known that he "had to be in my Father's house" (verse 49).

Now as the mature Servant of the Lord, Jesus again enters the temple area; he is distraught by what he finds. Within the temple courtyards are people selling sacrificial doves and changing foreign coin into the required currency to pay the temple tax. Far from being a house of prayer (Isaiah 56:7), the temple had become a den of robbers (Jeremiah 7:11). Profits had replaced prayer as the dominant feature of temple activity. Here is another example of bad stewardship.

Jesus acts in his role as King to purge the temple. He needed to do this so that he might use this as a place for teaching the Word of God. Mark's account of the cleansing of the temple is more detailed and places this event on the Monday of Holy Week (Mark 11:15-19). Luke's concern falls more with the following report of Jesus' teaching in the temple. It is not so much the cleansing which upsets the leaders as it is the teaching of Jesus.

Three opposition groups are mentioned. The chief priests had charge of all temple business and activities. The teachers of the law were interpreters and instructors of the Old Testament Scriptures. The leaders among the people refer to the elected elders and members of the Jewish high court, the Sanhedrin. They all wanted to kill Jesus, but the popular support that his teaching had among the people made this very difficult.

The authority of Jesus questioned

20 One day as he was teaching the people in the temple courts and preaching the gospel, the chief priests and the teachers of the law, together with the elders, came up to him. ²"Tell us by what authority you are doing these things," they said. "Who gave you this authority?"

³He replied, "I will also ask you a question. Tell me, ⁴John's baptism—was it from heaven, or from men?"

⁵They discussed it among themselves and said, "If we say, 'From heaven,' he will ask, 'Why didn't you believe him?' ⁶But if we say, 'From men,' all the people will stone us, because they are persuaded that John was a prophet."

⁷So they answered, "We don't know where it was from."

⁸Jesus said, "Neither will I tell you by what authority I am doing these things."

For a person to come from despised Galilee and take over the temple courtyard in Jerusalem as Jesus does is a challenge to those in charge. It alarms them that people come to hear this outsider teach. He proclaims the good news that the door of God's kingdom is open to all who repent and believe him. That the temple leadership should come and question Jesus about the source of the authority for his words and deeds surprises no one. In fact, one could say that they are only doing their duty.

Jesus responds to the official delegation with a counter question. He asks who gave the authority to John to baptize in the Jordan (3:1-18). Was this something that God authorized John to do, or did the Jerusalem leadership give him this right?

Those questioning Jesus find themselves in a dilemma. They are trapped by the choice that Jesus puts before them. If John was really God's prophet as the people took him to be, then they should have accepted him. But if they deny that John was from God, then the people may stone them for blasphemy. Moses had ordered that "anyone who blasphemes the name of the LORD must be put to death" by stoning (Leviticus 24:16). The best option for the temple leadership seems simply to express their ignorance. They confess they don't know where John got this authority—a rather embarrassing admission for them to make.

Jesus follows their lead and refuses to say by what authority he is teaching. His authority was not from a body of men like the chief priests but from God. Jesus had demonstrated that authority again and again during his earthly ministry (5:24,25). The crowds recognized his authority (4:32). It was an authority affirmed by the heavenly Father at the transfiguration (9:35). Even if Jesus had identified the source of his authority, his questioners still would not have believed him (22:67).

From now on, the conflict between Jesus and the official religious leadership of the Jews will intensify. There will be more verbal matches between Jesus and his interrogators.

Finally, there will be an arrest, a trial, and the cross. How true were the words of Jesus: "If you, even you, had only known on this day what would bring you peace—but now it is hidden from your eyes" (19:42).

The parable of the tenants

⁹He went on to tell the people this parable: "A man planted a vineyard, rented it to some farmers and went away for a long time. ¹⁰At harvest time he sent a servant to the tenants so they would give him some of the fruit of the vineyard. But the tenants beat him and sent him away empty-handed. ¹¹He sent another servant, but that one also they beat and treated shamefully and sent away empty-handed. ¹²He sent still a third, and they wounded him and threw him out.

¹³"Then the owner of the vineyard said, 'What shall I do? I will send my son, whom I love; perhaps they will respect him.'

¹⁴"But when the tenants saw him, they talked the matter over. 'This is the heir,' they said. 'Let's kill him, and the inheritance will be ours.' ¹⁵So they threw him out of the vineyard and killed him.

"What then will the owner of the vineyard do to them? ¹⁶He will come and kill those tenants and give the vineyard to others."

When the people heard this, they said, "May this never be!"

¹⁷Jesus looked directly at them and asked, "Then what is the meaning of that which is written:

"'The stone the builders rejected
has become the capstone'?

¹⁸Everyone who falls on that stone will be broken to pieces, but he on whom it falls will be crushed."

¹⁹The teachers of the law and the chief priests looked for a way to arrest him immediately, because they knew he had spoken this parable against them. But they were afraid of the people.

This parable Jesus tells to the people is a clear revelation of his impending death and the judgment that will fall on his killers. The prophet Isaiah had described the people of Israel as a vineyard which failed to produce fruit (5:1-7). In Jesus' parable the problem is not with the vineyard but with the tenants to whom the owner had rented his property. The tenants obviously represent the religious leaders of the Jews, as the leaders themselves recognize at the parable's conclusion. The comparison is fitting, seeing as they were trying to kill Jesus (19:47).

The owner is looking for fruit from his vineyard. Jesus earlier had told a parable about a tree that failed to produce fruit (13:6-8). Both Matthew and Mark report that on his daily trip from Bethany to Jerusalem, Jesus had cursed a fig tree for its failure to produce fruit (Matthew 21:18,19; Mark 11:12-14,20,21). These tenants who fail to give the owner the fruit due to him are another example of poor stewardship of what God gives for the use of his people.

Three servants of the owner are abused and sent away empty-handed by the tenants. These servants represent prophets like Elijah, Jeremiah, and John the Baptist. As a kind of last resort, the owner decides to send his beloved son, thinking that the tenants will respect him. He, however, suffers an even worse fate: the tenants throw him out of the vineyard and kill him. They imagine that since the heir is dead, they will inherit the vineyard. How mistaken they are! The owner comes and kills these tenants and gives the vineyard to others. The tenants suffer the same fate as the citizens who didn't want "a man of noble birth" as their king (19:11-27). Jesus is referring to the destruction that will befall the city of Jerusalem and the Jewish nation at the hands of the Romans in the year A.D. 70. By the "others" to whom the vineyard is given, he means the Gentiles.

The people also catch the drift of what Jesus is saying. The expression they use is found a number of times in the letters of Paul but only once here in the gospels. The NIV translates it as "May this never be!" The KJV says "God forbid." Either expresses a strong opposing reaction, or negation.

Jesus meets their objection by asking a question about the meaning of Psalm 118:22: "The stone the builders rejected has become the capstone." The rejected stone is Jesus himself, the son rejected by the tenants of the vineyard (see Acts 4:11 and 1 Peter 2:7, where this verse is applied to Jesus). That rejected stone ends up being the most important one in the entire building. The NIV translation has "capstone," the top stone of a structure or wall. More literal is the KJV "head of the corner." In ancient times this was the stone used at a building's corner to bear the weight or stress of the two walls. On Jesus rests the entire structure of God's kingdom.

And what of those who reject this stone? Divine retribution falls upon them. The rejected stone is not only important in the building; it is a stone which brings the judgment of God. The person who falls or trips over the stone will be broken to pieces; the person on whom the stone falls will be crushed. In either case, not the stone but the person is hurt. The effect is like that of the Jewish proverb "If a stone falls on a pot, woe to the pot. If the pot falls on the stone, woe to the pot. Either way, woe to the pot!" So also with anyone who dares to reject the stone that is Jesus the Savior.

Paying taxes to Caesar

20Keeping a close watch on him, they sent spies, who pretended to be honest. They hoped to catch Jesus in something he said so that they might hand him over to the power and authority of the governor. 21So the spies questioned him: "Teacher, we know that you speak and teach what is right, and that you do not show partiality but teach the way of God in accordance with the truth. 22Is it right for us to pay taxes to Caesar or not?"

23He saw through their duplicity and said to them, 24"Show me a denarius. Whose portrait and inscription are on it?"

25"Caesar's," they replied.

Paying taxes to Caesar

He said to them, "Then give to Caesar what is Caesar's, and to God what is God's." **²⁶They were unable to trap him in what he had said there in public. And astonished by his answer, they became silent.**

The enemies of Jesus, frustrated in their attempts to get rid of him due to his popularity among the people, now decide upon a new tactic. They hope to entice Jesus into making a statement that will get him in trouble with the Roman governor, Pontius Pilate. Matthew and Mark identify the spies sent to question Jesus as being Pharisees and supporters of the Herod family. They pretend to be honest by seeking to appear as if they really are interested in having an answer to the question of paying taxes to the Roman emperor. They preface their question with words of praise for Jesus, identifying him as one who teaches the way of God truthfully with no regard for human authority.

There were some groups within Jewish society who taught that it was wrong to pay taxes to the Romans. In A.D. 6, Judas of Galilee led an uprising of armed men who denounced the payment of Roman taxes. A sect known as the Zealots was strongly anti-Roman and promoted all things Jewish. For some Jews, to pay taxes with a Roman coin bearing the image of the Caesar seemed to be a form of idolatry. God had commanded his people to make no graven or molten image, and Jewish coins bore no figure of any human being.

Jesus was not fooled by his questioners. He saw through their duplicity; they were two-faced. This becomes evident when they are able to produce a Roman coin from their purse at the request of Jesus. The denarius was worth about a day's wage. It bore the image of the Roman Caesar with the inscription "Tiberius Caesar Augustus, son of the divine Augustus." If the spies were religiously opposed to paying tax to the Romans because of this idolatrous image and inscription, then they should not have been carrying the coin. This episode is an embarrassment for the spies.

The statement Jesus makes clearly indicates that it is proper to pay taxes to government, even if it is a foreign and heathen power. Paying such taxes does not interfere with the Christian's obligation to God. Just as the coin paid to Caesar carries his image, so people bear the image of God and have an obligation to him. We are able to be both good citizens and good Christians.

Despite the fact that Jesus here supports the payment of taxes to Caesar, this becomes one of the charges against him when he is brought for trial before Pilate (23:2). The enemies of Jesus will not be bothered with truth or honesty.

The resurrection and marriage

²⁷Some of the Sadducees, who say there is no resurrection, came to Jesus with a question. ²⁸"Teacher," they said, "Moses wrote for us that if a man's brother dies and leaves a wife but no children, the man must marry the widow and have children for his brother. ²⁹Now there were seven brothers. The first one married a woman and died childless. ³⁰The second ³¹and then the third married her, and in the same way the seven died, leaving no children. ³²Finally, the woman died too. ³³Now then, at the resurrection whose wife will she be, since the seven were married to her?"

³⁴Jesus replied, "The people of this age marry and are given in marriage. ³⁵But those who are considered worthy of taking part in that age and in the resurrection from the dead will neither marry nor be given in marriage, ³⁶and they can no longer die; for they are like the angels. They are God's children, since they are children of the resurrection. ³⁷But in the account of the bush, even Moses showed that the dead rise, for he calls the Lord 'the God of Abraham, and the God of Isaac, and the God of Jacob.' ³⁸He is not the God of the dead, but of the living, for to him all are alive."

³⁹Some of the teachers of the law responded, "Well said, teacher!" ⁴⁰And no one dared to ask him any more questions.

After dealing with a political question, Jesus is confronted with a question meant to show that the idea of a resurrection from the dead is ridiculous. The Sadducees appear here for the first time in Luke's gospel. This Jewish party took its name from the priest Zadok (2 Samuel 8:17). The Sadducees were generally supportive of Roman rule and no doubt were pleased with the previous answer of Jesus. The prominent men of Jerusalem, including many priests, belonged to this sect.

Josephus, the Jewish historian, says that the Sadducees do away with "the persistence of the soul, penalties in death's abode and rewards" in the afterlife. They believed that "the souls perish along with the bodies." Some of the Sadducees now pose a rather ludicrous chain of events to support their denial of the resurrection from the dead.

Moses had given Israel the law of the levirate marriage. *Levir* is the Latin word for "husband's brother, brother-in-law." If a woman should become a widow, her dead husband's brother was required to take her in marriage and seek to father children who would bear the dead man's name (Deuteronomy 25:5,6). The hypothetical example cited by the Sadducees has a woman marrying seven brothers before she herself dies childless. Now the question: "At the resurrection, whose wife will she be?"

Jesus solves the dilemma by distinguishing between two ages: the present age and the age to come. One of the purposes of marriage is to bring children into the world. But in the age to come, there will be neither birth nor death. And there will be no marriage. People will be like the angels (whose existence the Sadducees also denied). Those who by God's gracious judgment are privileged to live in that age are called by Jesus simply "God's children." Earthly family relationships will have become unimportant.

But Jesus is not content with simply answering the question posed by the Sadducees. He goes on to attack their unbelief. He recalls God's statement to Moses at the burning bush: "I am the God of your father, the God of Abraham, the God of Isaac and the God of Jacob" (Exodus 3:6). At the time of Moses all three of these patriarchs had been long dead physically. But the living God continued to speak of his relationship to them as being present. This means that they still live. Human relationships end with death, but the relationship a person has with God goes on eternally.

Jesus is commended for his answer by some of the teachers of the law. They may have been Pharisees who believed in the resurrection of the dead (see Acts 23:6). The answers that Jesus had given to a variety of questions demonstrated his authority and wisdom. The next time he is asked questions by his enemies will be at his trial.

Whose son is the Christ?

⁴¹Then Jesus said to them, "How is it that they say the Christ is the Son of David? ⁴²David himself declares in the Book of Psalms:

> **" 'The Lord said to my Lord:**
> **"Sit at my right hand**
> **⁴³ until I make your enemies**
> **a footstool for your feet." '**

⁴⁴David calls him 'Lord.' How then can he be his son?"

⁴⁵While all the people were listening, Jesus said to his disciples, ⁴⁶"Beware of the teachers of the law. They like to walk around in flowing robes and love to be greeted in the marketplaces and have the most important seats in the synagogues and the places of honor at banquets. ⁴⁷They devour widows' houses and for a show make lengthy prayers. Such men will be punished most severely."

One of the titles given by Jewish teachers to the Messiah was "Son of David." The blind beggar had addressed Jesus in this way (18:38). The angel Gabriel had told Mary that her son would be given "the throne of his father David" (1:32). To speak of Jesus as "Son of David" is proper (see Romans 1:3). But the title is inadequate and fails to fully convey the nature of the Messiah.

To prove this, Jesus quotes Psalm 110:1. In this psalm King David does not speak of the Messiah as his son but as his Lord. In the quotation the first use of "Lord" refers to God the Father. The second time the word occurs, the reference is to God's Son. He is given a seat at the right hand of the Father with the assurance that his enemies will ultimately serve as his footstool. Jesus does not answer his own question but implies that the Messiah is more than simply a son of David: he is David's Lord, who will rule at God's right hand.

Having demonstrated that the teachers of the law were faulty interpreters of the Scriptures, Jesus goes on to warn against some of their antics. Similar words of condemnation are found in 11:45-52. Matthew includes an entire chapter of woes against the Pharisees and scribes at this point in his gospel (23).

Jesus denounces the teachers of the law on various counts: vainly wearing showy robes, coveting people's praises, covering their financial pillaging of widows with pious prayers. Just how the lawyers were "devour[ing] widows' houses" is not spelled out. The following story may furnish an illustration of one method. Their fate will contrast sharply with that of the "children of the resurrection" (20:36).

The widow's offering

21 As he looked up, Jesus saw the rich putting their gifts into the temple treasury. ²He also saw a poor widow put in two very small copper coins. ³"I tell you the truth," he said, "this poor widow has put in more than all the others. ⁴All these people gave

their gifts out of their wealth; but she out of her poverty put in all she had to live on."

This poor widow who put "all she had to live on" into the temple treasury is often held up for praise. Jesus points out that her offering of the two smallest coins in circulation was really more than what the rich were putting into the treasury. As so often happens in Luke's gospel, Jesus is critical of the actions of the rich.

But this story might also be understood in a different way, especially in view of the context. At the end of the previous chapter, Jesus had warned against the teachers of the law who "devour widows' houses." One way this might be done is for religious leaders to so bind the conscience of a poor person that he gives an offering which God himself does not expect. Did God really want this poor widow to give all her money to support a temple that had become "a den of robbers" (19:46)?

In Mark 7:10-13 Jesus teaches that there are times when human need takes precedence over what might be offered to the Lord. If the story of the widow's offering is understood in this way, then Jesus is grieved by what he saw: another example of how the poor were being abused by the rich. The rich gave what they could easily afford; this poor widow gave what she could not afford.

Signs of the end of the age

⁵Some of his disciples were remarking about how the temple was adorned with beautiful stones and with gifts dedicated to God. But Jesus said, ⁶"As for what you see here, the time will come when not one stone will be left on another; every one of them will be thrown down."

⁷"Teacher," they asked, "when will these things happen? And what will be the sign that they are about to take place?"

⁸He replied: "Watch out that you are not deceived. For many will come in my name, claiming, 'I am he,' and, 'The time is near.' Do not follow them. ⁹When you hear of wars and revolutions, do not be frightened. These things must happen first, but the end will not come right away."

¹⁰Then he said to them: "Nation will rise against nation, and kingdom against kingdom. ¹¹There will be great earthquakes, famines and pestilences in various places, and fearful events and great signs from heaven.

¹²"But before all this, they will lay hands on you and persecute you. They will deliver you to synagogues and prisons, and you will be brought before kings and governors, and all on account of my name. ¹³This will result in your being witnesses to them. ¹⁴But make up your mind not to worry beforehand how you will defend yourselves. ¹⁵For I will give you words and wisdom that none of your adversaries will be able to resist or contradict. ¹⁶You will be betrayed even by parents, brothers, relatives and friends, and they will put some of you to death. ¹⁷All men will hate you because of me. ¹⁸But not a hair of your head will perish. ¹⁹By standing firm you will gain life.

²⁰"When you see Jerusalem being surrounded by armies, you will know that its desolation is near. ²¹Then let those who are in Judea flee to the mountains, let those in the city get out, and let those in the country not enter the city. ²²For this is the time of punishment in fulfillment of all that has been written. ²³How dreadful it will be in those days for pregnant women and nursing mothers! There will be great distress in the land and wrath against this people. ²⁴They will fall by the sword and will be taken as prisoners to all the nations. Jerusalem will be trampled on by the Gentiles until the times of the Gentiles are fulfilled.

²⁵"There will be signs in the sun, moon and stars. On the earth, nations will be in anguish and perplexity at the roaring and tossing of the sea. ²⁶Men will faint from terror, apprehensive of what is coming on the world, for the heavenly bodies will be shaken. ²⁷At that time they will see the Son of Man coming in a cloud with power and great glory. ²⁸When these things begin to take place, stand up and lift up your heads, because your redemption is drawing near."

²⁹He told them this parable: "Look at the fig tree and all the trees. ³⁰When they sprout leaves, you can see for yourselves and know that summer is near. ³¹Even so, when you see these things happening, you know that the kingdom of God is near.

³²"I tell you the truth, this generation will certainly not pass away until all these things have happened. ³³Heaven and earth will pass away, but my words will never pass away.

³⁴"Be careful, or your hearts will be weighed down with dissipation, drunkenness and the anxieties of life, and that day will close on you unexpectedly like a trap. ³⁵For it will come upon all those who live on the face of the whole earth. ³⁶Be always on the watch, and pray that you may be able to escape all that is about to happen, and that you may be able to stand before the Son of Man."

³⁷Each day Jesus was teaching at the temple, and each evening he went out to spend the night on the hill called the Mount of Olives, ³⁸and all the people came early in the morning to hear him at the temple.

The temple in Jerusalem was the center of Jesus' activities in the week before his crucifixion. After his triumphal entry into the city, Jesus went to the temple and drove out those who were using its courtyard for business purposes. Jesus uses that same courtyard for the purpose of teaching people the Word of God. The temple is the scene of the confrontations between Jesus and his opponents described in chapter 20. While in the temple, Jesus observes both rich and poor putting money into the treasury. This money was used to maintain the temple and support the daily routine of religious activities.

The temple was a beautiful building, as some of the disciples of Jesus note. The first temple, built by King Solomon, had been destroyed by the Babylonians in 586 B.C.

The second temple was completed about 515 B.C. King Herod the Great had decided to refurbish the aging temple, and this project continued even after his death. Josephus writes that "the exterior of the structure lacked nothing that could astound either mind or eye." Some of the stones of the temple were over 60 feet in length and 7 feet high. Yet this splendid building was doomed. Jesus says, "Not one stone will be left on another." He had said the same thing about the city of Jerusalem (19:44).

The fall of the city of Jerusalem and the destruction of the temple are for Jesus vivid reminders of the end of the present age. He had spoken earlier to the disciples of this event. In 12:35-48 he urges them to be watchful for that day. In 17:20-37 he stresses the suddenness and certainty of the coming of the day of the Son of Man.

As Jesus now sits on the Mount of Olives looking over the temple area (Mark 13:3), he speaks again to his disciples of the coming end of Jerusalem and of the world. This long discourse of Jesus is prompted by the disciples' double question: (1) When will these things happen? (2) What will be the sign that they are about to take place?

The first thing Jesus says in answer is "Watch out that you are not deceived." He had issued the same warning previously (17:23). There will be much talk about the coming end of this age, and some people will claim to be Christ returned to earth. "Do not follow them," warns Jesus. There will be wars and revolutions, but the disciples are not to be frightened. Jesus makes it plain that the end is not coming as quickly as many people thought. The Lord is patient (2 Peter 3:8,9).

Jesus adds others signs of the coming end besides war: earthquakes, famines, pestilences, fearful events, unusual signs in the heavens. Yet all of these are only general reminders of what is fully going to happen. These are signs that we continue to witness in our generation, sermons telling that the end is coming. But none answers the specific question of *when*.

Beginning with verse 12, Jesus turns away from the subject of signs of the end to focus on what the disciples will themselves experience in their own lifetimes. They must prepare for persecution as they carry the message of the gospel into the world. Being brought before kings and governors has a blessed result: the opportunity to be a witness for Jesus.

Jesus doesn't want his disciples to worry about what they will say when they are put on trial. They should not practice or memorize a speech ahead of time. Jesus assures his disciples that he will give them the right words to speak in the presence of their adversaries. Previously, he had promised that the Holy Spirit would teach them what to say (12:12). The work of the Spirit and the ascended Jesus are closely related.

The disciples will not only be opposed by worldly authorities. They will also find that family members and friends become enemies because of their allegiance to Christ. They will be surrounded by hatred. And some will be put to death. But even death will not separate the disciples from God's loving care. "The very hairs of your head are all numbered" (12:7). By standing firm the disciples will gain life (9:24).

The salvation that the disciples of Jesus will gain by firm witness to him is in striking contrast to the fate that awaits the sacred city of Jerusalem. Twice previously, Jesus had spoken of the sad consequences of that city's refusal to accept him and the peace he offered (13:34,35; 19:41-44). He tells his disciples that when they see the city surrounded by enemy armies, they will know that the threatened desolation (13:35) is at hand.

What Jesus describes here came to pass when the city of Jerusalem was put under siege by the Romans in the year A.D. 70. Great mounds of earth, or ramps, were set up, and the entire city was surrounded by a wall more than five miles long. Josephus reports that 1,100,000 Jews of Jerusalem and Judea were put to the sword and another 97,000 were taken to Rome as part of the triumphal procession into the capital. To illustrate the woe uttered by Jesus regarding women with children, one can point to the story recorded by Josephus about Mary, a woman from Perea, who was among the Jews starving in Jerusalem and who seized her child, an infant at her breast, slew it, and roasted it for food for herself. No wonder Jesus urges flight from the doomed city!

Jesus says that the desolation which Jerusalem will experience is punishment for her sins, in fulfillment of what was written in the Old Testament. One could point to passages such as Micah 3:12 and Jeremiah 6:1-8; 26:1-6 as examples of such prophecies. This Jewish city will be trampled on by the Gentiles until the time of punishment is complete.

Jesus moves from talk about the end of Jerusalem to an even more devastating event: the end of the world. This end will be marked by spectacular signs causing people to faint with terror. The heavenly bodies will be shaken, and the sea will toss and roar. It will seem as if creation is falling apart. And then the Son of Man will come in a cloud with power and great glory. His coming will not be in secret but like "the lightning, which flashes and lights up the sky from one end to the other" (17:24).

The events Jesus describes here are terrifying. Yet for the believer they have a comforting significance. The end means final redemption, final deliverance from all the evil of this world: sin, death, and the power of the devil. For good reason Jesus urges his disciples to lift their heads in hope when these end-time signs begin to unfold. The parable of the fig tree illustrates the truth that such signs mean that the kingdom of God is near.

Jesus' discourse on the end of the age was in response to the disciples' double question about the destruction of the temple: when and what signs? Jesus does not give them a precise answer as to when this will happen. However, he does assert in verse 32 that "all these things" will come to pass within the lifetime of his contemporaries. By "all these things" he is not speaking about the coming of the Son of Man and the catastrophic events of the end time. Even Jesus, according to his human nature while on earth, did not know when that day would be (Matthew 24:36; Mark 13:32). His statement here must be understood within the context of the disciples' double question. People living when Jesus spoke these words did witness the destruction of Jerusalem and the general signs which foreshadowed the end of the world.

The end of Jerusalem was a foretaste, a prelude, to the end of the age. Jesus gives the solemn assurance that "heaven and earth will pass away, but my words will never pass away." Nothing in this world, neither the temple nor the city of Jerusalem nor anything else, is abiding. Only the words of Jesus are eternal. His words were fulfilled about the destruction of Jerusalem; they will be fulfilled about the end of the world.

This thought leads Jesus to his concluding exhortation that his disciples "be always on the watch." The very fact that no precise date is given as to when the world will end is all the more reason always to be ready. Jesus warns against various activities that weigh people down and keep them from being alert. The expression "weighed down" means about the same as "depressed." "Dissipation" refers to a life of wasteful self-indulgence. This kind of life is often the result of depression, a symptom of lack of faith.

Watchfulness dictates a life of prayer. Jesus had provided for his disciples a living example of a person devoted to prayer. He urges them to pray that they might be able to escape the dreadful destruction coming upon Jerusalem and finally "be able to stand before the Son of Man" as faithful confessors of his name.

The last two verses in chapter 21 are a brief summary of the temple ministry of Jesus. They correspond to the report at the beginning of this teaching section, found in 19:47,48. Matthew and Mark report that Jesus stayed overnight in the village of Bethany, which is located on the Mount of Olives. Jesus continues to be very popular with the people. This fact creates a problem for the leaders who want to do away with Jesus.

Jesus suffers and dies

Judas agrees to betray Jesus

22 Now the Feast of Unleavened Bread, called the Passover, was approaching, ²and the chief priests and the teachers of the law were looking for some way to get rid of Jesus, for they were afraid of the people. ³Then Satan entered Judas, called Iscariot, one of the Twelve. ⁴And Judas went to the chief priests and the officers of the temple guard and discussed with them how he might betray Jesus. ⁵They were delighted and agreed to give him money. ⁶He consented, and watched for an opportunity to hand Jesus over to them when no crowd was present.

The chief festival of the Jews is the Passover. It is celebrated at the sundown that marks the beginning of the 15th of Nisan, the first month in the calendar year (roughly our March/April). The passover lamb was slain in the late afternoon of the 14th of Nisan and was roasted and eaten in a family circle at sundown. Not only was unleavened bread eaten with the meal, but unleavened bread continued to be eaten for seven days thereafter, hence the name "the Feast of Unleavened Bread." Since the Jewish month begins with the new moon, the Passover is always celebrated when the moon is full.

These holy days brought many pilgrims to Jerusalem. The chief priests and teachers of the law feared that this might make it all the more difficult to get rid of Jesus. He had the support of the common people, some of whom would be coming from his native Galilee. They are very pleased when one of the Twelve, Judas Iscariot, comes forward with the offer to betray Jesus. A deal is struck; Judas is paid thirty silver coins (Matthew 26:15), and he begins watching for an opportunity to hand Jesus over to the authorities when no crowd is present.

There has been much speculation over what prompted Judas to betray Jesus. Some suggest that he was disappointed in Jesus, thinking that Jesus had come to establish an earthly kingdom. Others wonder if perhaps Judas was just after the money. Luke puts his finger on the person behind the scenes: Satan. Jesus had resisted the temptations of the devil in the wilderness (4:1-13). But now Satan saw an opportune time to try again to overcome Jesus. He makes use of Judas to further his diabolical purpose.

The Last Supper

⁷Then came the day of Unleavened Bread on which the Passover lamb had to be sacrificed. ⁸Jesus sent Peter and John, saying, "Go and make preparations for us to eat the Passover."

⁹"Where do you want us to prepare for it?" they asked.

¹⁰He replied, "As you enter the city, a man carrying a jar of water will meet you. Follow him to the house that he enters, ¹¹and say to the owner of the house, 'The Teacher asks: Where is the guest room, where I may eat the Passover with my disciples?' ¹²He will show you a large upper room, all furnished. Make preparations there."

¹³They left and found things just as Jesus had told them. So they prepared the Passover.

¹⁴When the hour came, Jesus and his apostles reclined at the table. ¹⁵And he said to them, "I have eagerly desired to eat this Passover with you before I suffer. ¹⁶For I tell you, I will not eat it again until it finds fulfillment in the kingdom of God."

¹⁷After taking the cup, he gave thanks and said, "Take this and divide it among you. ¹⁸For I tell you I will not drink again of the fruit of the vine until the kingdom of God comes."

¹⁹And he took bread, gave thanks and broke it, and gave it to them, saying, "This is my body given for you; do this in remembrance of me."

²⁰In the same way, after the supper he took the cup, saying, "This cup is the new covenant in my blood, which is poured out for you. ²¹But the hand of him who is going to betray me is with mine on the table. ²²The Son of Man will go as it has been decreed, but woe to that man who betrays him." ²³They began to question among themselves which of them it might be who would do this.

²⁴Also a dispute arose among them as to which of them was considered to be greatest. ²⁵Jesus said to them, "The kings of the Gentiles lord it over them; and those who exercise authority over them call themselves Benefactors. ²⁶But you are not to be like that. Instead, the greatest among you should be like the youngest, and the one who rules like the one who serves. ²⁷For who is greater, the one who is at the table or the one who serves? Is it not the one who is at the table? But I am among you as one who serves. ²⁸You are those who have stood by me in my trials. ²⁹And I confer on you a kingdom, just as my Father conferred one on me, ³⁰so that you may eat and drink at my table in my kingdom and sit on thrones, judging the twelve tribes of Israel.

³¹"Simon, Simon, Satan has asked to sift you as wheat. ³²But I have prayed for you, Simon, that your faith may not fail. And when you have turned back, strengthen your brothers."

³³But he replied, "Lord, I am ready to go with you to prison and to death."

³⁴Jesus answered, "I tell you, Peter, before the rooster crows today, you will deny three times that you know me."

³⁵Then Jesus asked them, "When I sent you without purse, bag or sandals, did you lack anything?"

"Nothing," they answered.

³⁶He said to them, "But now if you have a purse, take it, and also a bag; and if you don't have a sword, sell your cloak and buy one. ³⁷It is written: 'And he was numbered with the transgressors'; and I tell you that this must be fulfilled in me. Yes, what is written about me is reaching its fulfillment."

³⁸The disciples said, "See, Lord, here are two swords."

"That is enough," he replied.

When Jesus was 12 years old, he had gone with Mary and Joseph to Jerusalem to celebrate the feast of the Passover. That was a memorable occasion for him, but it hardly compares in significance to the Passover meal that he celebrates with his disciples on the night before his death on the cross. He says as much to them as they recline at the table: "I have eagerly desired to eat this Passover with you before I suffer." This farewell meal has often been called the Last Supper.

This particular Passover is even more important for Christians today because during the meal Jesus instituted the Sacrament of the Altar. Each time we celebrate Holy Communion, this meal on the night in which he was betrayed comes to mind. In this sacrament Christ continues to give his true body and blood along with the bread and wine. Here is a preview of the heavenly banquet of salvation.

The Passover celebrates God's deliverance of the children of Israel from the slavery of Egypt. The Lord told the Israelites to slaughter a lamb at twilight on the 14th day of the month and to put some of the blood on the doorframes of their houses; the lamb was to be roasted and eaten by the families that evening (Exodus 12:1-13). During the night, the angel of death went through the land killing the first-born in every house of the Egyptians but passing over the Israelite homes that were marked with blood (12:29,30).

Jesus takes the initiative in planning this Passover meal with his disciples. He sends Peter and John into the city and directs them to follow a man carrying a jar of water who will lead them to a large upper room. The sight of a man carrying a jar of water would have been unusual since this was normally something only a woman did. Peter and John make all the preparations. The lamb is killed in the temple courtyard. The unleavened bread, wine, and herbs are obtained. At the appointed hour, Jesus and the rest of the disciples come to the upper room and recline on the couches around the table. The Passover meal consisted of four parts: (1) a preliminary course that included the first cup of wine and dish of herbs; (2) the recital of the Passover story and the drinking of the second cup of wine; (3) the meal proper, beginning with the blessing of the unleavened bread, the eating of the lamb with bitter herbs, and the cup of wine after the meal; (4) the conclusion, with the singing of Psalm 114 through Psalm 118.

Luke mentions two cups of wine. The first (verse 17) is probably the one that comes after the recital of the Passover story, prior to the meal proper. The second cup (verse 20) comes after the supper. What is altogether different about this Passover meal is the significance that Jesus gives to the bread and cup of wine. In giving his disciples the unleavened bread, Jesus says, "This is my body given for you; do this in remembrance of me." With the bread the disciples receive the true body of Jesus. In giving the second cup, Jesus says, "This cup is the new covenant in my blood, which is poured out for you." The Passover meal celebrated the old covenant in which the blood of a lamb was poured out to save people from slavery. The new covenant consists of the pouring out of the blood of Jesus for the sins of the world. Is it any wonder that Jesus desired to eat this meal with his disciples on the night before his sacrifice on the cross!

The disciples are hardly prepared for the words that Jesus speaks as he gives them the bread and wine. And they are even less prepared for the revelation that one of the Twelve will betray the master. That Jesus should die on the cross is part of God's plan of salvation. But this does not excuse the evil deed of Judas.

The disclosure that one of the Twelve is a traitor provokes a discussion among the disciples. They wonder who among them would do such a thing. Such questioning leads into a heated argument over the question of which of them was the greatest. This is not the first time they have discussed this subject (9:46). Even after having received the blessed Sacrament, they show themselves to be sinners. Only one of the Twelve actually betrayed Jesus, but all show themselves in need of a Savior.

Jesus certainly does not settle the dispute among the disciples by naming the one who is the greatest. Rather, he tells them how the greatest, or most important, should conduct himself. The disciples of Jesus are not to imitate the kings of the Gentiles and their style of rule. None of the disciples is to be given the impressive-sounding title "Benefactor," as was done by the Roman caesars. Jesus demonstrated what it meant to be a servant by washing the feet of his disciples at this Passover meal (John 13:3-16). This was only a faint symbol of the ultimate service he would perform by dying on the cross.

The kind of service urged on his disciples by Jesus is not often recognized or rewarded in this world. But Jesus gives the assurance that there will be a heavenly reward for those servants of his who will stand by him and faithfully witness to the good news of God's kingdom. Jesus makes three promises to his disciples: "I confer on you a kingdom . . . so that you may eat and drink at my table . . . and sit on thrones, judging the twelve tribes of Israel." We will have to wait until we reach heaven before we fully realize the significance of these promises.

Although Jesus does not designate one of the apostles as the most important, the history of the early church as recorded in Acts shows us that Peter soon is put into a leadership role (Acts 1:15). This man who left his boat to follow Jesus (5:1-11) now hears himself addressed with his birthname, "Simon." Jesus reveals that Satan had asked permission of God to test the faith of all the apostles ("sift you as wheat"). Jesus had prayed that Peter's faith would not fail and that after his repentance Peter would strengthen his brother apostles. Peter suggests that he needs no special prayers since he is ready to go to prison and even to die with Jesus. How little Peter knows his own weakness is revealed to him by Jesus: three times he will deny his Lord before a new day dawns. Only the prayers of Jesus saved his faith from failing totally.

The farewell speech of Jesus at the Last Supper is drawing to a close—but not without one more look at what the future holds in store for the apostles. When they were still in Galilee, Jesus had sent them out without provisions (9:3). They were taken care of along the way. But in the mission that will follow Pentecost, the going will not be so easy. The crowds will not be so supportive. They will need purse (money) and bag and swords. In fulfillment of Isaiah 53:12, Jesus will be numbered with outlaws. The apostles must be prepared to face the same kind of treatment.

The disciples at once pick up on the word "sword" that Jesus had used. They inform the Lord Jesus that they have two swords. This statement provokes a reply from Jesus that has been interpreted various ways. It almost sounds as if Jesus is saying that two swords are enough for the task at hand. But since Jesus prohibited the use of the sword at his arrest (Matthew 26:52), this can hardly be his meaning. His mention of the sword is meant simply to warn the disciples that hard and dangerous times lie ahead. His words "That is enough" must be understood as him saying to his disciples, "That is enough of talk like that." And with that concluding remark, Jesus and his band of followers leave the upper room and make their way to the Mount of Olives.

Jesus prays on the Mount of Olives

³⁹Jesus went out as usual to the Mount of Olives, and his disciples followed him. ⁴⁰On reaching the place, he said to them, "Pray that you will not fall into temptation." ⁴¹He withdrew about a stone's throw beyond them, knelt down and prayed, ⁴²"Father, if you are willing, take this cup from me; yet not my will, but yours be done." ⁴³An angel from heaven appeared to him and strengthened him. ⁴⁴And being in anguish, he prayed more earnestly, and his sweat was like drops of blood falling to the ground.

⁴⁵When he rose from prayer and went back to the disciples, he found them asleep, exhausted from sorrow. ⁴⁶"Why are you sleeping?" he asked them. "Get up and pray so that you will not fall into temptation."

The upper room in which Jesus ate the Passover with his disciples is traditionally located in the southwest section of Jerusalem. The walk from there took Jesus down through the Kidron Valley just east of the city and up the Mount of Olives. This was not the first time Jesus had gone here to pray. Luke has already told the reader that during the time Jesus was in Jerusalem, "each night he went out to spend the night on the hill called the Mount of Olives" (21:37). Now Jesus does nothing to throw Judas off his trail but rather goes as usual to his place of prayer.

When Jesus taught his disciples the Lord's Prayer, he included the petition "lead us not into temptation" (11:4). The disciples are now facing the most severe ordeal. The devil will tempt them to give up their faith in Jesus as God's promised Messiah. Satan has permission to sift them as wheat (22:31). Both before and after his own anguished emploring prayer to his heavenly Father, Jesus urges his disciples to pray so that they do not succumb to the evil power of Satan and fall into his trap. But, overwhelmed with sorrow, they seek escape from the impending crisis through sleep. They are not strengthened for the encounter that lies ahead.

The prayer of Jesus makes an appeal to his Father: "If you are willing, take this cup from me." This is the cup of God's wrath (Isaiah 51:17), the punishment for the sins of the world. Yet what ultimately matters to Jesus is not his own will but the will of his Father. The Father's answer to his Son is to send an angel to strengthen him. Still his anguish (the Greek here is similar to our word *agony*) continues, and sweat pours from his body to the ground like drops of blood gushing from a gaping wound. Here, as much as anywhere in the gospel record, the true human nature of Jesus is revealed. There is nothing fake about his sufferings. No human being can fully understand what agony he experienced. "He was crushed for our iniquities" (Isaiah 53:5).

Jesus arrested

⁴⁷While he was still speaking a crowd came up, and the man who was called Judas, one of the Twelve, was leading them. He approached Jesus to kiss him, ⁴⁸but Jesus asked him, "Judas, are you betraying the Son of Man with a kiss?"

⁴⁹When Jesus' followers saw what was going to happen, they said, "Lord, should we strike with our swords?" ⁵⁰And one of them struck the servant of the high priest, cutting off his right ear.

⁵¹But Jesus answered, "No more of this!" And he touched the man's ear and healed him.

⁵²Then Jesus said to the chief priests, the officers of the temple guard, and the elders, who had come for him, "Am I leading a rebellion, that you have come with swords and clubs? ⁵³Every day I was with you in the temple courts, and you did not lay a hand on me. But this is your hour—when darkness reigns."

Judas had left the Passover meal after receiving from Jesus a piece of bread dipped in the dish; the evangelist John notes: "And it was night" (John 13:26-30). The darkness is broken only by the shining of the Passover moon as Judas leads a crowd of priests, temple officers, and elders along the road to the place where Jesus is praying. Judas had given a sign by which Jesus could be recognized: he would greet Jesus with a kiss. Jesus' question to Judas calls attention to the hypocrisy of his act.

Seeing the band of armed men, the disciples are ready to put up a fight. They must have recalled the words of Jesus spoken in the upper room about providing themselves with swords (22:36). One of them (in John 18:10 he is identified as Peter) does not wait for a word from Jesus but strikes at once. The right ear of the high priest's servant Malchus falls to the ground. What Peter has done is a work of darkness. In compassion, Jesus reverses the evil and heals the ear with a touch. Jesus orders the violence to stop at once.

The nighttime mission of these religious authorities is to arrest someone who had been teaching daily in the temple courts. Jesus questions their need for swords and clubs as if they are dealing with the leader of an armed rebellion. He has an explanation for the entire course of events: "This is your hour—when darkness reigns." The prince of darkness is having his way for the moment.

Peter disowns Jesus

⁵⁴**Then seizing him, they led him away and took him into the house of the high priest. Peter followed at a distance.** ⁵⁵**But when they had kindled a fire in the middle of the courtyard and had sat down together, Peter sat down with them.** ⁵⁶**A servant girl saw him seated there in the firelight. She looked closely at him and said, "This man was with him."**

⁵⁷**But he denied it. "Woman, I don't know him," he said.**

⁵⁸**A little later someone else saw him and said, "You also are one of them."**

"Man, I am not!" Peter replied.

⁵⁹**About an hour later another asserted, "Certainly this fellow was with him, for he is a Galilean."**

⁶⁰**Peter replied, "Man, I don't know what you're talking about!" Just as he was speaking, the rooster crowed.** ⁶¹**The Lord turned and looked straight at Peter. Then Peter remembered the word the Lord had spoken to him: "Before the rooster crows today, you will disown me three times."** ⁶²**And he went outside and wept bitterly.**

After arresting Jesus on the Mount of Olives, the temple authorities take him to the house of the high priest. The traditional location for this house is in the southwest section of Jerusalem not far from the upper room where Jesus had eaten the Passover. Caiaphas was high priest in the years A.D. 18–36, but his father-in-law, Annas, who formerly had been high priest, continued to exert strong influence and took a hand in the interrogation of Jesus (John 18:12,13). Luke does not give the details of this nighttime questioning, which are found in Matthew 26:59-66 and Mark 14:55-64.

Peter had declared that he was ready to go to prison and even to die with Jesus (22:33). He had shown his willingness to defend Jesus with a sword. But he did not reckon with the power of the devil, which would cause him to fall into the trap of denying his Lord three times.

As Peter sits by the fire in the courtyard of the high priest's house, he is recognized by a servant girl. Peter denies that he knows Jesus at all. A second person links Peter with the band of disciples who follow Jesus. His assertion elicits an outright denial from Peter. About an hour later someone remarks that Peter's accent is that of a Galilean, the province from which Jesus originated. Peter's third denial is greeted with the shrill crowing of the rooster. A new day has dawned and the prophecy of Jesus has been fulfilled.

At that moment the Lord has the opportunity to look straight into the eyes of Peter. Peter remembers and goes outside and weeps bitterly. These tears of repentance are what Jesus meant by Peter's turning back (22:32). This entire incident made Peter a better man, one able to strengthen his brothers.

The soldiers mock Jesus

⁶³The men who were guarding Jesus began mocking and beating him. ⁶⁴They blindfolded him and demanded, "Prophesy! Who hit you?" ⁶⁵And they said many other insulting things to him.

The reign of darkness is clearly shown by the treatment accorded Jesus by those guarding him. They play a game of blindman's bluff to ridicule his claim of being a prophet (13:33). What Jesus suffers does fulfill his own prophecy: "They will mock him, insult him, spit on him, flog him and kill him" (18:32). Peter sought to avoid suffering by denying his Lord. Jesus accepts it with no word of complaint. "When they hurled their insults at him, he did not retaliate; when he suffered, he made no threats" (1 Peter 2:23).

Jesus before the Jewish council

⁶⁶At daybreak the council of the elders of the people, both the chief priests and teachers of the law, met together, and Jesus was

led before them. ⁶⁷**"If you are the Christ,"** they said, **"tell us."**

Jesus answered, "If I tell you, you will not believe me, ⁶⁸**and if I asked you, you would not answer.** ⁶⁹**But from now on, the Son of Man will be seated at the right hand of the mighty God."**

⁷⁰**They all asked, "Are you then the Son of God?"**

He replied, "You are right in saying I am."

⁷¹**Then they said, "Why do we need any more testimony? We have heard it from his own lips."**

Early Friday morning Jesus is taken from the house of the high priest where he had been interrogated to appear before the Jewish high council, called the Sanhedrin. This body consisted of 71 members including the high priest, who served as president. Its membership was divided between the elders, priests, and teachers of the law (mostly Pharisees). Its meeting hall was either in the southwest area of the inner court of the temple or in a place just west of the temple. The Sanhedrin possessed absolute power in religious matters but could not decree the sentence of death.

The council first questions Jesus as to whether or not he is the Christ. The Jews were looking for the promised Messiah and expected him to give them political freedom. Jesus is the Christ as Peter had confessed (9:20). But Jesus had forbidden the disciples to make this known since such a claim would be misunderstood. So also here at this trial, Jesus refuses to answer this question. Rather he says that "the Son of Man will be seated at the right hand of the mighty God." Jesus often used the title "Son of Man" to describe himself. He directs attention away from the false hope of an earthly Messiah to his heavenly rule as Son of Man at the right hand of God.

The suggestion that Jesus will be seated at the right hand of God provokes the entire council to ask, "Are you then the Son of God?" Jesus does not refuse to answer this question but replies, "You are right in saying I am." His affirmative answer takes us back to the very beginning of Luke's gospel when the angel Gabriel said to Mary, "So the holy one to be born will be called the Son of God" (1:35). For the Jewish council, this claim of Jesus constitutes the grossest form of blasphemy. They are not willing to consider the evidence that supports his assertion. They are intent only on bringing about his death.

Jesus before Pilate and Herod

23 Then the whole assembly rose and led him off to Pilate. ²And they began to accuse him, saying, "We have found this man subverting our nation. He opposes payment of taxes to Caesar and claims to be Christ, a king."

³So Pilate asked Jesus, "Are you the king of the Jews?"

"Yes, it is as you say," Jesus replied.

⁴Then Pilate announced to the chief priests and the crowd, "I find no basis for a charge against this man."

⁵But they insisted, "He stirs up the people all over Judea by his teaching. He started in Galilee and has come all the way here."

⁶On hearing this, Pilate asked if the man was a Galilean. ⁷When he learned that Jesus was under Herod's jurisdiction, he sent him to Herod, who was also in Jerusalem at that time.

⁸When Herod saw Jesus, he was greatly pleased, because for a long time he had been wanting to see him. From what he had heard about him, he hoped to see him perform some miracle. ⁹He plied him with many questions, but Jesus gave him no answer. ¹⁰The chief priests and the teachers of the law were standing there, vehemently accusing him. ¹¹Then Herod and his soldiers ridiculed and mocked him. Dressing him in an elegant robe, they sent him back to Pilate. ¹²That day Herod and Pilate became friends—before this they had been enemies.

¹³Pilate called together the chief priests, the rulers and the people, ¹⁴and said to them, "You brought me this man as one who was inciting the people to rebellion. I have examined him in your presence and have found no basis for your charges against him.

¹⁵Neither has Herod, for he sent him back to us; as you can see, he has done nothing to deserve death. ¹⁶Therefore, I will punish him and then release him."

¹⁸With one voice they cried out, "Away with this man! Release Barabbas to us!" ¹⁹(Barabbas had been thrown into prison for an insurrection in the city, and for murder.)

²⁰Wanting to release Jesus, Pilate appealed to them again. ²¹But they kept shouting, "Crucify him! Crucify him!"

²²For the third time he spoke to them: "Why? What crime has this man committed? I have found in him no grounds for the death penalty. Therefore I will have him punished and then release him."

²³But with loud shouts they insistently demanded that he be crucified, and their shouts prevailed. ²⁴So Pilate decided to grant their demand. ²⁵He released the man who had been thrown into prison for insurrection and murder, the one they asked for, and surrendered Jesus to their will.

The phrase "suffered under Pontius Pilate" has been spoken by confessing Christians for centuries. That the name of this man should have been included in both the Apostles' Creed and the Nicene Creed results from his governorship of the provinces of Judea and Samaria in the years A.D. 26–36. Little is known about Pilate except what is told in the gospels and in a few references by Josephus. However, because he is the judge who condemned Jesus to die, many writings developed claiming to chronicle his life before, during, and after the events recorded in the gospels.

Pilate was appointed by the Roman government as its representative, and he acted as the supreme judge in criminal cases. Usually the Roman governor resided in the seacoast city of Caesarea, but at certain critical times he came up to Jerusalem. The Passover festival was such a time when nationalistic feelings were high among the Jews, the city was crowded with pilgrims, and trouble was likely to break out. At least on this visit to the city, Pilate probably stayed in the fortress of Antonia, just north of the temple.

After Jesus had testified before the Jewish council early Friday morning, he is led off to Pilate. Three charges are leveled against him: (1) subverting (undermining) the nation; (2) forbidding the payment of taxes to Caesar; (3) claiming to be a king. Of these charges, Pilate seems unconcerned about the first two. He may have been aware that the second was a lie (20:20-25). Pilate perhaps knew that Jesus had ridden into Jerusalem on the previous Sunday and was hailed as a king by the crowds. So he asks Jesus directly, "Are you the king of the Jews?" Jesus' answer is not so positive as the translation of the NIV suggests. The Greek literally says "You say," with the *you* emphasized. Jesus must have answered with such a tone of voice that Pilate was convinced that the third charge was also false. He announces to the chief priests and people present that they have no case against Jesus. The trial should have ended at this point.

But the cry goes up that the teaching of Jesus is stirring up people throughout the land, starting in Galilee. With the mention of Galilee, Pilate cocks his ear. Galilee was a hotbed of revolutionaries. Perhaps the activities of Jesus need to be further investigated. Who better to do this than Herod, ruler of Galilee and presently in Jerusalem for the Passover festival. Pilate decides to send Jesus off to him. Herod was probably staying at the Palace of Herod built into Jerusalem's western wall.

This man is the son of Herod the Great, who had been king at the time of Jesus' birth. Herod had expressed an interest in seeing Jesus (9:9). He seems not to care about Jesus the teacher but rather Jesus the worker of miracles. Herod is totally disappointed in the performance he witnesses. Jesus answers none of the questions or any of the accusations. Herod and his soldiers end up playing games with Jesus before sending him back to Pilate dressed in an "elegant robe." It's not easy to say just what the robe symbolized. Some suggest that Herod may have dressed up Jesus to look like a clown. Others take the robe to either connote Jesus' innocence or perhaps to mock it. In any case, this little episode served to reconcile Pilate and Herod, who previously had been enemies. They are united in condemning to death a man in whom they find no fault.

Now the ball is back in Pilate's court. He calls together the chief priests and other leaders as well as the common people and for a second time declares Jesus innocent. He reports that Herod had made the same determination. Pilate proposes to punish Jesus and then release him. The punishment he has in mind is scourging with a whip containing pieces of metal. Such punishment is clearly unjust in the case of an innocent man, but Pilate hopes to appease the people.

After verse 16 some copies of the Greek text of Luke include the sentence: "Now he was obliged to release one man to them at the Feast." Very similar words are found in Matthew 27:15 and Mark 15:6. Some copyist probably included them in the text of Luke's gospel in order to introduce the request which is now made of Pilate that he release a man named Barabbas, who was in prison for some very serious crimes. It was a custom of Roman rule to grant pardon on some special occasions to a prisoner who was in custody. Pilate hopes to release Jesus, but the people demand the release of the dangerous Barabbas.

Now for the first time the word "crucify" is introduced into the proceedings. It comes not from the lips of Pilate but is shouted by the crowd that demands death for Jesus. For the third time Pilate declares Jesus innocent, but to no avail. He gives in to the Jewish leadership and surrenders Jesus to their will. He decides to keep peace in Jerusalem by sacrificing the life of one innocent person.

The crucifixion

²⁶As they led him away, they seized Simon from Cyrene, who was on his way in from the country, and put the cross on him and made him carry it behind Jesus. ²⁷A large number of people followed him, including women who mourned and wailed for him. ²⁸Jesus turned and said to them, "Daughters of Jerusalem, do not weep for me; weep for yourselves and for your children. ²⁹For the time will come when you will say, 'Blessed are the barren women, the wombs that never bore and the breasts that never nursed!' ³⁰Then

> 'they will say to the mountains, "Fall on us!"
> and to the hills, "Cover us!"'

³¹For if men do these things when the tree is green, what will happen when it is dry?"

³²Two other men, both criminals, were also led out with him to be executed. ³³When they came to the place called the Skull, there they crucified him, along with the criminals—one on his right, the other on his left. ³⁴Jesus said, "Father, forgive them, for they do not know what they are doing." And they divided up his clothes by casting lots.

³⁵The people stood watching, and the rulers even sneered at him. They said, "He saved others; let him save himself if he is the Christ of God, the Chosen One."

³⁶The soldiers also came up and mocked him. They offered him wine vinegar ³⁷and said, "If you are the king of the Jews, save yourself."

³⁸There was a written notice above him, which read: THIS IS THE KING OF THE JEWS.

³⁹One of the criminals who hung there hurled insults at him: "Aren't you the Christ? Save yourself and us!"

⁴⁰But the other criminal rebuked him. "Don't you fear God," he said, "since you are under the same sentence? ⁴¹We are punished justly, for we are getting what our deeds deserve. But this man has done nothing wrong."

⁴²Then he said, "Jesus, remember me when you come into your kingdom."
⁴³Jesus answered him, "I tell you the truth, today you will be with me in paradise."

The road to the cross has been christened by Christian tradition as the Via Dolorosa (way of pain/grief). The road begins at the fortress of Antonia and ends at the Church of the Holy Sepulchre, a distance of about one-half mile. Inside the church are the assumed sites of the crucifixion and burial of Jesus. In New Testament times this location was just outside the northwest wall of the city.

According to the Roman historian Plutarch, "each of the criminals carries forth his own cross" to the place of execution. Simon, a man from the North African city of Cyrene, is compelled by the soldiers to carry the cross behind Jesus. He literally follows in the footsteps of the Savior and is not so much the helper as the one helped. He is identified in Mark 15:21 as the father of Alexander and Rufus. It is likely that all three were early members of the church (a man named Rufus is also mentioned by Paul in Romans 16:13).

The procession of cross-bearers draws a crowd. Among these are women who weep for Jesus. On Palm Sunday the crowds had welcomed him into the city with shouts of acclamation; now there are tears as he is led out of the city. Jesus tells these daughters of Jerusalem that their tears would be better shed for themselves than for him. We are reminded that Jesus had himself wept over the city of Jerusalem (19:41).

The reason for the tears is the impending destruction of Jerusalem (21:20-24). That will be a time when children are no blessing from the Lord; rather, the barren woman will be regarded as blessed. That will be a time when people again cry out to the mountains and hills for protection from violent destruction as they did in the days of Hosea the prophet (Hosea 10:8). Jesus' concluding question is based on a bit of proverbial wisdom: if green wood burns, just think what a blaze will result from setting fire to dry wood. Jesus contrasts his own innocent suffering with the deserved suffering to befall the city of Jerusalem.

Jesus is crucified at the place called "the Skull." The Aramaic word for skull is *gulgulta* (Golgotha); the Greek is our word *cranium,* which was translated into Latin as *calvaria* (Calvary). This spot was given this name, no doubt, because of its particular shape.

Two criminals are crucified on either side of Jesus. The Jewish historian Josephus spoke of crucifixion as "the most pitiable of deaths." The Roman politician and author Cicero described it as "the worst extreme of torture inflicted on slaves." Jesus endured the pain of having nails driven through his hands and feet and then being hoisted into the air to die.

It is customary to say that Jesus spoke seven "words" from the cross. This is based on compiling his statements from the four gospels. No gospel contains all seven of these words. In Luke we find the first, second, and seventh. The first is Jesus' prayer asking forgiveness for those who are inflicting death upon him. They truly do not know what they are doing: killing the Son of God, by whose death the world is ransomed from sin.

Jesus is first crucified at 9 A.M. and dies six hours later. Not all the details of what happened during the time he hung on the cross are reported in every gospel. The division of Jesus' clothing among the soldiers is a fulfillment of Psalm 22:18. The crowd that had gathered along with the Jewish leaders and the soldiers made fun of Jesus. They mocked his ability to save others when he could not even save himself. Three titles are used with derision: Christ of

God, the Chosen One (see 9:35), and king of the Jews. Even the title on the cross written by Pilate is meant to poke fun: "THIS IS THE KING OF THE JEWS." The information included in the KJV that the title was written in Greek, Latin, and Aramaic was copied from John 19:20 and doesn't seem to be part of Luke's original text.

One of the criminals joined the onlookers in ridiculing Jesus. He mockingly asks to be saved but cares nothing for the salvation that Jesus gives. The other criminal experiences that salvation. He confesses his guilt and declares Jesus innocent. He pleads to be remembered when Jesus comes into his kingdom. The second word from the cross is the personal assurance Jesus gives to this repentant sinner: "Today you will be with me in paradise." The criminal's salvation is much nearer than he realized.

Jesus' death

[44]It was now about the sixth hour, and darkness came over the whole land until the ninth hour, [45]for the sun stopped shining. And the curtain of the temple was torn in two. [46]Jesus called out with a loud voice, "Father, into your hands I commit my spirit." When he had said this, he breathed his last.

[47]The centurion, seeing what had happened, praised God and said, "Surely this was a righteous man." [48]When all the people who had gathered to witness this sight saw what took place, they beat their breasts and went away. [49]But all those who knew him, including the women who had followed him from Galilee, stood at a distance, watching these things.

The death of Jesus Christ, Servant of God, is marked by three noteworthy occurrences and three responses from those looking on. First, there is the unusual darkness that hangs over the entire land from high noon till three o'clock. This darkness cannot be explained by an eclipse of the sun since such a thing is not possible when the moon is full, as is the case at the time of the Passover. Luke simply says that

The people beat their breasts

"the sun stopped shining" and leaves the matter there. All creation groans in darkness when the Light of the world is extinguished.

Next is the startling tearing of the temple curtain. There were large curtains in front of the Holy Place and the Holy of Holies. Once a year on the Day of Atonement, the high priest stepped through the curtain from the Holy Place into the Holy of Holies with the blood of a bull to sprinkle the mercy seat. No doubt this is the curtain torn in two by the death of the supreme High Priest whose blood cleanses all from sin (Hebrews 9:12). The tearing of the curtain opens the way into the heavenly sanctuary and marks the end of the old covenant.

Finally, through the darkness the voice of Jesus sounds from the cross, praying as he breathes his last: "Father, into your hands I commit my spirit." The words are from Psalm 31:5, used by Jewish people as a bedtime prayer. The Son entrusts himself into the hands of his Father, whose will he has done.

It is the Roman centurion, a Gentile, whose response to the death of Jesus is recorded first. He is moved to praise God and pronounce his own verdict on all that has taken place before his eyes: "Surely this was a righteous man." As people from Jerusalem turn away from this scene of death, they beat their breasts, as did the tax collector in the temple when he pleaded for God's mercy (18:13).

The third reaction is a silent one: the acquaintances of Jesus, both men and women, stand at a distance as they watch. They are not sure what the future holds for them. The women who had followed Jesus all the way from Galilee (8:1-3) will be first at his grave on the third day.

Jesus' burial

⁵⁰Now there was a man named Joseph, a member of the Council, a good and upright man, ⁵¹who had not consented to their

decision and action. He came from the Judean town of Arimathea and he was waiting for the kingdom of God. ⁵²Going to Pilate, he asked for Jesus' body. ⁵³Then he took it down, wrapped it in linen cloth and placed it in a tomb cut in the rock, one in which no one had yet been laid. ⁵⁴It was Preparation Day, and the Sabbath was about to begin.

⁵⁵The women who had come with Jesus from Galilee followed Joseph and saw the tomb and how his body was laid in it. ⁵⁶Then they went home and prepared spices and perfumes. But they rested on the Sabbath in obedience to the commandment.

The proper burial of the dead was a matter of great importance to people in Bible times. In the Law of Moses it is stated that the body of a person hung on a tree is not to be left overnight but should be buried the same day (Deuteronomy 21:22,23). There are many references to burials in the Bible, and thousands of tombs have been found and excavated by archaeologists. To provide burial for another person was considered a virtuous act; its lack, a great tragedy.

A man of prominence comes forward to ask Pilate for the body of Jesus. This is the first mention in the gospels of Joseph of Arimathea. Like Simeon and Anna, he was waiting for the kingdom of God. It is thought that the small village from which he came may be the same as Ramathaim, where Samuel was born (1 Samuel 1:1). As a member of the supreme council of the Jews, he was present for the trial of Jesus but did not agree with the verdict. The fact that he owned a tomb cut out of rock suggests that he was not a poor man.

The location of Jesus' tomb cannot be fixed with certainty. Since the fourth century, the traditional site is the place where the church of the Holy Sepulchre now stands. There are some factors which weigh against this location; the main question is whether it did indeed lie outside the walls of the city at the time of Jesus' death.

The burial had to be hurried along because at sundown the Sabbath Day began. Like the donkey on which Jesus rode into Jerusalem, the rock tomb into which his body is placed had not been previously used. Joseph wrapped the body in a linen cloth. (The claim that the so-called Shroud of Turin is this very cloth is questionable.) The burial of Jesus is evidence that he truly died.

Joseph did for Jesus what none of those who followed him from Galilee could have done so readily: he gave Jesus an honorable burial near the site of the crucifixion. For him to step forward and claim the body of Jesus from the cross must have blackened his reputation with the Jewish leaders. It was his way of taking up the cross and following.

The Galilean women who had watched Jesus' death follow Joseph and take note of the tomb in which the body is laid. Then they hurry off to prepare spices and perfumes intending to show their beloved master a last act of love after the Sabbath has passed. For Jesus, this Sabbath is a day of rest in the tomb. He waits for his day of triumph.

Jesus rises and ascends into heaven

The resurrection

24 On the first day of the week, very early in the morning, the women took the spices they had prepared and went to the tomb. ²They found the stone rolled away from the tomb, ³but when they entered, they did not find the body of the Lord Jesus. ⁴While they were wondering about this, suddenly two men in clothes that gleamed like lightning stood beside them. ⁵In their fright the women bowed down with their faces to the ground, but the men said to them, "Why do you look for the living among the dead? ⁶He is not here; he has risen! Remember how he told you, while he was still with you in Galilee: ⁷'The Son of Man must be delivered into the hands of sinful men, be crucified and on the third day be raised again.'" ⁸Then they remembered his words.

⁹**When they came back from the tomb, they told all these things to the Eleven and to all the others. ¹⁰It was Mary Magdalene, Joanna, Mary the mother of James, and the others with them who told this to the apostles. ¹¹But they did not believe the women, because their words seemed to them like nonsense. ¹²Peter, however, got up and ran to the tomb. Bending over, he saw the strips of linen lying by themselves, and he went away, wondering to himself what had happened.**

An aura of wonder hangs over this episode. The women come to the tomb of Jesus expecting to find his dead body. When they find the stone rolled away and the grave empty, we are told that "they were wondering about this." The KJV translates this as "perplexed." A feeling of puzzlement, almost doubt, comes over them. They don't know what to make of what they have seen. They need some interpretation.

Luke tells us that after Peter came to the tomb and saw the strips of linen lying by themselves, "he went away, wondering to himself what had happened." The Greek word here translated as "wondering" indicates that Peter is filled with awe, astonishment, and surprise. He senses that a miracle has taken place.

The empty grave does not prove the resurrection; there are other possible explanations why the body of Jesus was not found in the grave. Enemies of the Christian faith have long used these other explanations in an effort to discount the truth of the resurrection. If the women who came to the tomb, on the other hand, had found the dead body of Jesus, this would be certain proof that he is not alive. Both they and Peter found the grave empty and wondered. They needed an explanation.

The two men "in clothes that gleamed like lightning" provide the explanation: "He has risen!" The women are gently reminded that Jesus himself had prophesied both his crucifixion and resurrection (9:22). It took the words of these heavenly messengers to cause the women to remember. How difficult it is even for these close followers of Jesus to remember!

Luke waits to identify the women until after their visit to the tomb. Heading the list is the name of Mary Magdalene, from whom Jesus had cast out seven demons (8:2). She is prominent in John's account of the resurrection (John 20:10-18). Joanna the wife of Cuza, the manager of Herod's household (8:3), and Mary the mother of James are also named. Mark adds the name of Salome (Mark 16:1) whereas Luke simply speaks of others. These women had come from Galilee and had made it their special responsibility to minister to the needs of Jesus. Now they serve as the first human witnesses to the resurrection by telling the eleven apostles what they had experienced.

Their testimony is met with unbelief. The words of these women seem to the apostles to be pure nonsense. That God should choose women, whose testimony was generally regarded as unreliable in those days, to be the initial witnesses to the resurrection is another example of how he works in ways contrary to human thinking. Only Peter and an unidentified disciple (John 20:3-9) go to investigate the women's report. They find the grave empty. But they are not yet privileged to behold the risen Lord.

The women had come to the tomb "on the first day of the week." The resurrection of Jesus marks a new beginning in the history of the world. Just as the original act of creation began the first day of the week, so on Easter there is the dawn of a new day. Sin, Satan, death, and hell are vanquished! The body of believers continue to celebrate this decisive event each first day of the week. Sunday after Sunday, the words of Jesus are remembered; his body and blood is shared; his praises are sung. An early Latin hymn says it well:

257

"Welcome, happy morning!" Age to age shall say;
"Hell today is vanquished; Heav'n is won today!"
Lo, the Dead is living, God forevermore!
Him, their true Creator, All his works adore.
"Welcome, happy morning!" Age to age shall say;
"Hell today is vanquished; Heav'n is won today!"
(*Christian Worship* 163:1)

On the road to Emmaus

¹³Now that same day two of them were going to a village called Emmaus, about seven miles from Jerusalem. ¹⁴They were talking with each other about everything that had happened. ¹⁵As they talked and discussed these things with each other, Jesus himself came up and walked along with them; ¹⁶but they were kept from recognizing him.

¹⁷He asked them, "What are you discussing together as you walk along?"

They stood still, their faces downcast. ¹⁸One of them, named Cleopas, asked him, "Are you only a visitor to Jerusalem and do not know the things that have happened there in these days?"

¹⁹"What things?" he asked.

"About Jesus of Nazareth," they replied. "He was a prophet, powerful in word and deed before God and all the people. ²⁰The chief priests and our rulers handed him over to be sentenced to death, and they crucified him; ²¹but we had hoped that he was the one who was going to redeem Israel. And what is more, it is the third day since all this took place. ²²In addition, some of our women amazed us. They went to the tomb early this morning ²³but didn't find his body. They came and told us that they had seen a vision of angels, who said he was alive. ²⁴Then some of our companions went to the tomb and found it just as the women had said, but him they did not see."

²⁵He said to them, "How foolish you are, and how slow of heart to believe all that the prophets have spoken! ²⁶Did not the Christ have to suffer these things and then enter his glory?" ²⁷And beginning with Moses and all the Prophets, he explained to them what was said in all the Scriptures concerning himself.

The disciples on the road to Emmaus

²⁸**As they approached the village to which they were going, Jesus acted as if he were going farther. ²⁹But they urged him strongly, "Stay with us, for it is nearly evening; the day is almost over." So he went in to stay with them.**

³⁰**When he was at the table with them, he took bread, gave thanks, broke it and began to give it to them. ³¹Then their eyes were opened and they recognized him, and he disappeared from their sight. ³²They asked each other, "Were not our hearts burning within us while he talked with us on the road and opened the Scriptures to us?"**

³³**They got up and returned at once to Jerusalem. There they found the Eleven and those with them, assembled together ³⁴and saying, "It is true! The Lord has risen and has appeared to Simon." ³⁵Then the two told what had happened on the way, and how Jesus was recognized by them when he broke the bread.**

This story of the appearance of Jesus to the two disciples on the road to Emmaus is recorded only by Luke. The location of the village of Emmaus is disputed. The best known place by that name is located about 20 miles northwest of Jerusalem. But Luke says that Emmaus was about seven miles away (Greek measurement: 60 stadia). Josephus speaks of a village by that name lying roughly three and a half miles northwest of Jerusalem. Luke's mileage figure would then constitute a round-trip. Another site that is seven miles from Jerusalem was identified in later times as Emmaus, but there is no first century mention of this town. It seems likely that Luke is using the round-trip figure. So the two disciples had only a relatively short trip back to Jerusalem to tell their story to the assembled disciples.

One might aptly term this a "recognition story." Though the two disciples saw the risen Jesus, they were kept from recognizing him at first. Only after Jesus had served as host at their meal together were their eyes opened "and they recognized him." They later reported to the group that "Jesus was recognized by them when he broke the bread."

Some have wanted to interpret this meal as a celebration of the Sacrament of the Altar. It is argued that the term "the breaking of bread" in Acts 2:42 and elsewhere refers to Holy Communion. Though that is possible, the phrase "to break bread" with someone usually means to simply eat a meal together (see Acts 27:35, where there is obviously no celebration of the Sacrament). Since we are not told that Jesus shared the cup with the two Emmaus disciples, we cannot understand this meal as a celebration of the Sacrament.

There is something significant in the fact that these disciples did recognize Jesus in the breaking of bread. How many times had not the followers of Jesus experienced his presence in that very way: the feeding of the five thousand (9:16), the times he ate even with tax collectors and sinners (15:2), and also the Last Supper (22:19). Each time we Christians today celebrate the Lord's Supper, our faith recognizes him as the living Lord who is with us on our way.

One of the two disciples is named Cleopas. Luke possibly records the name because of his later activities within the early church. Who was the other person? A number of guesses have been made over the years, including the suggestion that the traveling companion of Cleopas was his wife (perhaps the name Cleopas is equivalent to Clopas, whose wife, Mary, was at the foot of the cross; John 19:25). They are privileged to become eyewitnesses of the risen Lord.

As the two walk along the road talking about the recent events in Jerusalem, they are joined by a third person. The reader of Luke's gospel is in on the secret as to the identity of this person, but the two disciples remain in the dark. They think it strange that anyone visiting in Jerusalem (or living in Jerusalem, as some translate) could be unaware of the happenings of the last few days.

Responding to Jesus' question, they relate to him their bitter disappointment over dashed hopes. It had seemed as if the mighty prophet from Nazareth would bring redemption to Israel, but his death by crucifixion plunged his followers into deep despair. Even the report of the women about the empty tomb and the angels' message failed to lift their spirits. One thing was missing: the risen Jesus had not been seen.

The women at the tomb had failed to remember the prophetic words of Jesus about his death and resurrection. These Emmaus disciples had failed to believe the prophetic Scriptures. Jesus admonishes the two for their foolishness in not believing what, for example, was written in Isaiah chapter 53. He asks the rhetorical question, "Did not the Christ have to suffer these things and then enter his glory?" The remainder of the journey to Emmaus turns into a Bible class with Jesus as both teacher and subject matter. Later Jesus' two students will inquire of one another about the marvelous burning they felt "while he talked with us on the road and opened the Scriptures to us." Searching the Scriptures is preparation for recognizing the living Jesus.

The two disciples are not about to let this dynamic stranger get away. With evening coming on, they urge him to stay with them. As they sit at the table, the guest becomes the host: he takes the bread, gives thanks, breaks it, and gives it to them. At the moment of recognition, the stranger disappears. The two hurry back to Jerusalem to report their encounter with the glorified Lord. They are met with the exciting news that Jesus had appeared to Simon. The mystery of the empty tomb is rapidly being solved. And with this comes a revival of hope.

Jesus appears to the disciples

³⁶While they were still talking about this, Jesus himself stood among them and said to them, "Peace be with you."

³⁷They were startled and frightened, thinking they saw a ghost. ³⁸He said to them, "Why are you troubled, and why do doubts rise in your minds? ³⁹Look at my hands and my feet. It is I myself! Touch me and see; a ghost does not have flesh and bones, as you see I have."

⁴⁰When he had said this, he showed them his hands and feet. ⁴¹And while they still did not believe it because of joy and amazement, he asked them, "Do you have anything here to eat?" ⁴²They gave him a piece of broiled fish, ⁴³and he took it and ate it in their presence.

⁴⁴He said to them, "This is what I told you while I was still with you: Everything must be fulfilled that is written about me in the Law of Moses, the Prophets and the Psalms."

⁴⁵Then he opened their minds so they could understand the Scriptures. ⁴⁶He told them, "This is what is written: The Christ will suffer and rise from the dead on the third day, ⁴⁷and repentance and forgiveness of sins will be preached in his name to all nations, beginning at Jerusalem. ⁴⁸You are witnesses of these things. ⁴⁹I am going to send you what my Father has promised; but stay in the city until you have been clothed with power from on high."

As evening came that first Easter Sunday, the eleven apostles and the other followers of Jesus, men and women, were more and more convinced that the grave was empty because Jesus had risen. But they had little understanding as to just what that meant. People in those days generally believed that the souls of the dead were able to roam the earth. There was a great fear of ghosts. However, it was unthinkable that a dead person could make bodily appearances.

Yet that is exactly what Jesus did: with his glorified body he appears to Mary Magdalene, to Peter, to the Emmaus disciples, and to the group that has assembled here. His greeting is the familiar "Peace be with you." It is a word they all need to hear, for they are understandably filled with fear.

Jesus first wants to convince his disciples that they are not seeing a ghost but rather a real, live person. He shows them his hands and feet still marked with the wounds he suffered. He invites them to touch him to demonstrate that he has flesh and blood and is no ghost. Finally, he eats a piece of broiled fish before their doubting eyes. There is a great struggle going on in their hearts between the joy of believing and the dread of being deceived. So faith wrestles with doubt in the Christian's heart.

Not only is this the same person who ate and drank with his disciples during his earthly ministry; his message is the same. Jesus reminds them of how his entire ministry is a fulfillment of the Old Testament Scriptures. The first public sermon preached by Jesus as recorded by Luke began with this thematic statement: "Today this scripture is fulfilled in your hearing" (4:21). Jesus moves through the various books of the Old Testament, opening the minds of his disciples to show how all has been fulfilled in himself. The Old Testament is promise; the New Testament is fulfillment. The message is the same: repentance and the forgiveness of sins.

When the rich man in hell requested that someone from the dead should go and speak to his five brothers, Abraham replied that "if they do not listen to Moses and the Prophets, they will not be convinced even if someone rises from the dead" (16:31). When Jesus appears here to his disciples, he does not simply show himself to be a living person; he opens their minds to an understanding of the Scriptures. Today we do not have the privilege of seeing the body of our risen Lord face-to-face, but we have the Old and New Testament Scriptures, which bear witness to him. These are sufficient for our faith and our witness.

Jesus concludes by giving to his followers a command and a promise. Their task will be to preach to all nations, witnessing to all they had seen and heard. It is an awesome assignment that Jesus gives, but along with it comes the promise that the disciples will be "clothed with power from on high." The book of Acts (also written by Luke) tells the story of how the Holy Spirit empowered the disciples to go with the gospel. The journey of Jesus ended in Jerusalem; the mission of the church will begin in that same city and finally reach to the ends of the earth.

The Ascension

⁵⁰When he had led them out to the vicinity of Bethany, he lifted up his hands and blessed them. ⁵¹While he was blessing them, he left them and was taken up into heaven. ⁵²Then they worshiped him and returned to Jerusalem with great joy. ⁵³And they stayed continually at the temple, praising God.

The gospel according to Luke ends on a note of blessing and praise: Jesus blessing his disciples with uplifted hands; the disciples worshiping him and praising God. In the Greek text, the word for "bless" and "praise" is the same. It is because we are blessed by God that we in turn praise him. This is the essence of Christian worship. Luke began his gospel with the priest Zechariah burning incense in the temple; the last verse finds the disciples in that same temple praising God for his Servant, Jesus Christ. Here is true recognition of the risen Savior.

After Jesus had blessed his disciples, we read that "he left them and was taken up into heaven." From the context in which this story is placed, it would appear that this ascension into heaven took place on Easter Sunday evening. In Acts 1:1-11 we have an account of Jesus ascending into heaven after spending 40 days with his apostles. Hence the church celebrates the Ascension of Jesus on the 40th day after Easter.

In a sense, each departure of the risen Jesus from his disciples during those 40 days was an ascension. Jesus was preparing his followers for that day when they would no longer have his visible presence to rely upon. Then, though Jesus was gone from their sight, their hearts were filled with the great joy of knowing him to be God's Servant, having come to rescue the world from sin and death. They were prepared to give their lives as his witnesses.